Richard Rodgers

Richard Rodgers

BY DAVID EWEN

illustrated with photographs

HENRY HOLT AND COMPANY, NEW YORK

First Edition

In Canada, George J. McLeod, Ltd.

Library of Congress Catalog Card Number: 57-10418

82625–0817
Printed in the United States of America

To Dick's three collaborators:
Larry Hart, Oscar Hammerstein II,
and Dorothy Rodgers

ACKNOWLEDGMENTS

Though the numerous articles in newspapers and magazines about Rodgers, and frequently by him, have been consulted for this book and tapped for quotation, the basic material for this biography comes from firsthand sources.

My subject, Richard Rodgers, has himself been, in numerous sessions, a bountiful reservoir of reminiscences and information. Such autobiographical data as Mr. Rodgers himself has been able to provide has been supplemented by the copious information contributed by his brother, Dr. Mortimer Rodgers; his wife, Dorothy; his collaborator, Oscar Hammerstein II; and his second cousin, Hannah Harris.

Many others have been cooperative with both recollections and documented material; without them this book would surely have been less complete and less accurate. I list these people alphabetically and express my gratitude to them in equal measure: George Abbott, George Balanchine, Robert Russell Bennett, Bennett Cerf, Richard Conried, Ralph G. Engelsman, Herbert Fields, Jules Glaenzer, Margot Hopkins, Theresa Helburn, Benjamin Kaye, Philip B. Leavitt, Lillian Leff, Howard Reinheimer, Dr. Albert Sirmay, and Jerome Whyte.

The facts of Lorenz Hart's life and personality which are available in published sources were richly supplemented by information graciously contributed to me by his brother, Teddy, and Teddy's wife, Dorothy; also by several of Larry's intimate friends, including Milton Bender, Irving Eisman, and Phil Charig; and by a few others whose wish for anonymity must be respected.

So many people have been contacted by wire, mail, and telephone for specific details—and they were so patient in the face of a barrage of queries—that I should like to thank them collectively. Also, I would be remiss if I did not express a measure of indebtedness to the scrapbooks so carefully compiled by the composer's father, the late Dr. William Rodgers; they facilitated the inevitable problems of research immeasurably, being an inexhaustible repository of basic facts.

I have been the recipient of many other kindnesses. Leonard Bernstein, Ira Gershwin, and P. G. Wodehouse wrote statements expressly for this book. The Music Division of the Congressional Library in Washington, D.C., provided an opportunity to inspect Rodgers' manuscripts; and the music and drama divisions of the New York Public Library gave access to valuable clipping files. The study of Rodgers' music was greatly facilitated by Columbia, Victor, Capitol, and Decca Records, who graciously supplied me with existing recordings of Rodgers' works; and by Williamson Music, Inc., which provided me with the complete scores of all the Rodgers and Hammerstein plays. My friend, Mischa Portnoff, repeated a service done for me when I worked on my Gershwin biography by spending several afternoons playing for me the vast library of Rodgers' songs, particularly those written in boyhood for which no recordings are available.

I am grateful for the permission to use quotations from the following lyrics by Lorenz Hart: "Any Old Place with You" (copyright 1919 by Jerome H. Remick & Co., copyright renewed, reprinted by permission); "I Feel at Home with You" (copyright 1927 by Harms, Inc., copyright renewed, reprinted by permission); "On a Desert Island with Thee" (copyright 1927 by Harms, Inc., copyright renewed, reprinted by permission); "Manhattan" and "Gilding the Guild" (copyright Edward B. Marks Music Corporation, used by permission).

I am also indebted to Chappell & Co., Inc., for permission to quote from several lyrics by Oscar Hammerstein II, and to Simon and Schuster, Inc., to quote some passages from *The Rodgers and Hart Song Book*, edited by Richard Rodgers, and *Lyrics*, by Oscar Hammerstein II.

A final word of gratitude goes to my brother, Dr. Frederic Ewen, and my friend, Heyman Zimel, for providing significant suggestions after a reading of the manuscript; and to Richard Rodgers and Oscar Hammerstein II for insuring accuracy of biographical information by plodding through the galley proofs.

DAVID EWEN

Little Neck, N. Y.
May 29, 1957

Contents

PART TWO : RODGERS AND HAMMERSTEIN

APPENDIXES

Richard Rodgers

INTRODUCTION

Since 1925 with his first Broadway success, *The Garrick Gaieties,* and his first song hit, "Manhattan," Richard Rodgers has dominated the American musical theater. He has written the scores for thirty-four stage productions—thirty-five, if we include the television musical, *Cinderella.* Sixteen were major successes, two of them establishing box-office records which to this day remain unequaled by any other musical production. First with Lorenz Hart and Herbert Fields, then with Hart (occasionally supplemented by George Abbott), finally with Oscar Hammerstein II, Rodgers has written plays which are surely the proudest achievements of the musical theater of our generation: *Dearest Enemy, A Connecticut Yankee, Peggy-Ann, On Your Toes, I Married an Angel, Babes in Arms, The Boys from Syracuse, Pal Joey, By Jupiter, Oklahoma!, Carousel, Allegro, South*

Pacific, The King and I. Plays like these led Ira Gershwin to say: "I am certain that musicologists, present and future, will have to agree that Rodgers is not only one of our most successful composers of theater music but also one of exquisite taste and resourcefulness; and as a composer-showman, one of integrity and courage."

For this long string of plays, Rodgers has written over one thousand songs. At least two hundred have been substantial hits, and about a hundred have become classics in the popular-music repertory. "Here in My Arms," "Where or When?", "My Heart Stood Still," "With a Song in My Heart," "Oh, What a Beautiful Mornin'," "You'll Never Walk Alone," "A Fellow Needs a Girl," "What's the Use of Wond'rin' "—the man who wrote such songs, and many others like them, is a musical creator without peer. "He is, perhaps, the most imitated songwriter of our time," writes Leonard Bernstein. "He has established new levels of taste, distinction, simplicity in the best sense, and inventiveness." Today it can be said that nobody in the past forty years has written as many good songs for the stage over such a sustained period as he; nobody writing music for the popular theater has been heard and loved by so many people in so many different parts of the civilized world.

For his achievements Rodgers has been bountifully compensated by material rewards as well as public acclaim. He gained both fame and fortune when he was comparatively young, only twenty-three. From then on his success has continued to mount, with only negligible lapses, up to the present-day peak, where he sits atop the world of music and the theater, at the height of both his prosperity and creative power. He is now not only a world-composer, a master in his field, but also, with Hammerstein, the head of a theatrical empire that includes a Broadway and London producing firm, a publishing house, and a motion-picture company.

Success of such magnitude finds few parallels, if any, in American music.

Such a record of achievement is remarkable enough. Yet Rodgers' importance transcends even such formidable accomplishments. No less important than the consistently high standard of his musical writing through the years—and the measure of success he has gained through his writing—is the influence he has exerted upon an entire generation. The fact is that the history of the American musical stage since 1925 is also the history of Richard Rodgers. Its evolution from the now-dated musical comedy of the early 1920's to the vital and vibrant musical play of the 1950's can be traced step by step in the successive stages of Rodgers' career.

In the early Rodgers musicals, in which he collaborated with Hart and Fields, there was a conscious attempt to be freed from stereotyped boy-meets-girl themes. Such early plays as *Dearest Enemy* (1925) and *A Connecticut Yankee* (1927) went for their texts to American history on the one hand and Mark Twain on the other. Soon the iconoclasm grew bolder. *Peggy-Ann* (1927) not only was created from the then exotic fabric of dream psychology but even dispensed with some of the ritual which the musical comedy had followed so religiously for so long a time, such as an opening and closing chorus. In *Chee-Chee* (1928) music became integral to the stage action through the introduction of all kinds of incidental musical episodes.

Then in later Rodgers and Hart musicals a new concept of musical comedy was realized; indeed, the term "musical comedy" was discarded in favor of "musical play." These later plays included *Babes in Arms, On Your Toes, I Married an Angel, The Boys from Syracuse, Pal Joey,* and *By Jupiter.* Songs, dances, and humor (and at moments even tragedy) arose naturally from the situation of the play; each musical number now became a "plot number." Music, no longer an obstruction to the stage action as it so often had been in the past, became a contributing force to carry that action onward. It was no longer a decorative ornament to the play but an essential element to emphasize emotion and atmosphere and dramatic conflict. The chorus also now became basic to the plot; the dances not only acquired validity within the text but also achieved some of the artistic amplitude of ballet. And so the climate was prepared for the wonderful musical plays of Rodgers and Hammerstein which followed immediately—plays in which the musical comedy finally became a native art form: *Oklahoma!, Carousel, Allegro, South Pacific,* and *The King and I.*

Some have said that the American musical comedy at its best is perhaps the greatest single contribution we have made to the theater of the world. Others have written that when great American operas are finally written they will resemble more closely musical plays like *South Pacific, Carousel,* and *The King and I* than the stylized productions American composers have been presenting at the Metropolitan Opera. In any event, the artistic importance of the American musical play is now an established fact, both in this country and abroad. And it is Richard Rodgers, above all others, who established this fact. More than any other single composer of our era he has helped to change the destiny of our musical theater.

That he should have always been willing to work with the unusual texts and techniques which his collaborators frequently provided him in their plays is remarkable in itself. For Broadway composers have been notoriously reluctant to associate themselves with any kind of play or stage method that does not cling to the tried and accepted formulas, particularly in the 1920's. But more remarkable still is the fact that Rodgers did not merely submit to such new procedures.

In those conferences in which these fresh ideas were first projected, he was often the one to introduce them. Then in writing his music he continually kept pace with the ever-increasing demands made upon him by his texts—growing all the time musically even as his plays were becoming more mature and adult, continually broadening his musical canvas, enlarging his artistic horizon, giving his music ever greater scope, freedom of movement, articulateness.

Within the past quarter of a century most writers of popular songs and music for the stage have been influenced by him. But his influence has reached beyond the practitioners of music to embrace even the public. Since no living composer has had a larger audience for his music than Rodgers, and since in his writing he has adhered to a high level of musical and dramatic aesthetics, he has succeeded in elevating the prevailing taste for popular music in general, and music for the theater in particular. The ready acceptance that musical plays with extended and often complex and subtle scores find today with so many people everywhere has surely been made possible by the indoctrination that these people have received through the years from Rodgers' musicals.

In a professional career that spans almost forty years, Rodgers has worked intimately with only two writers, Lorenz Hart and Oscar Hammerstein II. It is neither accident nor coincidence that in selecting writing partners Rodgers should turn to collaborators who are not only adept at creating lyrics for songs but who also are keen and trenchant intellects of the theater, who know the theater in all its facets, and who have had the will and the talent to write for it with fresh and independent thought. For Rodgers is a man of the theater. His musical talent has its roots in the theater. He can work fruitfully only with those collaborators to whom the theater is as much a vital and ever-growing and ever-changing art as it is to him. And his creative strength is drawn for the most part from the theater: he finds abstract musical composition difficult. Without the stimulation of a play, or a situation, text, or character, his artistic inspiration is slow in coming. Most composers get thematic ideas which they jot down in a notebook for future use. Rodgers does not have such a notebook—a handy reservoir of musical materials—because ideas simply do not leap into his mind when he does not have a specific assignment to complete. "Songs never come to me," he confesses. "I have to go after them."

Given a play that arouses his imagination, Rodgers becomes singularly fertile. He then produces music quickly and easily, turning on his inspiration as if it came from a faucet. The more artistically ambitious a play is, the greater become the dimension and depth of Rodgers' musical writing. It is for this reason Rodgers' talent was able to blossom so fruitfully and quickly in such early musicals as *Dearest Enemy, Peggy-Ann,* and *A Connecticut Yankee,* with their provocative texts and often novel procedures. And it is the reason why, associated with the beauty and poetry of Oscar Hammerstein's plays, he has so often touched musical greatness.

The productive years that lie ahead of Richard Rodgers can only strengthen the position he has acquired in our musical theater. They cannot undermine it or basically change it. Whatever else he may yet do, he is already a creative figure of first importance both in the American theater and in American music—with few if any rivals.

Part One

RODGERS AND HART

"Tuneful and tasteful

Schmaltzy and smart

Music by Rodgers

Lyrics by Hart."

IRVING BERLIN

1

"PEOPLE HAVE MADE A PRODUCTION OF ME"

Richard Rodgers is a genius who has few of the personal attributes we often associate with genius—the volatile moods, idiosyncrasies, deviations, and quirks. Those who meet him for the first time often find it hard to associate the trim, efficient, practical, and well-adjusted man before them with the one who has written so much wonderful music.

In appearance he looks like a prosperous banker. His dress is always neat but never suggests the dandy. The cut of his clothes is conservative, setting off to advantage his well-built, five-foot-seven figure. His hair, now streaked with gray, has modified the boyishness which characterized him well into his middle years, bringing him added dignity and softening the finely chiseled features of his oval face. This is the face of a doer, not a dreamer. There is strength in the assertive jaw and the firm lips. The eyes are alert and expressive, registering each of his varying moods—whimsy, shrewdness, strong purpose, skepticism, defiance—as if they were windows on his deepest and innermost feelings and thoughts.

He speaks in a quick, clipped voice, emphasizing a remark with an abrupt nod of the head. A quiet wit, refreshing turns of a phrase, deft puns spice his conversation; he is highly articulate. He has a droll way of referring to people or punning on their names. One of his former orchestrators—a nervous, restless Middle European—was baptized by him "the bouncing Czech." Lea Morse, a musical-comedy star given to repentant moods, was always referred to by him as "Re-morse." He knew that Leif Erickson had difficulty in getting people to pronounce his first name correctly. One day, at rehearsal, while Erickson was struggling with a Rodgers song, the composer told him, "Well, Life, I'll try to make Leaf easier for you."

In his social and business associations Rodgers plays the sophisticate—probably to conceal or keep in check both his extreme sensitivity and his capacity for emotion. A key to his personality may perhaps be found in the way he plays his own songs at the piano. He appears to be unemotional and is undemonstrative; he brings to his music detachment and objectivity, as if composer and performer were two different people.

When he ponders a problem he withdraws deeply into himself, becomes moody and unapproachable. But even on other occasions he is often remote and forbidding. Many have called him cold and aloof; very few of those who know him are actually able to penetrate the shell of his reserve. The number of his friends is legion; he is fond of them, and they of him. But those with whom he is completely communicative can be counted on the fingers of a single hand, with some fingers to spare. There is, first and foremost, his collaborator, Oscar Hammerstein II. Then there is Howard

Reinheimer, Hammerstein's classmate at Columbia College and after that his lawyer; since Hammerstein and Rodgers teamed up for *Oklahoma!* Reinheimer has also been Rodgers' lawyer. There is Jerome Whyte, who first became associated with Rodgers when he served as stage manager for *The Boys from Syracuse;* subsequently he was associated with *Oklahoma!* mainly as casting director for its various companies, and later became producing supervisor of the Rodgers and Hammerstein London office. Hammerstein, Reinheimer, and Whyte are all business associates—but they are also the friends who have Rodgers' ear and heart, who are closest to him.

For all his self-containment, he has a deep vein of tenderness for those he likes; and when he lets himself go emotionally he becomes so sentimental that he can burst into tears. "He is a man," says Robert Russell Bennett, his orchestrator, "with a beautiful warmth somewhere deep in his blood." He has always conducted his affairs on such a high ethical plane, and with such fairness to all concerned, that in the fifteen years Reinheimer has been his lawyer, there has not been a single legal suit against Rodgers—a remarkable fact when one recalls the extent and range of his business dealings. He has always been extremely generous with money, help, friendship, praise. His colleagues in the theater know he is sincere when he tells them how much he likes their work—which he frequently goes out of his way to do—because they know he is fiercely honest in all his judgments and completely free of envy or malice.

Even more admirable is his tolerance to unknowns in the theater, his receptivity to new talent. His office is open to anyone seeking a legitimate hearing. "Rodgers," says Dorothy Fields, who has known him for his entire career, "is gentle to everybody. If some kid gets up and sings half of *Aïda,* he will sit there and listen with interest, and never cut him short or walk out. He has put a quality of humanity in the theater. When he hires people he protects them and takes an interest in their personal affairs." (It is this protective attitude toward his employees that has encouraged them to refer to him affectionately as "Pops.") The files in the Rodgers and Hammerstein office are the most extensive in America for names and qualifications of young performers; they number about four thousand. Someday a few of them may be lifted to stardom in a Rodgers and Hammerstein production, even as many unknowns have been in the past. "If the telephone operator says she knows a guy who would do fine as a Bowery bum," Rodgers explains, "that's fine with me. If a doorman wants to bring me his cross-eyed uncle, that's all right with me, too. You never can tell. No business can thrive without new blood." It is, then, no accident that in collaboration with Hart, and then with Hammerstein, he has through the years found obscure players who became in his productions stars of the first magnitude: Alfred Drake, Yul Brynner, Lisa Kirk, June Cochrane, Gene Kelly, Desi Arnaz, Wynn Murray, Vera Zorina, Bambi Linn, Celeste Holm, Joan McCracken, Howard Keel, John Raitt, Isabel Bigley, Florence Henderson, Shirley Jones, Betta St. John, Judy Tyler, among many others.

Yet he can also be hard. Frequently, when he and Hammerstein are feted, he explains that in their partnership the tall Hammerstein is the "big boy" who is a "softy," while the comparatively short Rodgers is the "small guy" who is tough —and this is sometimes the case. Rodgers can be strong-willed and dictatorial, especially in connection with one of his shows. When confronted with anybody who is careless about his work, indifferent to it, or inept, he is callous to that person's feelings. He does not lose his temper, but his sardonic remarks have the sting of acid. He feels resentment so keenly that often he continues to harbor a grudge long after the damage has been inflicted and repaired. But anybody who works under him respects him even during periods of such ugly moods because they know he is driven not by ego or eccentricities but by a severe integrity and artistic conscience. Because he demands the most and the best of himself, he expects everybody around him to give of his most and best.

It is sometimes difficult to remember that Rodgers is a musician. He does not conform to any stereotype of what a musician is like or should be. Musicians are often temperamental, volatile, unstable, irresponsible, but Rodgers is none of these. To his daily life and work he brings a sound respect for what is practical and pragmatic, and he brings to his decisions a quick and searching intelligence that depends more on cold calculation than impulse. In contrast to the many quixotic characters who populate the world of music and the theater, he is the last word in sobriety; in contrast to their often frenetic existences, his is well ordered. He is that rarity among artists, a man who has no need for stimulants, sedatives, tranquilizers, or a psychiatrist's couch to get from one day to the next.

Rodgers is always so methodical and systematic, with such a healthy respect for exactitude and detail, that Oscar Hammerstein insists he would have made a wonderful surgeon. These same qualities in him have led many writers to describe him as a wonderful businessman. Legends die hard, and it is difficult to put to final rest one built up by so many and for so long a time. But the truth of the matter is that Rodgers has little sympathy for business affairs and does not involve himself actively in the multifarious details involving the conduct of the fiscal affairs of the Rodgers and

Hammerstein office. He insists on leaving contractual matters, bookings, and other negotiations to men he has hired for this purpose.

However, it is quite true that he brings to composition the discipline and stability a businessman carries to his work. There are never any tantrums or histrionic displays of temperament as he gets his musical ideas down on paper. His results are achieved with the quiet and competent dispatch that a good craftsman or artisan brings to his workbench.

Possibly because success came so early and remained a habit, he wears it lightly and with grace. "People have made a production of me," he has said concerning the literature flattering his personality, "and I can't live down the casting." But the truth is that he lives up well to such a production. His friends agree that he has been untouched by arrogance, snobbery, or smugness. While he possesses a healthy ego that can value and find both pride and joy in his accomplishments, he does not allow himself to assume a pompous attitude or indulge in self-glorification. Possibly he has too much of a sense of humor to do that. As a matter of fact, he seems to take his great native gifts with a surprising degree of casualness, seems at times almost to deprecate them. Many have spoken of him as a genius, but in his own candid self-analysis he is more apt to consider himself only as an efficient, well-functioning, skillful, knowledgeable workman. "I'm a commercial-theater kid," is one way he has evaluated himself. "I don't write for posterity."

He is remarkably free of unpleasant and undesirable traits and habits. He never drinks excessively, his only indulgence being an occasional social cocktail or a Scotch and water before dinner. At a party after the première of *Oklahoma!* he was asked why he did not celebrate the occasion with drink.

His answer provides an insight to his personality: "And miss the fun I get from a wonderful occasion like this? No—thank you!" Gambling holds as little attraction for him as drinking; he never indulges in games of chance, even for small stakes. He does not even smoke. He used to, but it affected his throat and he decided to give it up. Night clubs bore him to tears; the only time he goes is to seek out talent. But large parties, swarming with celebrities, continually fascinate him. Through the years he has come to know well people in the highest spheres of social, political, and artistic life—people like Margaret Emerson, Governor Averell Harriman, Herbert Bayard Swope, Noel Coward, Jules Glaenzer, Deems Taylor —but he has never outgrown a boyish delight in moving among the elite on personal terms. He is in his element, and at his charming best, at gala affairs that crop up so frequently either to honor him for one reason or another, or to celebrate an important première.

He is indifferent to all sports, either as a participant or as a spectator—even to golf, to which so many of his friends are so partial. The only exception is croquet, which in the Rodgers family is very serious business indeed. "Dick takes croquet more seriously than anything outside his work," reports his wife. "At a party he is the soul of effortless charm, but on the croquet field he can be as stern and as unyielding as granite. He gets mad at himself, his opponents, the wickets, a passing breeze. He can compose music with all hell breaking loose around him, but let one leaf move within his peripheral vision during a shot and he explodes." In 1953 he and his wife won against George S. Kaufman and Moss Hart in a bitter Connecticut-Bucks County competition. But sometime later the Rodgerses lost in an important Long Island tournament because, his wife tells us, "I go to pieces in the finale while Dick, who cares even more, can summon up an icy calm."

Rodgers does not have strong religious convictions. His membership at Temple Emanu-El in New York, and his occasional attendance at services, is partly a concession to his wife's deeper religious feelings and partly sentimental attachment to his racial background. His feeling is that his tie to other Jews everywhere is social rather than religious. Besides he believes strongly that "when anybody who is a member of a minority can accomplish something important, he should declare himself so that this minority can become a little less minor."

In politics, his leanings are liberal, and he has often supported the platforms of the Democratic party. His wife usually echoes his own political beliefs, but during the 1940 elections the Rodgers family was divided against itself: Dick was for Roosevelt; his wife, for Willkie. Because of his personal associations with Dwight D. Eisenhower, which began in 1948, Rodgers originally supported him for the Presidency in 1952. But when during the early part of the campaign Candidate Eisenhower made his rapprochement with Senators McCarthy and Jenner, Rodgers publicly announced a shift to the Democratic fold. This change of political heart did not interrupt the personal friendship of the two men. Eisenhower never bore Rodgers any ill feeling and even entertained him as a dinner guest at the White House. Notwithstanding Rodgers' high regard for the President, he still insisted on supporting the Democratic party in the 1956 election.

Rodgers has always been appreciative of woman's physical charms. "I had my first date when I was eight," he confesses, "and I have been in love ever since." Beginning with his grandmother, women have always played a prominent role in his life and through the years have often had a share in his major decisions. Some of his girl friends were from the musical-comedy stage, others from families of high social station. All were beautiful, intelligent, dynamic in personality.

But this was before 1930, when he married Dorothy Feiner. He was madly in love with her then, and he both adores and respects her now. Dorothy, for her part, has saved every letter, card and message Rodgers ever sent her—even the back of a bar check on which he once hurriedly scribbled his name, address, and telephone number. "He's the sweetest guy in the world," she says, and the marriage "is getting better all the time." She is habitually the one who first hears the songs he writes. Her response—"very good, Dick darling" when she does not like it; silence and tears when she does—is a barometer he watches carefully.

Dorothy Rodgers is a remarkably handsome woman—fair, slender, willowy. She wears her dark hair simply, with a part in the middle and drawn back into a knot in the back of her head. That is the way Dick likes it best. Her brown eyes are gentle, and there is repose in the delicate features of her face. She carries herself with dignity and with an air of tranquillity no matter what she may be doing. She can engage in the most heated arguments without raising her voice. Her temper (like that of her husband) often reveals itself in frigid silences.

That tranquillity and serenity of hers are deceptive: the slow and casual air she assumes is a cover-up for an extraordinary energy. The raising of her two daughters; the personal and social demands made upon her by a busy and famous husband; her own delight in entertaining in the grand manner—all this, apparently, is not enough to occupy her. Until May, 1951, when she became seriously ill, she alone kept a methodical accounting of all the household finances, personally supervised the running of her two large homes, and attended to all the personal correspondence.

Since then, however, she has been assisted in many of these details by an efficient secretary, Eileen Minich.

When Dorothy married Rodgers she gave up her own career as sculptress, for which she had shown talent, because, as she explains, "I figured that one creative artist in the family is enough." But she had too much intellectual and physical energy to abandon a career of her own indefinitely, especially after the girls grew up. Just before World War II she organized a firm called "Repairs, Inc.," which specialized in fixing broken furniture, glass, china, knickknacks. This firm patched up the murals in the Sert Room of the Waldorf-Astoria, and set Helen Hayes' cuckoo clock running. It filled many kinds of outlandish requests, such as building a Lucite stand to hold the jawbone of somebody's grandfather. When "Repairs, Inc." became a profitable venture, Dorothy's restless vitality sought other avenues of activity; the firm expanded into interior decoration, its first assignment being a nursery for Raymond Massey's children.

But during World War II Dorothy gave up her business activities to engage in war work. She became a first-aid instructor for the Red Cross, and a member of the Writers War Board, which supplied material for servicemen's entertainments. After the war she not only continued but even extended her community interests. She has been active in the affairs of the Museum of Modern Art; has been involved in trying to establish a school of the theater at Barnard College; has devoted herself to the Public Education Association, dedicated to raising the educational standards of the New York public school system; and has been on the board of the New York Red Cross.

In addition to all this activity, Dorothy is a patent-holding inventor. She sold an idea to Macy's for a file for receipts and canceled checks that looks like a book and can be kept on the bookshelf. She received from Personal Products Corporation an initial payment of $10,000 as an advance against royalties for a device to clean bathroom bowls, patented as "Jonny Mop." (Appropriately, the canceled check hangs framed on a wall in the Rodgers bathroom.) For some time she has been working on a small air-conditioning unit to be worn inside the clothing during hot weather.

Her passion is directed not toward clothes, jewels, or furs, but activity; her extravagance, buying beautiful things for her homes, especially paintings.

The Rodgerses have two daughters. Mary was born in 1931, went to Wellesley College, and is now married to Julian Bonar Beaty, Jr., a young lawyer. The Beatys have three children: Richard Rodgers Beaty, born in 1952; Linda McKay, in 1953; and Constance Peck, in 1955. Whenever he is asked whether having grandchildren makes him feel old, Rodgers replies: "On the contrary—I find it very invigorating. It's kind of a family flattery, and good for the ego. You see, it's wonderful to know that you can have grandchildren and still be as active and as young as I am."

Mary has the driving ambition for success of her father— and in his own field. She wants to be a composer. She has written some delightful children's tunes to her own lyrics. A number of these have been published by Chappell under a title provided by her father, *Some of My Best Friends Are Children,* and were recorded by Golden Records. Her productivity was temporarily arrested by the business of bringing three children into the world, but she has by no means lost the will or the hope of creating music professionally.

Linda is four years younger than Mary. After a year at Smith College, when Richard and Dorothy Rodgers went to California for the filming of *Oklahoma!* Linda went with them. There she met and fell in love with Dan Melnick, a young television producer, whom she married in February, 1955. Like her sister, Linda has a talent for music, particularly the piano.

The Rodgers winters are spent in New York City in a handsomely furnished duplex apartment in the East 70's, attended by three servants besides Mrs. Minich. Summers and odd week ends throughout the year are spent at "Rockmeadow," their country place in Southport, Connecticut. The large gray-shingled house with huge white chimneys is situated on a forty-acre tract that includes a tennis court, swimming pool, croquet field, and a greenhouse that through the year supplies both Rodgers establishments with all their flowers. Dorothy Rodgers is responsible for the furnishing of both places. The New York apartment, mostly English, Empire, and French Provincial in decoration, has stateliness and formality. The walls are covered with paintings by Matisse, Sisley, Braque, Toulouse-Lautrec, Renoir, Rouault, Vuillard among others (the Rouault and Vuillard being gifts the Rodgerses exchanged on the twentieth anniversary of their marriage). Both love art deeply; buying pictures is their greatest single extravagance. "If ever I am eager to earn more money than I do now, and it is not often, it's not to buy a yacht or a villa in Cannes. After all, Dorothy gets seasick, and I don't like to travel. But I would like to own a few more paintings." There are, however, few pictures in Rockmeadow. Both Dick and Dorothy prefer that the center of interest there be focused on the beautifully landscaped grounds which are brought into the room through the large picture windows.

Rodgers loves that Connecticut house deeply—particularly when he is surrounded by his family and several intimate friends. In contrast to the New York place, it is informal in every respect. It is furnished in French Provincial and literally bursts with bright colors, mostly gay greens, yellows, and pinks.

Of all his musicals, Rodgers is most partial to *Carousel*. "It tries to say the most and says it the best." He does not like to single out those of his songs he prefers. "A composer," he explains, "may like some of his songs for reasons that have nothing whatsoever to do with their musical value— the circumstance under which he wrote one; the person to whom he wrote another; the associations a third might bring up." Dorothy, however, has no hesitancy in picking out her favorites: "Hello, Young Lovers," "You'll Never Walk Alone," "Little Girl Blue," and "Dear, Dear"—the last not for its musical interest but its sentimental association, being the first love song Rodgers wrote after their marriage.

As for his future ambitions, Rodgers says simply, "I'd like to continue living as I do now for the rest of my life, enjoying the things I enjoy now, keeping on doing work for the theater, and writing one or two more shows that will leave an impression."

But his aims are probably not quite so modest. The dominant drive that has swept him from triumph to triumph has by no means been slackened. He is as restless today as yesterday for new worlds to conquer. He is like a mountain climber who, despite the towering heights he has already scaled, is dissatisfied as long as he has not won Mount Everest. To Rodgers, the achievements of the past—however impressive—can never hide the unscaled peaks of his own Mount Everest, beckoning ever through the distant clouds.

2

BACKGROUNDS

There is nothing whatever in Richard Rodgers' first compositions to indicate that here, in the making, was one of
America's foremost song writers. From his first completed
song, everything he wrote has been carefully preserved and
can today be consulted in neatly bound volumes arranged
chronologically. One searches in vain through the first songs
for some hint of later creative powers. The melodies are
pleasing enough. A few numbers have charm and freshness.
The harmonizations are sometimes neat, though not particularly inventive. A detail here or there—sometimes a sudden change of key, sometimes the enlargement of a melodic
idea—may betray a conscious attempt at originality. This,
coming from a boy in his early teens, bespeaks precocity, to
be sure, and proves the powerful attraction that making
music had for him. But between precocity and genius there
is a yawning chasm.

He cannot remember the time he did not want to be a composer. He had no visions of becoming another Mozart, Beethoven, or Wagner. When he began writing his first melodies, at the age of nine, he knew virtually nothing about these composers or their works, his musical environment and experience consisting exclusively of some grand-opera excerpts and some songs from American and European operettas. He simply wanted to be allowed to put down on paper or to play on the piano the many tunes that were crowding into his head. This activity gave him the delight and satisfaction other boys of his age derived from mechanical toys or from playing with their friends in the street.

Even after he started writing songs he was not driven by lofty ideals—to make an art out of his melodies or to try to open new horizons for American popular music. Getting a melody that pleased the ear and stuck in the memory was for him an end in itself, an end that brought him infinite joy.

The pattern of his personality was crystallized as early as his ambition to write music. In boyhood, as now, he managed to maintain an outward calm that often concealed inner turmoil. When upset, he rarely gave way to emotional outbursts but lapsed into moody silences. He early developed the habit of fingernail-biting that remained with him up to his early teens. Then, as today, he was fastidiously neat; none of those who remember him as a boy recall his ever passing through that phase of sloppiness and indifference to personal appearance to which almost all youngsters at one time or another succumb. He was well organized in his habits, and in his thinking.

Most interesting of all in view of his later development, the boy revealed an outlook that was unusually practical and down-to-earth; and, surprising for one of his years, he betrayed from the outset a hunger for success. With an undemonstrative, inoffensive but nevertheless strong determination, and with an almost coldly scientific calculation, he set about first to get his songs heard; then to get them heard in influential places; finally to get these songs to open up the doors to success to him. What he was aiming for as a boy was not the posthumous immortality that awaits so many significant composers, but the more tangible rewards of public acceptance and wealth.

Financial stability was contributed to the Rodgers family by Dick's maternal grandfather; culture, by his grandmother.

His grandfather, Jacob Levy, had come to this country from Poland. When he arrived in New York he found a menial job with Klingenstein Brothers, a small textile jobbing house at 111 Greene Street. He remained with that firm the rest of his life, growing with it and eventually becoming Klingenstein's partner. By the time Dick was born, Levy was a man of considerable means, since Klingenstein Brothers was then not only a powerful jobber and factor house but also had several mills as subsidiaries.

The first room Jacob Levy rented in New York was in a house owned by the Lewines, whose daughter Rachel became Jacob's wife in 1869. In later years Rachel was an extraordinarily well-read and well-informed woman. She loved music devotedly, attended concerts frequently, and had a weekly subscription for the Metropolitan Opera. To this day Dick feels that she was one of the most brilliant women he has known. For years, whenever a question of information arose in the Rodgers household, he heard it said, 'Don't consult the encyclopedia, ask Grandma." In religion she was a freethinker; her husband—while not strict in fulfilling the ritual—insisted on attending synagogue occasionally and observing the major holidays.

The Levys had three children, two sons and a daughter.

Mamie, who came between Lester and Louis, was the core of her parents' existence. Born in Rutgers Place, in downtown New York, in 1873, she was educated in the city public schools. Being talented in music, she was also given intensive instruction on the piano with private teachers.

Dick's father, William Abraham Rodgers, was born in Holden, Missouri, in 1871, the oldest of seven children. Of Alsatian extraction, his name, at birth, was William Abrams, but while he attended college his family changed its name legally to Rodgers.

He came to New York when he was only five years old. The death of his father twelve years later placed much of the burden of supporting a large family squarely on his shoulders. While pursuing his studies, he held various jobs; one of the most important was that of customs officer on the New York docks.

His first ambition embraced not medicine but the army. He loved the panoply of the military career—the uniforms, ribbons, medals—and he was intensely patriotic. A Brooklyn congressman recommended him for West Point, and Rodgers was chosen as alternate for admission. The selection of his rival was one of Rodgers' major disappointments.

Nobody in the family remembers how he came to study medicine. He first attended the College of the City of New York, where he was a classmate of Bernard Baruch in the class of 1889. From there he progressed to Bellevue Medical School, while still supporting himself in his customs-officer's job. Today, on Richard Rodgers' desk in his New York apartment, rests a framed telegram dated March 29, 1893. It reads: DEAR MOTHER. I AM A DOCTOR NOW. AFFECTIONATELY, WILL.

He had been in practice about three years, and was still a struggling practitioner, when he met and fell in love with Mamie Levy. She was twenty-four, two years younger than

Will—petite, sensitive, soft-spoken, and withdrawn. They were married on November 24, 1896, at the Levy home at 816 Lexington Avenue, and a European honeymoon followed. Returning to America in 1897, they set up house with Mamie's parents.

As long as the Levys lived, the Rodgerses continued to share a home with them. (Rachel died in 1920, Jacob eight years after that.) At first, financial necessity dictated this arrangement, for it was some time before William's practice was large enough to pay the expenses of an office and the support of a family. After he began doing well, his arrangement with his in-laws was continued partly through inertia, partly because Mamie's parents were reluctant to be separated from her and Mamie was incapable of hurting them in any way.

Dick has only the warmest and most tender recollections of his grandparents. But beneath the placid surface there were minor disturbances. Both grandparents were people of strong will and purpose—if not autocrats, then people who liked to have the control of things well in their hands. Wealth on the one hand and education on the other had given them confidence in their decisions. Mamie, who after her marriage should have been a queen in her own realm, was always subservient to dominating parents. They loved her completely and devotedly; but they also ruled her, and as time passed, she became increasingly reserved, self-contained, fearful of making decisions, reluctant to change her environment, haunted by all kinds of inexplicable and groundless fears. In the last years of her life, Mamie confided to Dorothy Rodgers that her failure to set up her own home immediately after marriage had been one of the great mistakes of her life.

She was a gentle woman, lavish with gifts to everybody around her, and wonderfully tolerant. Money or social position meant nothing to her, and although she lived to see Dick achieve adulation and wealth, she took these triumphs in her stride—content that Dick was doing what he wanted to, and doing it well. But the amount of space he could command in the newspapers, or the amount of money he could earn, never really excited her. What would have made her excessively proud and happy were the endowments and benefactions that Dick has given in recent years; but, regrettably, these came after her death.

William Rodgers and his father-in-law had a healthy respect for each other, a respect that was blended with genuine affection. Thus two men of strong will, each somewhat dictatorial by nature, each stubborn, were able to live harmoniously together. But William disliked his mother-in-law intensely, finding her too overbearing and opinionated for his tastes, and despite the close proximity with which they lived, there were weeks at a time when he refused to talk to her.

William Rodgers was red-haired and strikingly handsome. He stood almost six feet tall, was lithe and slim, and had a dignified bearing which for many years was accentuated by his goatee. (When he finally disposed of the beard he continued for the remainder of his life to wear a dapper mustache.) He always dressed in impeccable taste, spoke exceedingly well, had charming manners and an engaging wit. Though he could be surly and explosive when things did not go well for him, or when he was crossed, he could be irresistible when in the proper mood. Dick's father was an exceedingly practical man who appreciated the value of money and wanted his sons to do so too. Nevertheless, it was his basic philosophy of living that each man must be permitted to select his own future, wherever his inclinations or abilities might lead. Today, Dick says that the most significant influence in his early development probably was his father's tolerance toward his musical proclivities, even though Dick floundered about in the musical profession until his twenty-third year without any visible means of support. The truth of the matter was that, while encouraging Dick in his music, his father was deeply and vitally concerned over his future.

Dick's career and success satisfied something deep within William. He himself had once had yearnings to be a writer; at the College of the City of New York he was an editor of its Year Book. He also loved music profoundly and was a devoted theatergoer. He and his wife used to attend all the leading musical productions on Broadway—particularly the operettas of Victor Herbert and Reginald De Koven and the comic operas of Gilbert and Sullivan. Whenever the Rodgerses came home from a performance, they invariably brought back with them the printed sheet music, and sometimes even the complete vocal and piano score, and found renewed delight in reviewing the musical highlights. William sang in a pleasing baritone voice to Mamie's piano accompaniment. Consequently, to have his son associated with the stage as a successful composer was one of the richest rewards of his life, possibly greater than any his own profession brought him. He loved all the trimmings of Dick's career— the publicity, the applause of audiences, rubbing elbows with theater people.

Just how much Dick's career meant to William can be measured by the way he bound up his own life with it. When Dick was a boy getting a few lines in camp or school papers, his father meticulously saved every clipping (from the very first one!), including every program on which the name of Richard Rodgers appears. These he pasted neatly into a scrapbook. As Dick's career grew and developed, William continued to cut out and preserve all the programs and clippings, even during the last year of his life, when the clippings became voluminous and gathering and pasting them became a formidable task. Just before his death, when he was too ill to attend to them any longer—they filled several boxes—he telephoned Lillian Leff, Rodgers' secretary at the Rodgers and Hammerstein office, to instruct her how the work should proceed. And besides being the keeper of Dick's scrapbooks, he also maintained a strict ledger of Dick's income and expenses with the exactness of a trained accountant. Only after Dick married Dorothy did William surrender this chore to her.

When Rodgers went out to Hollywood in 1931 and worked there for several years, Dr. William Rodgers felt a sudden emptiness in his own life which his medical practice could not fill. His desire to be with his son, to remain a part of his son's career, was perhaps the greatest single factor in deciding him to retire from his practice and to go out to California. A mild heart attack, previously suffered, provided him with a convenient excuse for doing what he really wanted to do.

William Rodgers was a good and conscientious doctor, dedicated to his calling. In fact he was the inspiration for *A Man to Remember,* a motion picture about a general practitioner directed by Garson Kanin in 1938. "Many times during the course of the preparation of the shooting of *A Man to Remember,*" Garson Kanin wrote to Richard Rodgers in 1938, "I thought of your father and how deeply I was impressed . . . by his quiet, unassuming and yet very knowing manner and I remember thinking at the time how, though comparatively unknown, he had done so much for his fellow man."

Part of the vacuum created by Dr. Rodgers' retirement was filled by his increased preoccupation with Dick's expanding activities in the theater. But as the years passed, William grew restive and seemed eager to return to medicine. When, in the early 1930's, he went out to California, he took the state medical board examinations. His reason was that, since he was staying in California for several years, an emergency might arise which might make a demand on his professional services, and he wanted to be ready. During World War II, when his lifelong patriotism was inflamed by his hatred of the Nazis, he wanted desperately to get into uniform as a doctor. He was turned down because of his age, but he did manage to find work as assistant medical director of the draft board and ultimately received a medal for his contribution to the war effort. After the war, he brought his background and experience to the Police Athletic League (P.A.L.) by helping them select doctors for the boys. And in the middle 1940's, during the threat of a smallpox epidemic, he set up a free clinic in his New York hotel room to give inoculations to whoever wanted them.

3

LIFE BEGINS ON SATURDAY AT 2:30

William and Mamie Rodgers had two children, both sons. Mortimer was born on January 13, 1898, at the brownstone house on Lexington Avenue where his parents had made their first home. Richard Charles Rodgers followed Mortimer by four and a half years. During this period, before the Levys had bought a summer house of their own in Long Beach, the Rodgerses and the Levys rented a summer house in or near Arverne, Long Island, each season. It was in one of these rented houses—a beautiful and spacious place with a private tennis court—on Brandreth Avenue in Hammels Station near Arverne that Richard Rodgers was delivered by Dr. Bernard Sauer on the morning of June 28, 1902.

A year after Dick was born, the house on Lexington Avenue was sold and the Levys now acquired a five-story brownstone building at 3 West 120th Street, near Mount Morris Park. The ground floor was assigned to Dr. Rodgers' office and waiting rooms. On the second floor were the dining quarters and a spacious living room with a Steinway piano. The various bedrooms occupied the third and fourth floors. This was Dick's home for the next seven years.

Both Mortimer and Dick had normal childhoods, given to play, school, and the problems of growing up. Of the two boys, Mortimer was the more outgoing, boisterous, active, and mischievous. Dick was his mother's son—quiet, self-contained, gentle, and a complete conformist. But both boys differed from their friends in one significant way. Each seemed to know what he wanted to become and could not be shaken from his resolve; and each ultimately fulfilled that childhood ambition.

Mortimer, who in temperament and personality was like his father, aspired to imitate him in one other respect—by becoming a doctor. As a child, Mortimer was comparatively indifferent to the expensive toys given him by fond relatives. He preferred to play with his father's medicine bottles and bandages, and—greatest treat of all—to accompany his father on a case and carry his bag. He was not yet thirteen when he told his aunt with conviction that he would someday be a doctor. A psychiatrist might possibly venture the opinion that this drive to be a doctor was the boy's way of winning the favor of his father, who continually lavished his admiration on Dick and proudly exhibited him at family gatherings and parties as a musical prodigy.

When Mortimer reached manhood, his father tried to dissuade him from going into medicine. The older man pointed out that, while the profession promised a good social and financial position, it also denied one a normal domestic life and was a huge drain on one's physical resources. But Mortimer was intransigent. After attending Columbia College in the class of 1918, he went to Bellevue College, where his father had also received training. In 1928 Mortimer began to practice. Today he is a successful gynecologist, director of gynecology and obstetrics at Lenox Hill Hospital and clinical professor of gynecology and obstetrics at New York University College of Medicine.

Like Mortimer, Dick took an undeviating path toward his own chosen field—music. His interest in it, and his aptitude, were early evident. As a baby, he would identify songs by the colors on the sheet music. He often asked his mother to play for him one song after another of his choice by picking out the favorite from a pile of music sheets on the piano or inside the piano bench. When he was four he could piece together on the piano bits of melodies, using two fingers. One of the songs he remembers trying to play came from Victor Herbert's *Mlle. Modiste,* which his parents saw early in 1906 and the music of which they used to sing and play continually.

By the time he was six, Dick played the piano by ear with both hands, the right carrying the melody, the left providing a support with tonic-dominant chords. An attempt was now made to teach him music formally. Dr. William Rodgers enlisted the services of his sister, Tillie, to instruct both Dick and Mortimer. Tillie herself, unfortunately, was not very far advanced as a pianist, and she was not a particularly inspiring teacher. Despite their tender years, both Mortimer and Dick were wise enough to recognize the fact that if they were to learn the piano they would have to seek instruction elsewhere. Their parents had nothing to do with this decision. They were not even aware that the two children went on their own, one day, to contact a local music school on Lenox Avenue between 120th and 121st Street. There they acquired a replacement for Tillie. This new period of study lasted less than two years. Curiously enough, it was Mortimer who was the conscientious and dedicated pupil, while Dick was haphazard about his practicing habits. He disliked trying to read music from the printed page, loathed finger exercises and scales. Instead of devoting himself to formal practice he would spend hours either improvising melodies or trying to perform the songs he had heard his parents sing and play. He became an expert ear-executant, while his ability to read printed music left much to be desired. Often he came to his lessons without having once looked at the music he was supposed to practice. "But even then he was the supreme diplomat," Mortimer recalls. "When the lesson began he would ask his teacher to play through the piece because he wanted to know what the correct tempo was, or the correct phrasing, or what have you. Then, with those sharp ears of his, he would be able to play his lesson through more from memory than by looking at the music."

This preoccupation with the piano was interrupted for a full year when he was eight by osteomyelitis of the right index finger. For a while it was feared that amputation would be necessary. A delicate operation was performed at Mount Sinai Hospital in which the infected bone was removed, saving not only the finger but also the hand. Not until a full year later, after a plastic operation (one of the earliest of its kind), did normalcy of movement return to the stricken finger, enabling Dick to play the piano once again. A deep scar across the tip of his finger is still visible as a reminder of a childhood experience that almost proved emotionally traumatic but which fortunately was not crippling in any way.

The first play that made an impression on Dick was *Pied Piper,* a musical starring De Wolf Hopper, which he saw in a theater on 125th Street when he was six years old. But this was not the first time he had been inside a theater. He was an infant in arms when his nurse took him and Mortimer one afternoon to the gallery of a 125th Street theater to see a play called *Parisian Romance,* through all of which he slept blissfully.

But *Pied Piper* was an emotional experience he never forgot. "The moment the curtain went up I was carried into a world of glamour and beauty I had never known existed," he recalls.

A few months later, a family celebration brought him downtown into a Broadway theater for the first time, to a performance of Victor Herbert's *Little Nemo,* at which the Rodgerses and the Levys occupied a box. Two songs stirred Dick. To this day he cannot hear "Won't You Be My Playmate?" or "Give Us a Fleet" without experiencing a slight thrill.

From this time on, the theater became the focal point of his existence. "Life for me began on Saturdays at two-thirty." Each visit to an operetta downtown in the company of his parents or grandparents, or to the 125th Street theater for a Saturday matinee, represented for him an occasion he could not forget. Mortimer recalls that Dick's joy in the theater came not only from the songs and the performers but even from things which Mortimer himself rarely noticed: staging, scenery, costuming, an unusual bit of stage business. No detail of a show, not even a negligible phase of the production, seemed to elude Dick's alert eye. For days after a performance he continued to review its unusual features.

Dick remembers some of the musicals he saw in boyhood. *Snow White,* in 1911, was unforgettable because he fell madly in love with its star, Marguerite Clark—"not because she was so beautiful, but because she was smaller than I, a fact of not inconsiderable importance to me at the time." Also in 1911 he saw *The Quaker Girl,* starring Ina Claire. Going to this play had particular significance for him because his grandfather allowed him to play hooky from school one weekday afternoon so that they might see a matinee.

Then came a musical whose impact on him was shattering, which suddenly made him lose interest in foreign operettas and in operetta composers like Victor Herbert. The musical was *Very Good, Eddie*—book by Guy Bolton, lyrics by P. G. Wodehouse, and music by Jerome Kern. Rodgers first saw it at the Standard Theatre on upper Broadway in 1916, then revisited it about half a dozen times.

Very Good, Eddie represented a new genre in the American musical theater which Bolton, Wodehouse and Kern had introduced in 1915 with *Nobody Home*. This was a more intimate kind of musical entertainment than was then generally produced—a radical departure from the extravagant sets and costumes, elaborate staging, and large casts employed by operettas. Everything in *Very Good, Eddie* was on a small scale. There was only a handful in the cast, and very little dancing; few changes in sets were required; the costuming was the last word in simplicity. When one of the characters sang a song, the spectator almost had the feeling that it was being performed for him exclusively, and in his own living room. *Very Good, Eddie* was so informal and had such homespun warmth that critics described it as "kitchenette production" and "parlor entertainment." This new approach to musical playwriting became a Broadway institution, henceforth identified as the "Princess Theatre Shows" after the small theater in which they were seen.

This was something fresh and new, as even young Rodgers could appreciate, something authentically American. Then there was the music of Jerome Kern, which was like nothing else then being heard in the theater—songs like "Babes in the Woods" and "Nodding Roses" vibrant and vital in their melodic language. Kern now became Rodgers' idol. "The influence of the hero on such a hero-worshiper is not easy to calculate," Rodgers wrote many years later, "but it was a deep and lasting one. His less successful musical comedies were no less important to a listener of thirteen or fourteen. I know that for a large part of one winter most of my allowance was spent for a seat in the balcony of the Maxine Elliott Theatre listening to *Love o' Mike*." Rodgers goes on to pay tribute to Kern, who has remained one of his favorite composers. "Kern was typical of what was, and still is, good in our general maturity in this country in that he had his musical roots in the fertile Middle European and English school of operetta writing and amalgamated it with everything that was fresh and clear in music writing in the world. Actually he was a giant with one foot in Europe and the other in America. Before he died, he picked up the European foot and planted it squarely alongside the American one. . . . I have never felt that enough has been said about Kern's contribution to American music through his influence on subsequent writers of music in this country." The most ingratiating quality of Rodgers' best songs—the expressiveness and tenderness of the lyricism as well as the simplicity and directness of all other musical accessories—betrays the influence that Kern has had upon him.

Rodgers' sixth year, in which he saw his first play, also marked the beginning of his academic schooling, at the Model School on 119th Street between St. Nicholas and Seventh Avenues. A year later, Rodgers was transferred to P.S. 10, on 117th Street and St. Nicholas Avenue. There his facility at playing melodies on the piano received some recognition. One day at assembly, the school principal, Dr. Birkens, asked which children could perform or sing. Rodgers was one of those who volunteered. At one of the assemblies he played a potpourri of opera arias which he had managed to learn by ear after having heard his parents sing them, and which he himself had assembled into some sort of continuity. (He now recalls with some amusement that this potpourri ended with the "Pirate's Chorus" in the mistaken belief that the Gilbert and Sullivan comic opera *The Pirates of Penzance* was an opera.) Winning for the first time through his piano both the approval of his teachers and the plaudits of his schoolmates became a powerful stimulus for more music making, both in public and in private.

In 1911, the whole family moved to a large fifth-floor apartment at 161 West 86th Street, which would remain their home for the next decade or so. (Dr. William Rodgers' office and waiting rooms were now downstairs in the same building.) Dick was transferred to P.S. 166 on 89th Street between Amsterdam and Columbus avenues. Here, too, he found some encouragement for his piano playing. He was in the seventh grade when Miss Elsa Katz, a first-grade teacher in charge of the school's musical activities, discovered he could play the piano. She arranged for him to play at assemblies. These performances in the assembly hall, and the enthusiasm he won from both Miss Katz and the school principal, John F. Reigart, proved such a booster shot to his ego (he was only a run-of-the-mill student in the classroom) that to this day he remembers Miss Katz affectionately. Unfortunately she cannot return the compliment. Now living in retirement in New York City as Elsa K. Franklin, she is compelled to confess that she does not remember Richard Rodgers at all. "How proud I would have been," she writes, "to have had my name go down to posterity as one who had been an influence in the life and career of the now world-famous Richard Rodgers. But alas! my memory won't help me." Through the influence of Miss Katz, Rodgers was chosen to play during the exercises when he was graduated from P.S. 166 on January 28, 1916. As the eleventh number of the program, he once again performed his opera potpourri.

From his tenth year on, until confirmation, Dick received religious instruction at a Sunday school at Temple Israel on 120th Street near Lenox Avenue. Neither of his parents had sympathy for formal religious training, but Dick's grandfather was insistent that the boy be made conscious that he had been born a Jew. Dick's confirmation was a formal religious ceremony at Temple Israel. A family party followed in which he was the recipient of the customary *bar mitzvah* gifts of fountain pens, books, and gold coins. This religious schooling was his only awareness in boyhood and youth of his origins. He did not live in neighborhoods where Jewish boys were made acutely, sometimes painfully, aware of their religion; at home he did not see much of Hebrew ritual or rule.

In and out of school, Dick (except for his bent for music and the theater) was a normal but not particularly distinguished boy, and there was little to single him out from the others. He was not at all studious; his marks at school were only fair; and he did very little reading, not even the nickel paperbacks devoured by his schoolmates. His athletic activities were, except for tennis and swimming, negligible.

Like many children, he had his early crushes on girls. The first was in 1910 for Edith Marcus, an eight-year-old whom he met in a Harlem dance school where his parents sent him to learn social dancing. One year later there was Janet Greenberg, also eight, who lived in Washington Heights and who attended Sunday school with him. One Sunday afternoon Dick took the subway to her house to take her out to the movies. Janet's mother, taken aback to find her child going on a date with a nine-year-old, sent her maid along as chaperon. This friendship lasted several years; Rodgers still sees her occasionally since, as a friend of Lillian Leff, Janet sometimes drops in at the Rodgers and Hammerstein office.

Bennett Cerf, the publisher and compiler of humorous anecdotes, remembers Richard Rodgers as a boy. Cerf attended Columbia, where he was not only Mortimer's fraternity brother but also one of his closest friends. The first recollection Cerf has of Dick was seeing him try persistently to intrude into the living room when Mortimer was entertaining his friends, and being gruffly chased away. Then one summer in 1910 Cerf visited the Rodgerses at their Long Beach house. "The night I arrived in Long Beach I remember for two reasons," he has written in his column in the *Saturday Review*. "One, Morty's father was summoned to attend the ailing Miss Norma Talmadge, who represented for me at the time absolute perfection and the unattainable in woman-kind; and, too, the household was awakened in the middle of the night by a violent thunderstorm. At the height Dick appeared suddenly in pajamas, white as a sheet, and trembling with fear. 'What the blank are you doing here?' barked Morty with characteristic graciousness. 'I w-w-w-wanted to be sure you f-f-f-fellows were O.K.,' quavered Dick."

Dick was about nine years old when he started inventing melodies of his own. He would sit at the piano and for hours at a time would work out original tunes. His father's delight and pride in these sessions was immeasurable. He would often write little jingles which Dick set to music at the piano, and the excitement Dr. Rodgers exhibited would have done justice to a Mozart *père* seeing his *Wunderkind* writing a piano sonata. Whenever there were visitors at the Rodgers apartment, they would usually be treated (or subjected) to Dick's piano playing and improvisations. His mother, herself a fine pianist, was no less proud of Dick than her husband, but being a retiring person sometimes resented his father's making an exhibition of the boy. His father, however, refused to be denied his pleasure.

It was not long before Dick began putting his musical thoughts down on paper. He learned to write music the way he had learned to play the piano, partly by ear, partly by trial and error. His two years of piano study had taught him how to put down on paper a simple melody in a consistent tonality. For a while all he wrote down was the melodic line.

But this primitive practice soon displeased him, and before long he provided his simple tunes with equally simple chordal backgrounds. These chords he would first try out on the piano with the left hand, while the right traced the melody; when a chord pleased his ear, he would write it down.

Piano playing dominated Dick's time and interest when, in the summer of 1914, he went to Weingart's, a boy's summer camp in Highmount, New York. While he enjoyed swimming there, and was good enough in tennis to win a gold medal in a tournament, the piano seemed to have been his principal activity. This fact was noted in the *Weingart Review* of that summer. "We have quite a pianist in our midst, a noteless wonder," it remarked proudly. Then it went on to praise Rodgers in verse:

> Ragtime Dick is full of tune
> Ragtime bangs the box,
> He's always banging the thing for us,
> That's why he gets no knocks.

Dick wrote his first two complete songs—verse as well as chorus, harmony as well as melody—when he was fourteen. One was "Campfire Days," a camp song. This was written in the summer of 1916 at Camp Wigwam, in Harrison, Maine, where Rodgers was then spending the summer. (At one time or another, this camp was attended by many boys who later became celebrities—Arthur Loesser, the pianist; Richard Simon, the publisher; Mortimer J. Adler, the educator; Arthur Mendl, the musicologist.) The music counselor was Robert Lippmann, now a distinguished orthopedist, who influenced Dick strongly. Besides being exceedingly kind and friendly, and possessed of the tact to treat Dick as an equal, Lippmann played the piano beautifully—and for all these reasons Dick admired him profoundly. It was Lippmann who urged Dick to write his first complete song. The lyric was

typically corny ("Campfire days, campfire days, cheery old
pals around the blaze"); and so is the melody, which Dr.
William Rodgers faithfully preserved in his scrapbook.

Rodgers' second song was "The Auto Show Girl," lyrics by
David Dyrenforth. Rodgers no longer remembers under what
circumstances he came to write it. In any event, the song was
not only written but even multigraphed for private distribution, and a few copies are still around. It is a bouncy tune in
the style of the one-steps then so popular; surprise chromaticisms and sudden changes of key without proper transitions
provide interest to an otherwise stereotyped tune.

In February, 1916, Rodgers entered Townsend Harris
Hall, a high school affiliated with the College of the City of
New York. Since this school compressed the usual four-year
high school curriculum into three, its scholastic requirements
were of the highest, and the most exacting demands were
made of the students. Rodgers was either unwilling or unable to meet such demands. He did much better outside the
classroom than in it. He was a good swimmer who, in February, won first place in a novice meet held by the New York
Athletic Club. He was also liked well enough by his fellow
students to receive two elective posts at school—one term as
corresponding secretary of the athletic association, the other
term as treasurer of the General Organization.

After a year at Townsend Harris Hall, Rodgers transferred to De Witt Clinton High School. It was then that he
made important contacts with the world of serious music.
One day at school he described to Mr. Clark, his English
teacher, his reaction to his first visit to the opera a few years
earlier, when his grandmother had taken him to the Metropolitan to see *Carmen* with Caruso and Farrar. "What I saw
there was not only the stage," he told Mr. Clark, "always
enough to make me wide-eyed, but the stage combined with
some of the most wonderful music and singing I had ever

heard. I left the opera house as if I had been hit by a sledge-hammer." Mr. Clark told Rodgers that on Saturday evenings the Metropolitan Opera presented performances with regular casts but at popular prices. Encouraged by his teacher, Rodgers bought a Saturday evening subscription for $17.00 and, during the 1918-1919 season, went to the opera every Saturday evening.

His first association with serious orchestral music came about a year after that. He took a girl on a date to the Capitol Theatre, which had then been recently opened as a new movie palace. One of the theater's attractions was a large symphony orchestra, providing background music for the motion picture. "Wouldn't it be wonderful," Rodgers asked his friend, "if there were not movies here at all, and one could just listen to the music?" The girl explained as tactfully as she could that there actually was such a place in New York and that its name was Carnegie Hall.

Rodgers soon began visiting the auditorium regularly to hear orchestral performances by the New York Philharmonic Orchestra under Josef Stransky and the New York Symphony Society under Walter Damrosch. One concert is still vivid in his memory: that of the New York Philharmonic with Josef Hofmann as soloist in the Tchaikovsky B-flat Minor Piano Concerto. Rodgers was in the standing-room section behind the parquet seats when he heard the concerto's first majestic chords, Hofmann's tone and sonority as rich and vibrant as those of a pipe organ. "I suddenly felt so weak that if I hadn't been holding on to the rail at the time I probably would have fallen down." For years after that, whenever he heard those opening measures he always recalled the way Hofmann played them that day.

His musical life now became a dichotomy. Serious music was relegated to his listening experiences and popular music to his creative. He came to love serious music deeply—most of all the works of Beethoven, Bach, Mozart, Brahms, and Chopin. But once away from the concert hall, his musical interest embraced only the popular music of the day. "I just never felt the urge to write serious piano pieces or orchestral works," he explains. "That kind of melody simply did not come to me when I started writing."

And the writing of popular songs was a major occupation. Sometimes Mortimer wrote the lyrics for him, sometimes his father, most often friends of the family.

Then came Rodgers' first chance to write a score for a musical comedy. Mortimer belonged to a neighborhood boys' athletic group, the Akron Club, which in 1917 decided to produce an original musical in order to contribute to the "Tobacco Fund" then being raised by the New York *Sun* for men in the service. One of the members, Ralph G. Engelsman, wrote book and lyrics; Milton Bender, an outsider, was asked to stage and produce it. At this point Mortimer suggested that his brother Dick be recruited to provide the music. Some of the members protested, feeling that a fifteen-year-old boy was too young to be entrusted with such an important assignment. Nevertheless, Dick was finally chosen. He contributed seven numbers. One was his first creation, "The Auto Show Girl." Six others were written directly for the production, one of them being a gay, sophisticated little number, "The Vampire Song."

The writing of these seven songs, plus having them sung in a show, was not enough for young Rodgers. With a drive and a determination for success which were henceforth to characterize him, he felt impelled to try to get them published. Through the mother of one of his girl friends he managed to get an introduction to Max Dreyfus, head of the publishing house of Harms and a major power in Tin Pan Alley. When Dick finished playing his songs for him, Dreyfus asked him,

"What do you do besides writing songs?" The fifteen-year-old composer explained he was attending De Witt Clinton High School. "Then," Dreyfus added icily, "I strongly suggest you go back to school, for that's where you belong." Dreyfus subsequently reversed this frigid reaction; he later became Rodgers' publisher, partner, and lifelong friend.

Just before the Akron Club performance, someone suggested that the songs be printed and sold in the lobby. The idea was at first quickly rejected. Some of the boys argued that if Max Dreyfus did not find them good enough to publish, why then should the public want to buy them? When Dr. Rodgers offered to pay the cost of multigraphing, about twenty-five dollars, the opposition crumbled. These copies sold well enough not only to restore to Dr. Rodgers his initial investment but also to realize a little profit.

The Akron Club show, *One Minute Please,* was given in the grand ballroom of the Hotel Plaza on December 29, 1917. This was one of the coldest days in New York history, several degrees below zero. That afternoon the New York *Sun* ran a special article entreating its readers to support the production in spite of the freezing weather. By curtain time only a scattered handful was in the audience, and the rise of the curtain was delayed. But by 9 P.M. the ballroom was filled up. The show was a great success—and so were Rodgers' songs. Each was roundly applauded, and after the performance not only the friends of the Rodgers family but many strangers came up to him to congratulate him warmly. The Akron Club was able to contribute about three thousand dollars to the New York *Sun* fund.

This assignment for the Akron Club led Rodgers to write music for a second amateur show, *Up Stage and Down,* given in the grand ballroom of the Waldorf-Astoria on March 8, 1919, for the benefit of the Infants Relief Society. Several members of the club were in the cast, and Dick himself conducted. This was Rodgers' first experience with the baton. Since he had never studied conducting, he performed mostly by ear and through an innate feeling for rhythm. He beat the simple time values of his songs methodically and accurately, and the instrumentalists and singers followed him easily. (He never did study conducting; he finally acquired both a consummate command of baton technique and a sure ability to convey his interpretative demands to players and singers through his remarkable ability to learn quickly from direct experience.)

Rodgers' score comprised twenty numbers. Two were outstanding for their delightful lyricism: "Love Me by Parcel Post," lyrics by Mortimer, and "Prisms, Plums and Prunes," lyrics by Benjamin Kaye, a close friend of the Rodgers family. All the others were just run-of-the-mill. About two months later, this same show, renamed *Twinkling Eyes,* came to the 44th Street Theatre under the auspices of the Brooklyn Y.M.H.A., the proceeds going to the Soldiers and Sailors Welfare Fund.

From a practical point of view, Rodgers' first two shows did nothing to advance his career, since they went completely unnoticed by professional music circles. But even though Rodgers had a sound appreciation for practical values and the importance of commercial success, he was not disappointed. He now felt he was a composer, a composer of two musical shows, no less (even though amateur productions), which had played in such places as the Hotel Plaza, the Waldorf-Astoria, and the 44th Street Theatre before audiences numbering several thousand. Success, he felt confidently, was around the next corner.

4

"A CAREER, A PARTNER, A BEST FRIEND"

The scores for his two amateur shows had completely won both the confidence and the admiration of the members of the Akron Club for young Dick Rodgers. One of these members was particularly enthusiastic about him. This was Philip Leavitt, son of a successful paint merchant, and in 1917 and 1918 Mortimer's classmate at Columbia College. "I liked those early Rodgers songs so much—they all fell so pleasantly on the ear—that I learned them all and can still sing them to you," Leavitt recalls today.

In an effort to advance Rodgers' career, Leavitt one day tried to convince the young composer that it would be to his advantage to establish a permanent working arrangement with some gifted lyricist instead of haphazardly setting to music any lyric that happened to come along. When Dick proved sympathetic, Leavitt told him that he had such a man in mind. His name was Lorenz Hart. Leavitt had known him for many years and had always regarded him highly for his deftness in writing verses and for his trenchant intellect. Leavitt went on to explain that Hart was a lyricist in search of a composer.

One Sunday afternoon in 1918, Leavitt brought Rodgers to Hart's brownstone house on 59 West 119th Street in Harlem. Lorenz opened the door for them and ushered them into the overstuffed Victorian living room. Hart was one of the shortest men Rodgers had ever seen. He was only five feet tall, and his feet and fingers were as tiny as those of a child. A normal-sized head gave him the appearance of being deformed. But he had a handsome face, with deeply set, intense eyes, delicate lips that frequently broke into an ingratiating smile, and an impressively high forehead.

At first Rodgers was self-conscious in Hart's presence, painfully aware of the gulf that separated them. Hart was a young man of twenty-three whereas Rodgers was a boy of sixteen. Hart had already left Columbia College, after spending three years there, and was a professional writer who earned money translating foreign operettas for the Shuberts. Richard, on the other hand, was a high-school boy, still to earn his first dollar. To Rodgers, Hart seemed a man of the world, a man who smoked, drank liquor, had been to Europe, had played in one of his own skits in a Columbia varsity show Rodgers had seen, and whose conversation betrayed a vast cultural background as well as an impressive experience in living. The cynicism and wit with which Hart always flavored his remarks contributed further to his worldly airs.

Hart's cat, Bridget, strolled into the room. Hart made a wisecrack, Rodgers laughed—and the ice was broken. From that moment on, they hit it off remarkably well. At that they had several things in common. Lorenz had once attended De Witt Clinton High School briefly and had been a pupil at

Weingart's Institute, at whose summer camp Dick had spent a season. But binding them even closer together than such coincidences was the fact that both were in love with the "Princess Theatre Shows." Larry could sing Jerome Kern's songs by the dozen, verses as well as choruses, the unfamiliar tunes as well as the popular ones. And Larry, like Dick, was a devotee of the opera.

Their mutual admiration and respect increased when Dick played some of his melodies for Hart and Hart read some of his verses to Rodgers. Hart liked the easy way Rodgers had with a pleasing melody and said so; and to Rodgers, Hart's lyrics were a revelation. As they discussed the problems of song writing, Hart vigorously denounced the then current lyrics with their sloppy versification, sophomoric diction, clichés, maudlin sentiments, hackneyed verbiage. He wondered why it was not possible to write a lyric with the meticulous care, good taste, refinement and verbal sensitivity that a good poet brings to a poem. "I heard for the first time," Rodgers recalls, "of interior rhymes, feminine rhymes, false rhymes. I listened with astonishment as he launched a diatribe against songwriters who had small intellectual equipment and less courage, the boys who failed to take every advantage of every opportunity to inch a little further into territory hitherto unexplored in lyric writing."

Then and there both of them reached the decision to work together. As Rodgers left Hart's house and walked down the street he kept telling himself, "I have a lyricist. I have a lyricist." Actually, though he hardly knew it at the time, he had found in Hart much more than a collaborator. "In one afternoon, I acquired a career, a partner, a best friend—and a source of permanent irritation."

Like Rodgers, Hart came from a middle-class family. His father, Max Hart, was a promoter whose interests through the years covered coal mines, railroads, and real estate. A short, heavily built man, he was an earthy character who drank heavily, cursed heartily, enjoyed Rabelaisian humor, and liked noisy parties. His wife Frieda (née Isenberg) was, by contrast, as petite and exquisitely pretty as a Dresden figurine. Lorenz was their first child. He was born in an apartment on 111th Street near Lexington Avenue in New York on May 2, 1895. A second son, Teddy, came two years later.

In 1904, the Harts acquired the brownstone house on 119th Street in Harlem which remained their home for about a quarter of a century. The house became famous for its conviviality. There were always large crowds there, and gay all-night parties. Liquor flowed generously, for the Hart cellar was always well stocked. (The father early taught Larry to be a drinker and thus, innocently, set the stage for his son's final destruction.) And wherever Max was there too could be found an inexhaustible repertoire of bawdy tales. The overcrowded living room sometimes included people from the theater. Teddy Hart recalls an evening when Lillian Russell was a Sunday evening guest.

The Hart family prided itself on being directly descended on the father's side from Heinrich Heine, the German lyric poet. But of all the Harts only Lorenz showed his famous ancestor's influence. Max, while possessing a keen mind for business and even for law, which he studied by himself, was actually a coarse, uncouth personality impervious to culture. (Though he tried to conceal it, Lorenz was always a little ashamed of his father, just as he was excessively fond of his mother.)

Teddy, from childhood on, hated the smell of school and books and was a perpetual problem to his teachers. Larry, however, was of a different stripe. Without direction or encouragement he became, even as a boy, an omnivorous reader

—his favorites always being the classics. By the time he was ten he could quote poetry by the stanza and Shakespeare by the page. He would spend half the night reading. At school he was excellent in all subjects and especially brilliant in languages. But he was no grind. An alert and spongelike intelligence enabled him to learn with facility and to retain what he learned. Except for a brief stay at De Witt Clinton High School, his elementary and secondary schooling took place in private schools: at the Weingart Institute on 120th Street and then at Columbia Grammar School.

He was interested in arts other than literature too. In his early teens he started going regularly to the opera. Through his real-estate interests, his father came to know Oscar Hammerstein I, the distinguished opera impresario, who provided him with tickets for the Manhattan Opera House. Larry, who used the tickets, thus came to know the French and Italian repertory and to admire stars like Mary Garden, Tetrazzini, and Bonci. Operas in a lighter vein—the comic operas of Gilbert and Sullivan, and later the musical comedies of Jerome Kern—became his passion, too.

He was also a devout theatergoer. He saw his first play when he was seven at the German Theatre on 14th Street. After that he frequently went to the Star Theatre on 107th Street, where melodramas were featured. His interest in the stage made it impossible for him to remain merely a passive spectator. On one of his birthdays he was given a toy theater, the first of several. This instantly became his favorite plaything, for he was now able to contrive little plays of his own invention and to produce them the way they were being done at the Star. The toy theater gave him the idea of entertaining his friends in his living room (one-man routines) with his own material. (He remained an acting "ham" ever after; a natural and effective performer, he enjoyed to the full singing his own songs for his friends.)

The streets in Harlem in the early 1910's seemed to swarm with children who later became famous in the theater. Hart came to know a few of them well. Herbert Fields not only lived near Hart but, in the summer of 1910, also was his partner in producing shows at Camp Paradox, which both attended. Herbert was the son of the veteran showman Lew Fields, who for a generation had been the partner in the celebrated burlesque team of Weber and Fields. Others with whom Hart played on 119th Street were Morrie Ryskind and Edwin Justus Mayer, both of whom became playwrights, and the brothers Herman and Joseph Mankiewicz, who became famous in Hollywood.

In 1913, after a holiday in Europe with his family, Larry entered Columbia College. There his preoccupation with literature, poetry, and the theater took precedence over all other studies and led him, after a single year, to transfer to the school of journalism, even though he had no intention of becoming a newspaperman. He was already writing smart little verses which he circulated in and out of class among such friends as Howard Dietz, Morrie Ryskind, and Irwin Edman—later famous as lyricist, musical-comedy librettist, and philosopher, respectively. One of Hart's professors, Walter B. Pitkin, thought highly of his work, particularly of a revealing study of Charles Chaplin which Professor Pitkin read in class as an example of astute critical analysis. Other professors were less enthusiastic. For one of them Hart had written on assignment a portrait of the Lew Fields family. The opening paragraph represented a negation of good journalistic practice. "Mr. Hart," the professor said sternly, "this is not newspaper prose!" From across the room came Hart's high-pitched query: "Poetry maybe?"

Actually, as he himself once said, what he majored in at Columbia was not literature or journalism—but varsity shows. The annual Columbia Varsity Show was an institution toward which most undergraduate writers, actors, and composers aspired. The basic theme of each production might vary yearly, but the main center of interest of each remained the same: men dressed up and acting like girls. Hart's first association with the show—in 1915 and 1916—was as a female impersonator. In 1915, for *On Your Way,* he wrote a skit satirizing Mary Pickford in which he played the part of the movie queen. One year later he was seen as a flirtatious maid in *Peace Pirates.*

He left Columbia in 1917 without a degree, impatient for a career in the theater. For several summers he went to Brant Lake Camp, a boys' summer camp, where he helped Arthur Schwartz (later to become a famous popular composer) produce the shows. One of the songs which Schwartz wrote at this time to Hart's words became famous several years later; with a new set of lyrics by Howard Dietz, it became "I Guess I'll Have to Change My Plan," introduced by Clifton Webb in the *Third Little Show.*

Hart was twenty-three, still drifting aimlessly in theatrical waters and seeking a harbor, when he met Richard Rodgers. For all his outward worldly airs and sophistication, apparent intellectual self-assurance and *savoir-faire,* he was really uncertain of himself and his direction. Nor did he realize that this casual Sunday afternoon meeting with a sixteen-year-old composer was to prove the turning point in his life.

When Rodgers confided to Mortimer and Bennett Cerf that he was about to collaborate with Hart, both did their best to discourage him. They said they knew Hart well, that he was shiftless, disorganized, and undependable. "He'll never amount to anything," Cerf said, "and neither will you if you hang around him." Dick said nothing, but, as Cerf remembers, "there was a look in his eye that seemed to tell both of us where we could go."

In any event—and in spite of well-intentioned advice—Rodgers started working at once with Hart. In a few weeks they completed about fifteen songs. Sometimes they worked at the Rodgers apartment but mostly (in deference to Hart's seniority) in the Hart living room. They would first sit around for several hours exchanging ideas for possible songs. Most frequently the melody came first. Dick would sit at the piano tossing off melodies. When one struck Larry's fancy, he would have Dick repeat it several times until some catching poetic line or phrase came to mind.

Of these songs, Hart was partial to a piece called "Venus," while Dick favored something called "Little Girl, Little Boy," a sweet and sentimental tune which he still recalls nostalgically. But both Rodgers and Hart agreed on the merits of "Any Old Place with You." Hart felt that he had arrived at a lyric that was smart and glib, moved gracefully, and was thoroughly adult:

> I've got a mania for Pennsylvania
>   Even ride in London hacks,
> I'll call each dude a pest, you like in Budapest
>   Oh, for far Peru!
> I'd go to hell for ya, or Philadelphia
>   Any old place with you!

Dick was proud of the secondary seventh chords which he rightly felt gave his melody an arresting dash; and he experienced the excitement of a pioneer in defying the standard practice of preceding a thirty-two bar chorus with a sixteen-bar verse by reversing this procedure.

"Any Old Place with You" carried Rodgers and Hart for the first time into the professional theater. Once again it was Philip Leavitt who was the catalyzing agent. Having successfully brought Rodgers and Hart together, and seen them enter into a permanent working arrangement, Leavitt now hoped to become a liaison agent between the song writers and a professional theatrical manager. One of Leavitt's intimate friends was Lew Fields, who was also his neighbor in Far Rockaway, where the Leavitts were spending the summer of 1919. Fields, after having made theatrical history with Weber, had since 1915 been producing musical comedies, in some of which he himself starred, and some of which he wrote.

Leavitt arranged for Rodgers to visit the Lew Fields summer place on Franklin Avenue in Far Rockaway one Sunday afternoon in 1919. Almost every account of this meeting reports that Hart went with Rodgers—an expected circumstance since Hart was a good friend of Herbert Fields, and since Hart liked singing his songs with Rodgers at the piano. But to the best recollection of not only Rodgers himself but also of Herbert Fields and his sister Dorothy, both of whom were present at the meeting, Rodgers went alone. And it was he who sang his own songs while accompanying himself on the piano.

Lew Fields praised some of Rodgers' songs. Then he announced undemonstratively that he would put "Any Old Place with You" in one of his shows. Leaving the Fields house somewhat dizzy with success, Rodgers rushed to the nearest telephone to relay the good news to his father. In an attitude that was now customary with him, he began his conversation in a facetious vein. "Father," he said, "I have some *terrible* news to tell you." Then, after a dramatic moment's pause, he broke the news that Fields was taking his song for his show. Dr. William Rodgers answered sternly: "Never again, as long as you live, begin a telephone conversation with 'I have some terrible news to tell you,' even if this is actually the case." Then, having duly admonished Dick, he could freely share his delight.

"Any Old Place with You" was interpolated into *A Lonely*

Romeo, then running at the Casino Theatre, on the evening of August 26, 1919, sung by Eve Lynn and Alan Hale. This not only became Rodgers' first song heard in the professional theater, but also the first to be published commercially. Remick, Lew Fields' publisher, issued it in 1919. "What I earned from both the performance and the publication couldn't buy me a suit, but the appearance of one of my songs in a Broadway show was certainly a big moment in my life."

Rodgers and Hart worked on a complete score together for the first time for one of the Columbia varsity shows.

Columbia became the logical choice for Rodgers when—after a summer session in 1919 to acquire enough entrance credits—he had to select a college. Both his brother and his collaborator had attended Columbia. But more significant still was the fact that Columbia was the place where varsity shows were put on annually by student talent. And, already, Dick had set his heart on writing the music for one of these shows.

In 1915 Mortimer had taken Dick to see one of these varsity shows, *On Your Way,* in which Larry Hart did his take-off of Mary Pickford and in which Oscar Hammerstein II sang some songs and acted in some comedy sequences. In one of the latter, Hammerstein was a long-haired poet *à la* Bunthorne in Gilbert and Sullivan's *Patience.* After the show, while the floor was being cleared for dancing, Mortimer introduced his brother to Hammerstein, explaining that the boy wrote songs. "As we were being introduced," recalls Hammerstein, "I noted with satisfaction young Richard's respectful awe in the presence of a college junior whom he had just seen playing one of the chief parts in the Varsity Show. I, too, was conscious of my current glory, and, realizing what a treat it must be for a child to meet me, I was my most gracious and courteous self—a man about nineteen trying to be man about town. . . . In my memory of him, during this period he wore short pants. He tells me now that by that time he had already put on long pants. This impression—or illusion—is never quite absent from my current conception of him. Behind the sometimes too serious face of an extraordinarily talented composer and a sensationally successful theatrical producer, I see a dark-eyed little boy in short pants. The frequent overlapping of these two pictures is an element in what I consider to be my sound understanding of Dick and my affection for him."

Hammerstein adds that, soon after this first meeting, he saw Richard Rodgers at the fraternity house and heard him play some of his tunes on the old battered piano there. But Hammerstein is mistaken; actually this happened a few years later, after Dick had entered Columbia and joined the fraternity.

A month or so after Dick entered Columbia College, in the fall of 1919, an announcement appeared in the *Columbia Spectator* calling for student scripts for the following year's varsity show. Rodgers and Hart met at Philip Leavitt's house to discuss possible ideas. Herbert Fields (though he was not a Columbia man) was also there to join the discussions and to contribute some useful suggestions. At last, Rodgers and Hart worked out a complete play—text, lyrics, and music—which they submitted to a Players Committee comprising Richard Conried (son of the onetime Metropolitan Opera impresario Heinrich Conried), Ray Perkins, and Oscar Hammerstein II. The committee agreed that all of Rodgers' music, and most of Hart's lyrics and dialogue, were acceptable. However, it had a suggestion to make regarding the book. It had considered a second entry, by Milton Kroop, a satire on Bolshevism called *Fly with Me*, set on a Soviet island in 1970. The committee proposed that this script be combined with that of Rodgers and Hart; that all of the Rodgers and Hart songs be adapted for the new play. In revising Kroop's play to suit the new requirements, Hart had some assistance from Leavitt; then Hart revised his own lyrics to meet the new material. However, all of Rodgers' music was retained. The new show now received the unanimous approval of the committee. In accepting Rodgers' contribution, the committee broke tradition: this was the first time that the work of a freshman had been accepted.

Fly with Me was given the first of several performances in the grand ballroom of the Hotel Astor on March 24, 1920. Dick conducted. His score had thirteen numbers, all published by William R. Stewart. One, "Peek in Pekin," had a delightful Oriental tang; another, "Gone Are the Days," was a slick patter song; a third, "Moonlight and You," had touches of winsome sentimentality. All in all this was a skillful score filled with catchy tunes—a fact duly noted by a well-known newspaper columnist, S. Jay Kaufman, in *The Globe* on March 25. "Several of the tunes are capital," he wrote. "They have a really finished touch and will, if transplanted, be whistled. We had not heard of Richard Rodgers before. We have a suspicion we shall hear of him again."

Lew Fields attended one of the performances of *Fly with Me* and announced that he was willing to use a few of the songs for his next Broadway musical. Fields, with George Campbell, had just written the text for a new show, *Poor Little Ritz Girl,* relating the adventures of a Southern belle in New York who had come to seek her fortune in the theater but who found it by marrying a wealthy bachelor. Fields planned to produce this play immediately and felt that some of the Columbia Varsity Show songs could fit in nicely. Fields knew his Broadway audiences and knew the kind of songs that had a direct and immediate appeal. The easy flow of Rodgers' melodies made for such an appeal. When he officially announced his intention of using Rodgers' music for his new play, Fields publicly expressed his enthusiasm for the young composer by telling an interviewer: "Rodgers has real talent. I think that within a few years he will be in a class by himself."

Poor Little Ritz Girl opened at the Central Theatre on July 28, 1920, the cast including Eleanor Griffith, Charles Purcell, Andrew Tombes, and Lulu McConnell. During that summer, Rodgers and Herbert Fields were working as counselors at Camp Paradox. Both received special permission to go to New York for the première. For Rodgers this première was not the unmixed blessing he had expected. He had come believing the whole score was his. Only after arriving in the theater and glancing through the program did he learn to his chagrin that only seven of the fifteen numbers in the play were his. The other eight were by a veteran of Shubert musicals and operettas, Sigmund Romberg.

Nevertheless, Rodgers' official initiation as a Broadway composer went off well. The critics liked the show. The New York *World* said that it had "a real plot, humor, a good-looking chorus, and a tuneful score . . . so dexterously blended that the farce did not interfere with the musical comedy and the musical numbers are never allowed to interfere with the progress of the plot." H. T. Parker, the eminent music and drama critic of the Boston *Transcript,* had some particularly kind words for Rodgers' music (even though he seemed to detect in one of the songs a suspicious hint of Offenbach's "Barcarolle" from *The Tales of Hoffmann*). Mr. Parker wrote: "He writes uniformly with a light hand; now and then with neat modulations or pretty turns of ornament; here and there with a clear sensibility to instrumental voices; and once again with a hint of grace and fancy."

Poor Little Ritz Girl ran for 119 performances and netted a profit to its producer, launching the career of Rodgers and Hart on Broadway with a hit, even if only a modest one.

5

AMATEUR KNIGHTS

A song in one Broadway show, half a score of another, was a creditable beginning for a professional career in the theater. Unfortunately, however, these songs failed to make any impression upon those who were in a position to advance Rodgers in his career. However much Rodgers and Hart tried to break down the indifference of producers and music publishers by repeatedly bringing them their new songs, all these important people of the theater ignored them with disconcerting unanimity.

After their first success it was five years before Rodgers and Hart appeared again in the professional theater. Meanwhile they took on any assignment that came along. Some of Rodgers' activity, without Hart's assistance, was directed toward the musical shows the Akron Club was now producing regularly. *You'd Be Surprised,* an extravaganza, facetiously subtitled "An Atrocious Musical Comedy," book by Milton Bender, was presented at the Hotel Plaza on March 6, 1920, the cast including Dorothy Fields, for whom Dick was now beginning to have romantic leanings. Rodgers' score had "Mary, Queen of Scots," fetchingly sung by Dorothy Fields, a number soon to be lifted for *Poor Little Ritz Girl;* also a song with a fragile lyrical line and unusual modulations, particularly in the verse—"Princess of the Willow Tree," lyrics by Bender.

In 1921 the Akron Club again called on Rodgers, this time for an ambitious undertaking. Each year, the Brooklyn department store Oppenheim Collins presented a vaudeville show for its employees at the Brooklyn Academy of Music. An enterprising parent of one of the members of the Akron Club sold the idea to the department store that the club should put on one of its shows for the store. Half of the program was assigned to the club, the other half was still to consist of vaudeville entertainment. Since Oppenheim Collins paid a fee, the Akron Club could afford to reimburse its writers, and at one of the club meetings the decision was reached to pay $250.00 each to Rodgers and Hart for writing the songs, and an additional $250.00 to Herbert Fields for directing the production.

The show, *Say Mama,* came to the Brooklyn Academy of Music on February 10, 1921, and two days later was repeated at the Hotel Plaza for the benefit of the Akron Club itself. Of the sixteen numbers by Rodgers and Hart, three aroused interest because of their jaunty, sophisticated air: "Chorus Girl Blues," "Watch Yourself," and "Wake Up, Priscilla." "Mr. Rodgers," reported the *Theatre World* of March, 1921, "will some day be among our great composers."

Although *Say Mama* was the last Akron Club show in which Rodgers had a hand, his association with the club has continued up to the present time. Once every five years the club holds a reunion at the Hotel Plaza. Rodgers attends these reunions faithfully. One of their attractions is to have Rodgers sit at the piano and evoke nostalgic memories of the past by playing many of the songs he wrote long ago for the old club shows.

Say Mama was an event of some consequence in Rodgers' career because it marked the first occasion in which Herbert Fields collaborated actively with him and Hart; and it was with the cooperation of Fields that Rodgers and Hart were soon to achieve their first significant triumphs on Broadway.

Herbert Fields was two years younger than Hart, five years older than Rodgers. From his famous father he had inherited a love for the theater and the determination to make it his lifework. But originally his ambition lay not in writing or producing but in acting. He had an appealing stage presence and a flair for dialect roles that encouraged his father to find for him a minor role in *A Lonely Romeo* and a few other plays.

Herbert Fields, as we have seen, had known Hart from boyhood on, had collaborated with him on camp shows. Fields came to know Rodgers well immediately after their first meeting in Far Rockaway. But the idea that the three might work together did not materialize for several months. One night in 1919, at Larry Hart's house, Rodgers asked Fields, "Why do you want to be an actor? You can't sing and you aren't too handsome. You'll end up as you began— in bit parts. Now if you were to write a book for a musical comedy, with us doing the songs, then we might all get somewhere quick." The fact that Fields had never before written for the theater was immediately brushed aside as irrelevant. In all candor it should be said that this faith in Fields' literary potential was dictated by expediency. Rodgers and Hart felt that if Fields were to collaborate with them on a musical comedy then it might be possible to get his father to produce and finance the show.

Their first opus, an extravaganza called *Winkle Town,* was hopefully submitted to Lew Fields, who read the book patiently, listened to the songs, and firmly rejected it. Several other producers were approached; none of them was impressed. Only Laurence Schwab of the producing firm of Schwab and Mandel saw enough promise in Rodgers' music to ask him to come down to Max Dreyfus' office for a professional opinion. Dreyfus, in this second meeting with the young composer, was hardly more encouraging than he had been before. "There's nothing here," he said curtly when Rodgers finished playing and singing his music. Then with a callous disregard for Rodgers' presence, he tried to interest Schwab in another composer "who can *really* write music" —a young and then still unknown hopeful by the name of Vincent Youmans.

It is not easy to understand, nor can Max Dreyfus explain today, why he was unable to discover in Rodgers' early songs the composer's future potential. In the best songs there was enough originality of approach and technique to suggest an alert creative mind, and the lyricism was both fresh and inventive. Dreyfus' keen scent for latent talent had in the past enabled him to discover such major composers as Rudolf Friml, Jerome Kern, and George Gershwin among others; but that scent had failed him in the case of Rodgers. Not until Rodgers first became successful was Dreyfus to be won over to the composer—and in one instance to a song he had previously dismissed.

In a last desperate effort to salvage *Winkle Town,* Rodgers and Hart called on Oscar Hammerstein II to help them; by now Oscar was working in the professional theater for his producer-uncle, Arthur. When Hammerstein told them as gently as he could that there was nothing he could contribute to the play, Rodgers and Hart finally resigned themselves to the disagreeable fact that their first shot had been a dud.

A feeling of dissatisfaction with himself and his slow progress as a professional composer; the immediate impact of his disappointment in *Winkle Town;* finally, the influence of one of his girl friends, who one day convinced him he should return to the study of music—all these combined to bring about a major decision. Rodgers was to abandon his current musical activities, leave Columbia College for good, and concentrate on a formal musical education. When he conveyed this decision to his father, he argued that he felt he was wasting his time at Columbia on subjects like mathematics and history, which had no interest for him, when what he really wanted and needed was to acquire the basic tools of his trade. "If that's what you feel you must do, then you must proceed to do it," his father told him. Though Richard Rodgers is convinced his father was in full sympathy with his own plan—and though his father had made every effort to convince his son of his enthusiasm for it—the older man was nevertheless deeply disturbed. For some time now he had been confiding to his friends his doubts about the wisdom of allowing Dick to drift along aimlessly in music instead of channeling him into another direction. The doctor was too soundly practical and valued material things too highly not to ask himself whether, now that Dick was no longer a boy, he should not compel his son to abandon music for a more profitable and secure profession. Yet he was also a man of strong principles. Dick's passion for music making was unmistakable, and Dr. Rodgers believed implicitly in his son's right to choose his own future. Wisely, he never gave Dick any inkling of his doubts and concern when he consented to Dick's leaving Columbia and enrolling at the Institute of Musical Art.

Dick's two-years stay at the Institute was to prove an unforgettable experience. It gave him a lift he needed badly at the time. More important still it provided him with the basic tools of his profession, which he was to acquire for the first time. Up to now instinct and experiment had served him in his harmonization and instrumentation, and had led him to make only elementary use of these sciences. His studies at the Institute were to give him the materials which henceforth would enable him to bring plan and design to his musical writing. He was in these two years transformed from an apprentice and amateur into a trained musician. At the Institute he developed a new spaciousness of form which would soon enhance a song like "Gilding the Guild," the new agility of rhythm soon to be found in "The Girl Friend," the new and calculated effects in melodic writing through unusual intervals soon to appear in "Here in My Arms." Thus in two years was his musical talent permanently deepened and enriched.

His studies at the Institute also opened up for him new and wonderful vistas of musical appreciation. Teachers like Percy Goetschius in harmony, George Wedge in ear training, and Henry Krehbiel in music history brought new point and meaning to the music he heard. He still remembers the overpowering emotional effect derived from a Beethoven concert after he had attended a Beethoven lecture by Krehbiel, for Krehbiel's analysis had suddenly brought him a new understanding of Beethoven's thematic and architectonic construction. "I get a little religious about the whole thing," Rodgers says in recalling this period of his life.

While attending the Institute, Dick had a hand in three of its musical productions. The first, on June 1, 1921, was *Say It with Jazz*, a take-off on Rimsky-Korsakov's *Le Coq d'or*, highlighting a battle between jazz and classical music. Except for two songs by William Kroll and Gerald Warburg, both to become respected musicians, Dick was not only responsible for the complete score but also for the stage direction. On June 2, 1922, *Jazz à la Carte* was produced at the Institute; on May 31, 1923, *A Danish Yankee in King Tut's Court.* In the stage direction of the last, Rodgers was helped out by Herbert Fields.

Rodgers was also active outside the Institute. In 1922, he took a leave of absence from the school to tour the Shubert vaudeville circuit as conductor of a tabloid musical produced by Lew Fields, *Snapshots of 1922.* In the same year he also wrote a few songs for Laurence Houseman's *The Chinese Lantern,* presented by the dramatic art class of the Benjamin School for Girls, a private school then attended by Dorothy Fields. And early in 1923 he contributed three numbers to the Columbia Varsity Show, *Half Moon Inn.*

He left the Institute of Musical Art in June, 1923. He was gone but not forgotten. Throughout 1924, *The Baton* —the Institute newspaper—carried a series of satirical sketches by Rodgers about musical prodigies entitled "The Diary of a Prodigy."

After Rodgers left the Institute, his collaboration with Hart was continued. Sometimes with Herbert Fields, frequently without him, they wrote amateur shows for schools, churches, synagogues—for anybody who would promise a fee or extend the hope of opening a door to Broadway.

One of their assignments was to put on an entire show for the Benjamin School for Girls. This brought no fee, but Rodgers and Hart agreed they could use the school as a showcase to introduce their work to Broadway producers. They made a musical adaptation of J. H. McCarthy's romance about François Villon, *If I Were King,* and presented it at the Maxine Elliott Theatre on March 25, 1923.

Several important producers were invited. One of them approached Rodgers after the show to tell him how much he liked it and to inquire if he and Hart owned the musical adaptation rights. When Rodgers confessed he did not, the producer made a discreet exit. Sometime later, this producer made his own arrangements for the adaptation of *If I Were King* into an operetta—but with other writers. As *The Vagabond King,* music by Rudolf Friml, it was first seen at the Casino Theatre on September 21, 1925, and became a classic of the American operetta theater.

A similar experience occurred a second time the following year, and also at the Benjamin School. This time Rodgers and Hart adapted *The Prisoner of Zenda.* Shubert was so impressed that he bought the rights to Anthony Hope's novel for Sigmund Romberg. Renamed *Princess Flavia,* it was presented by the Shuberts at the Century Theatre on November 2, 1925.

The circuitous route to Broadway, then, was proving a dead-end street. Rodgers and Hart now decided on a more direct path. Calling in Herbert Fields as collaborator, they planned a comedy tailor-made for Lew Fields' gifts as an actor. They wrote a satire on Tin Pan Alley, with Lew Fields cast as a serious Austrian composer employed in Tin Pan Alley whose ambitious Dresden Sonata is revamped as "Moonlight Mama." (A second song in the show, "I'd Like to Poison Ivy," was also a parody of Tin Pan Alley methods.) Lew Fields tried out the play in Bethlehem, Pennsylvania, on March 24, 1924; in the cast he was joined by Sam White, Eva Puck, and in a minor role of a student violinist a young unknown by the name of Fredric March. The authorship of the play was credited to "Herbert Richard Lorenz," a pseudonym that succeeded in fooling nobody.

As *The Melody Man,* this show was launched at the Ritz Theatre on May 13. The critics were divided. Alexander

Woollcott liked the comic interludes, and Quinn Martin considered it one of the surprises of the season. Percy Hammond, on the other hand, thought it "feeble, immature, meandering," while John Corbin felt it could amuse only those who were easily amused. The "nays" won out. The play folded after only fifty-six performances—and Rodgers, Hart, and Fields were amateurs again.

6

SUCCESS

Dr. William Rodgers was growing increasingly impatient over his son. Dick was now twenty-two years old, subsisting on the small allowance his father was giving him. He gave no indication of making any headway with music or of even hoping to earn a living from it.

The father was torn between his idealistic desire to allow Dick to pursue his ambition without parental obstruction and a sound practical sense which dictated that he must compel his son to think of a way to prepare for the future. In this dilemma he sought out the advice of one of his patients, Benjamin Kaye, an attorney for a New York bank. Kaye had friends in the theater and enjoyed writing verses and sketches for it; he could perhaps provide some advice on the best course to follow regarding Dick.

One evening in 1924, Kaye came to the Rodgers apartment on 86th Street to discuss the problem with Dr. Rodgers. Kaye insisted that Dick had exceptional talent which must be allowed to develop; he also felt that eventually Dick might win for himself the same prestige and financial gains that men like Irving Berlin and Jerome Kern had acquired in Tin Pan Alley. It was Kaye's studied judgment that the *status quo* must be maintained. Dick must be allowed to proceed as he had done up to now, writing songs and trying to get them performed.

But Dr. Rodgers' anxiety was not relieved by Kaye's optimism, nor was he completely convinced by his friend's logic. Even after hearing Kaye's advice he felt Dick must now be made to seek a field other than music for his livelihood; a few years more might be too late.

What Dr. Rodgers did not know was that at this period Dick himself was tormented by doubts about his ability and by lack of faith in his future. His spirits were at their lowest ebb. The amateur shows were getting him nowhere. His few brief flurries on Broadway had failed to interest a single publisher or producer. Larry Hart had also lost courage and was beginning to talk of abandoning their collaboration for more fruitful endeavors. Discouraged and broke, Dick began suffering from insomnia, a condition that lasted almost a year and which he carefully concealed from his family.

At last Dick made up his mind. He would try to find a place in business. Through one of his friends he was able to contact a Mr. Marvin, a successful manufacturer of children's underwear. Marvin agreed to hire Rodgers as a salesman for $50.00 a week. If Rodgers showed any aptitude for business, Marvin promised he would then create a more responsible and better paying post for him in his organization.

Dick never did take on the job. A telephone call from Benjamin Kaye one Sunday evening brought him back into the theater even before he had had a chance to desert it.

All through the fall of 1924, Benjamin Kaye had been meeting with a group of youngsters who hung around the Theatre Guild and played bit parts in its productions. Now at Kaye's apartment in Greenwich Village, now at actress Edith Meiser's place on 72nd Street, Kaye and the youngsters discussed the idea of producing a small, sophisticated revue in the style of the *Grand Street Follies,* which was then drawing the carriage trade to downtown New York.

The first time they thought of such a revue was when they saw Sterling Holloway convulse parties with his imitations of Emily Stevens, then a Theatre Guild star in *Fata Morgana.* Holloway had other imitations, as well as ideas for smart skits—all of which, it was soon felt, could provide refreshing material for a revue. Among those who were consulted early in 1924 were Paul Moss and Benjamin Kaye, both of whom proved enthusiastic. Kaye could be particularly helpful since he liked writing sketches that satirized current plays.

By fall they had begun planning their revue seriously, and by the end of the year they had a practical reason for wanting to put on the production. The Theatre Guild had just built a new home on 52nd Street. Why not put on a show to raise funds for two tapestries for the theater? The youngsters, and Kaye with them, were certain they could get the co-operation of the Guild itself.

But the lack of a composer was a stumbling block. This problem was being discussed one Sunday evening at Kaye's apartment when Kaye suddenly suggested the name of Richard Rodgers. Kaye had been looking for some opportunity to advance Dick's career in the theater since speaking with Dr. Rodgers. An intimate revue sponsored by the Theatre Guild would be the opportunity he was looking for.

He telephoned Richard Rodgers at once. Rodgers told him of his plan to give up music for business, but Kaye, while sympathizing with Rodgers' feelings, carefully pointed out the advantages of working with a group of youngsters with fresh ideas and the courage of their youth; and of being associated, even if by remote control, with an organization like the Theatre Guild. "You can never tell what this sort of thing can lead to," he said over the phone. "Hop into a cab and come down here and let us tell you what we have in mind."

Rodgers came that evening, listened, and was won over. One of the youngsters, Edith Meiser, had some lyrics which could be used for songs and these Rodgers took home with him. A week later he called Kaye to say that, while he admired Edith Meiser's lyrics, he still preferred working with Larry Hart. If the group was willing to accept Hart as his lyricist he would be happy to work on the music.

Once Rodgers and Hart began to work on the new assignment, all thoughts Rodgers had of taking on a salesman's job vanished. In about two weeks they completed half a dozen numbers; an additional one, "Manhattan," was resurrected from their ill-fated *Winkle Town,* because both had always been partial to it. An appointment was then arranged for them to play the songs for Lawrence Langner and Theresa Helburn, directors of the Guild. Helburn clearly remembers the effect the songs made on her as, on the bare stage of the empty Garrick Theatre, Larry sang them to Richard's piano accompaniment. "Manhattan" made a particularly strong impression. The melody had sentiment without being sentimental, sweetness without being cloying. And the lyric was slick and smart.

> We'll go to Greenwich
> Where modern men itch
> To be free.
> And Bowling Green you'll see with me.

> Our future babies,
> We'll take to Abie's
> Irish Rose.
> I hope they'll live to see it close.

The songs decided Langner and Helburn to sponsor the project. They promised to provide the necessary financing—the total budget came to $5000.00—and to offer the free use of the Garrick Theatre for two Sunday performances.

Philip Loeb was chosen to produce, Herbert Fields to direct the dances, and Harold Clurman to serve as stage manager. The youngsters went to work with a will. The girls of the cast all helped to make the costumes, while the boys lent a hand in painting the scenery and building the sets. Several young writers (including Newman Levy and Morrie Ryskind) were invited to provide material to supplement some already written. When the cast was finally assembled it included not only those who had been among the first to conceive the project but also other fresh talent whose presence in the theater would someday be felt strongly: Romney Brent, June Cochrane, Betty Starbuck, Lee Strasberg, and Elisabeth (Libby) Holman.

To assist Rodgers in rehearsing the musical numbers, a young pianist named Margot Millham (now Margot Hopkins) was engaged. She was a pupil of Ernest Hutcheson. Margot visited Rodgers at his apartment for an interview; the composer played "Manhattan" for her and asked her if she could learn such a number quickly. Margot, possessed of a remarkable ear and memory, sat down at the piano and played the song with Rodgers' own harmonies. She was immediately engaged. This partnership has continued up to the present time. Through the years Margot has served as a pianist of Rodgers' music at rehearsals and various auditions, sometimes solo, sometimes with the composer at a second piano.

The revue, now officially called *The Garrick Gaieties,* was scheduled for two performances—a matinee and an evening— at the Garrick Theatre on Sunday, May 17, 1925. A modest admission price was charged, $2.00 for the orchestra, and $1.00 for the balcony; well before performance time the house was sold out. That first performance did not begin without incident. Before curtain time, the police appeared at the theater to stop the show on a complaint from the Sabbath League. Only after Benjamin Kaye had convinced the police that the show was being put on for charity and not for profit —benefit shows were permissible on Sundays—was the restriction removed.

A sprightly note in the program set the tone for the entire production. *"The Garrick Gaieties* is distinguished from all other organizations of the same character . . . in that it has neither principals nor principles. *The Garrick Gaieties* believe not only in abolishing the star system; they believe in abolishing the stars themselves. The members of *The Garrick Gaieties* are recruited, impressed, mobilized, or drafted from the ranks of *Caesar and Cleopatra, The Guardsman* . . . and other Theatre Guild productions—a few rank outsiders being permitted to appear; proving we do not intend to become a monopoly."

The production had vivacity, freshness, and the impertinence of youth.

> We like to serve a mild dish,
> Of folklore quaintly childish,
> Or something Oscar Wildeish,
> In pantomime or dance.
>
> Our one great contribution
> To art is revolution!
> Our mood is very "Roosh-in"
> You can tell it at a glance.

> Our bare stage may look funny,
> But it saves us lots of money
> And we know just what we do,
> Because we always take a chance!

So ran Hart's lines nimbly in the opening Rodgers and
Hart number, "Gilding the Guild." After that came a rapid
procession of funny skits, sparkling parodies, freshly conceived songs and dances. The parodies were on such current
productions as Michael Arlen's *The Green Hat* ("The Green
Derby"), Sidney Howard's *They Knew What They Wanted*
("They Didn't Know What They Were Getting"), and *Fata
Morgana* ("Fate in the Morning"). Among the skits and
sketches were a delightful imitation of the *diseuse* Ruth
Draper, by Hildegarde Halliday, and a hilarious comedy
about the New York police written by Newman Levy. The
seven Rodgers and Hart songs included two which became
standout hits: "Manhattan" (sung by June Cochrane and
Sterling Holloway) and "Sentimental Me" (Cochrane, Holloway, James Norris, and Edith Meiser). Rodgers and Hart
also introduced a one-act burlesque on opera in the jazz
idiom, with a department-store setting, called "The Joy
Spreader," the idea for which came from Gilbert Seldes.

The critics were enchanted. Alexander Woollcott described
it as "fresh and spirited and engaging . . . bright with the
brightness of something new minted." Robert Benchley said
it was "the most civilized show in town." Gilbert Gabriel
called it "a witty, boisterous, athletic chowchow."

The songs of Rodgers and Hart came in for special attention. To Gilbert Gabriel they were "fitting and enlivening"
and to Bernard Simon, "an irreverent revel." The critic of
the *Daily News* considered them "well above the average
Broadway product." "They clicked," commented a critic on

Variety, "like a colonel's heels at attention." The songs were published by Edward B. Marks, who announced in midsummer that the demand for the sheet music was unusually heavy.

The accolade of both the critics and the public encouraged the Guild to put on four additional performances in June, all matinees. All four performances sold out, even though an unprecedented heat wave then afflicted the city. It was apparent that the show had box-office attraction, a fact that led Rodgers to appeal to Theresa Helburn to put it on a regular run. Helburn was sympathetic, but she pointed out that *The Guardsman* was then running at the Garrick and she had no other house for their show. "Why not close down *The Guardsman?*" Rodgers asked as discreetly as he could. "I understand its weekly gross has fallen down to about five thousand dollars, and the *Gaieties* can easily do twice that." Helburn promised to consider the matter seriously. When she learned that Alfred Lunt and Lynn Fontanne the stars of *The Guardsman*—were not averse to closing their show, she made her decision. *The Garrick Gaieties* started on a regular run the Monday after *The Guardsman* closed—on June 8. It stayed on for twenty-five weeks.

Each of the principal collaborators now received a small percentage of the gross. The share of Rodgers and Hart amounted to about fifty dollars each a week, not counting the royalties from the published sheet music. In addition, since he filled the job of conductor, Rodgers drew the weekly union scale wage of $83.00.

For the first time Rodgers was drawing a regular income from his music. But equally significant was the fact that *The Garrick Gaieties* had suddenly made him a Broadway celebrity and a composer whose music had become a salable commodity. The story is told that several years after *The Garrick*

Gaieties, Rodgers and Hart visited the Garrick Theatre. Pointing proudly to the tapestries, Hart said: "Dick, *we* are responsible for them." Rodgers replied: "Hell, no, Larry. They are responsible for *us.*"

7

TRIUMVIRATE

Before *The Garrick Gaieties* was produced, Rodgers and Hart had completed a musical comedy called *Dearest Enemy,* book by Herbert Fields. This was the first of several musical comedies written collaboratively by Rodgers, Hart, and Fields which were to make them the outstanding triumvirate of the musical comedy in the 1920's.

This triumvirate brought a welcome infusion of fresh techniques and approaches into a musical theater which for a generation had experienced little basic change. Productions might be slicker than they had been a decade earlier, the trappings more ornate—but the formulas and conventions that had prevailed in the 1900's and 1910's had not been abandoned.

On the one hand the American musical in 1925 consisted of operettas which imitated the European patterns.

They created an unreal world of unreal people. Against an exotic background or a mythical-kingdom setting, elegant ladies and fine-plumed gentlemen became enmeshed in intrigues from which the virtuous always emerged triumphant, in which evildoers met their just punishment and the hero invariably captured the heroine. Costumes, settings, lavishly mounted scenes were of primary interest. Of relatively minor importance was the usually sentimental plot, which served merely as the thread on which to bead the pearls of song (usually in three-quarter time) and the swirling dances.

Victor Herbert, who for a generation had dominated the American operetta, had been dead a year in mid-1925. But to the European traditions which he had carried into the American theater there were others still faithful, notably Sigmund Romberg, whose *Student Prince* had begun a run of 608 performances on December 2, 1924; and Rudolf Friml, whose *The Vagabond King* opened triumphantly on Broadway three days after *Dearest Enemy*. Like the operettas of Herbert, the *Student Prince* and *The Vagabond King* were synthetic theater, belonging to another age and to other lands; in the America of the 1920's they were almost anachronistic.

Then there were the musical comedies whose relation to everyday life and people was hardly any closer. Stereotyped boy-meets-girl stories and stock characters served a single purpose: to present songs, dance routines, comedy, and large production numbers. The formula was invariable. A chorus usually opened and closed each act. The songs and dances were interpolated at definitely set points in the story. The concern of the musical comedy was exclusively to entertain, and it had little traffic with values treasured by other branches of the theater.

If the musical comedy of this period had any vitality at all it was mainly because there were composers who could bring

to their writing melodic and rhythmic inventiveness and creative freshness even while adhering rigidly to the ritual of the
musical-comedy stage. Jerome Kern, whose "Princess Theatre Shows" in the late 1910's made such a strong attempt to
break with standard practice, had in 1920 returned to the
older and more conventional aesthetics with *Sally;* and in
1925 he was still working within the more formal and accepted mold in *Sunny.* Nor was the *status quo* disturbed by
George Gershwin in *Lady Be Good* in 1924 and *Tip Toes*
in 1925, or by Vincent Youmans in *No No Nanette* in 1925.

Until 1925 (though he was then being represented on
Broadway by the Four Marx Brothers farce, *The Cocoanuts*),
Irving Berlin had made his principal musical contributions
to the stage in revues—particularly his own *Music Box Revue,* which he wrote and produced annually between 1921
and 1924. This was even truer of the then still unknown
Cole Porter in 1925, whose last appearance as a Broadway
composer had been in the *Greenwich Village Follies* of 1924,
and whose first musical comedy was still three years in the
future.

But in 1925 the musical comedy was beginning to stir
restlessly within, and trying to break loose from, its constrict-
ing and time-honored format. And the triumvirate of Rodgers, Hart, and Fields—beginning with *Dearest Enemy*—first
helped to bring this change about.

The idea for *Dearest Enemy* had come to them before
The Garrick Gaieties made Rodgers and Hart famous. One
afternoon in 1924—soon after *The Melody Man* had opened
—Rodgers, Hart, and Fields were strolling on Lexington
Avenue discussing projects for musicals. They stopped in
front of a building on 37th Street which had a plaque reading: "Howe with Clinton, Tryon, and a few others, went to
the house of Robert Murray, on Murray Hill, for Refresh-

ment and Rest. With Pleasant Conversations and a Profusion of Cake and Wine, the good whig lady detained the gallant Britons almost two hours. Quite long enough for the bulk of Putnam's division of four thousand men to leave the city and escape to the heights of Harlem by the Bloomingdale Road, with the loss of only a few soldiers."

It was Larry Hart who first recognized in this incident the seed for a fruitful idea.* Herbert Fields wrote the book, expanding the Murray Hill incident of the Revolutionary War and adding a secondary plot, the romance of Betsy Burke, the pert little Irish niece of Mrs. Robert Murray, and the redcoat captain Sir John Copeland.

Lew Fields, to whom the script was submitted, did not like it. "Who ever heard of a musical based on American history?" he asked. "The public won't buy it." Other producers were equally wary. Some of them even refused to look at the play, arguing if the play was not good enough for Fields' father it was certainly not good enough for them.

Rodgers found an ally in Helen Ford, star of musical comedy. Primarily because she wanted to play the role of Betsy, she promised to do everything in her power to get this musical produced. She scurried about to get the necessary financing; she interested her husband, George Ford, in becoming its producer; she enlisted her friend, John Murray Anderson, to do the staging. All this took considerable time, and for a while it seemed to the authors that the play would never be performed. Meanwhile, *The Garrick Gaieties* had come and conquered New York and stirred the interest of the theatrical world in Rodgers and Hart. Now that they were known, they were certain to attract attention with their

---

* Over a quarter century later, the same episode was used by Robert Sherwood for his last play, *Small War on Murray Hill*. Produced on Broadway early in 1957, it was a failure.

next effort. *Dearest Enemy* suddenly became a valuable property demanding immediate exploitation.

With a cast headed by Helen Ford, Charles Purcell, and Flavia Arcaro, *Dearest Enemy* was tried out for a week in Baltimore. Just before the opening night there, Rodgers, who was to conduct the performance, rushed into a nearby delicatessen for a sandwich. As he ate, a large can of peaches fell off the shelf on his head and knocked him out. He was, however, revived in time to conduct the overture.

This accident was no omen of unhappy things to come. *Dearest Enemy* went over well in Baltimore and even better in New York, where it opened at the Knickerbocker Theatre on September 18, 1925. It was a feast for the eye, as Alexander Woollcott reported, "an endlessly lovely picture. The parade of damsels clad in Reynolds costumes past the fine, white balustrades of the old Murray staircase, all footing it neatly in measures rehearsed by John Murray Anderson, this alone is worth the price of admission." The pictorial appeal was further heightened by an intermission curtain designed by Reginald Marsh depicting old New York.

But *Dearest Enemy* had much more to recommend it than just its handsome mountings. It was "an American musical play," as the program described it, a page from American history set to music. Fresh in subject matter, spontaneous in treatment, and full of vivacity, it had both wit and nostalgic appeal. Its gaiety was spiced by a discreet salaciousness. ("Hooray, we are gonna be compromised," sing the young Continental ladies on learning that the British troops are on their way. Then they add philosophically: "War is war.") It was also deeply stirring, as in the patriotic finale in which George Washington makes his only appearance.

Here for the first time Rodgers had to write music for a play which, in its originality of subject matter and develop-

ment, made exacting demands upon him. He now possessed
the technique to write lucidly and articulately within more
extensive designs than those provided by the thirty-two-bar
song. But most significant of all he now revealed those dramatic sensibilities and instincts which were soon to make him
the foremost composer of the popular theater.

The score for *Dearest Enemy* was studded not only with
songs but also with duets, trios, and choral numbers. Probably as a gesture of admiration for its musical spaciousness,
Percy Hammond described *Dearest Enemy* as "a baby grand
opera." The grace of the eighteenth century was evoked in a
gavotte that opened the second act; a stirring martial note
was sounded in the song "Cheerio"; an insouciant, impudent
attitude was expressed in "Old Enough to Love." And in
the song hit, "Here in My Arms," sung by Helen Ford and
Charles Purcell just before the first-act finale, Rodgers endowed the words with wings. There is skill as well as beautiful lyricism here.

Dearest Enemy ran almost a year and served to focus the
limelight on Rodgers. Max Dreyfus called him and welcomed him ceremoniously into his office. "Why didn't you
come to *me* with 'Manhattan'?" he inquired with irritation.
"It's a grand number and I would have been proud to publish
it." Tactfully, Rodgers did not remind him that when last
he had been rudely dismissed by Dreyfus he had played for
him the music of *Winkle Town,* one of whose numbers was
"Manhattan." Dreyfus was now ready to contract for the publication not only of the principal songs of *Dearest Enemy* but
also for all of Rodgers' future songs, at a royalty of three cents
a copy. Dreyfus was thereafter to remain Rodgers' friend and
publisher, but it cannot be said of the man who helped
discover Friml, Gershwin, and Kern that he had done a
similar service for Rodgers.

Suddenly Rodgers and Hart were very much in demand. Rodgers had waited too long for success not to enjoy its sweet taste fully. Success to him meant the opportunity to work. Now he took every assignment that came along, then went hunting for more. His drive and his capacity for work seemed limitless; he pushed Hart on to produce more and more lyrics for his abundant music making.

In 1926, five Rodgers and Hart shows played on Broadway, three of them simultaneously, and four of them proved successes. While *Dearest Enemy* was still doing well at the Knickerbocker, and soon after *The Garrick Gaieties* had completed its run at the Garrick, a new Rodgers-Hart-Fields production opened at the Vanderbilt Theatre, which for the next few years was to be the home of the best musicals of this prolific triumvirate. It was *The Girl Friend*, produced by Lew Fields on March 17, an intimate musical Rodgers and Hart had promised to write for Sam White and Eva Puck when they were playing in *The Melody Man*. A routine plot involving professional cyclists, corrupt gamblers, and a fixed six-day bike race was flexible enough to permit interpolations of rousing burlesques on grand opera and on minstrel shows, and to highlight a brilliant eccentric dance by Dorothy Barber. It also enabled June Cochrane, previously one of the lesser performers in *The Garrick Gaieties,* to achieve stardom.

At first business was slow for *The Girl Friend;* for a time it seemed as though it would have to close down. But two songs —the title number and "The Blue Room," both sung in the first act by Sam White and Eva Puck—began to catch on outside the theater. The interest of "The Girl Friend" lay in its rhythmic vitality, and in a charming release in the chorus; that of "The Blue Room," exclusively in its melodic invention, to which a most sparing and economical harmony was completely subservient. Both songs became so popular (the newspapers reported on May 10, 1926, that "The Girl Friend" was the best-selling song in the country) that they started to draw attention to the play, and soon capacity houses became the rule. *The Girl Friend* was finally such a hit that it ran for over four hundred performances and had a second company on the road at a time when second companies were not usual.

The Girl Friend had already established itself solidly when the second edition of *The Garrick Gaieties* was produced by the Theatre Guild at the Garrick on May 10. Like its happy predecessor, the newcomer was a source of endless amusement; more satires on current plays (this time, *The Dybbuk, Lulu Belle,* and *The Goat Song*); more gay take-offs, the most felicitous being that of Queen Elizabeth by Edith Meiser; more brilliant sketches by Newman Levy, one of them about George Washington, the other on society ladies. The contribution by Rodgers and Hart included not only one of their best songs of this period—"Mountain Greenery," sung by Bobbie Perkins and Sterling Holloway—but also a burlesque on musical comedy, *Rose of Arizona,* in which several different popular-song styles of the period were gaily parodied. "Young Rodgers," wrote Frank Vreeland, "more than fulfilled the promise of yesteryear, radiating melodies that it would be hard to beat, except say in *The Girl Friend* and *Dearest Enemy,* which also happen to be his compositions. In the freshness and spontaneity of his work he is the most auspicious young composer for musical comedy in our midst, and should develop into the Irving Berlin of the future."

The next two Rodgers-Hart-Fields musicals did not appear until the end of the year. But other chores awaited Rodgers. With Hart he wrote songs for a one-act musical which Renée Robert and Jay Velie (billed as "Terpsichore and Troubadour") played at the Palace Theatre the week of January 4, and after that in other leading vaudeville houses. His songs were also heard in the *Fifth Avenue Follies,* a Billy Rose production at the Fifth Avenue Club, the first such night spot on the Avenue. And besides writing new songs, Rodgers completed arrangements to reproduce some of his old ones on piano rolls for Ampico. "The Blue Room" and "The Girl Friend" were released in April; "Here in My Arms," "Manhattan," and "Sentimental Me," a few months later; "My Heart Stood Still," early in 1927.

There was an assignment in London, their first—a show which Jack Hulbert planned both to star in and to produce. Intending to combine business with an extended holiday, Rodgers, Hart, and Fields set sail on the *Conte Biancamano.* They docked in Naples, then traveled north leisurely and were joined in Milan by Mortimer Rodgers. They rented a car and motored through the Dolomites to Venice, then proceeded to Switzerland and France. This was Richard Rodgers' first sight of Europe. While sight-seeing experiences excited him, he did not like the continual movement of travel; and he was lonesome for New York.

When they arrived in London, Rodgers and Hart rented an apartment at 29 Saint James's Street. They were not happy with developments in England. Jack Hulbert was too aloof and distant a person for their gregarious taste, and they found it difficult to get along with him. Besides, they did not like the book of the musical he gave them—a thing called *Lido Lady,* by Guy Bolton, Bert Kalmar, and Harry Ruby. And they were shocked to discover that the leading role of a beautiful tennis champ was to be played by a middle-aged actress. They could not wait to finish the job and get back to New York, where a new production of theirs was being planned. After completing their score for

London, and without waiting for rehearsals, they set sail for home on the *Majestic.*

A delightful surprise awaited them as the boat nosed its way into New York Harbor. As they were having breakfast on their last morning aboard ship, Rodgers happened to look out of the porthole and to his amazement saw a banner reading: GARRICK GAIETIES. The cast of the show had come down the bay on a tug to welcome them home.

While they were beginning to work on a new Broadway play, *Lido Lady* opened at the Alhambra Theatre in Bradford, England, on October 4. The show prospered better than they had expected. After a tour of the English provinces, it opened at the Gaiety in London on December 1, where it amassed the respectable run of over 259 performances. A second company was then formed for Edinburgh. *Lido Lady,* then, was a profitable financial venture, and it was well received by the English critics. The Rodgers and Hart score included nine numbers. The only real winner in this group was one of their old numbers, plucked out of *Dearest Enemy,* "Here in My Arms."

Peggy-Ann—the new Rodgers, Hart, and Fields musical—was the most unorthodox they had thus far attempted. It was based on *Tillie's Nightmare,* a comedy by Edgar Smith in which Marie Dressler had starred on Broadway in 1914, and was built around the dream fantasies of the heroine.

Years before the invasion of dream psychology into Broadway and Hollywood—fourteen years before Moss Hart's psychoanalytic musical comedy, *Lady in the Dark*—*Peggy-Ann* was a Freudian play. It had a Debussy-like, impressionistic quality in which fantasy became confused with reality; where the absurd, outlandish and the impossible frequently became plausible. The scene shifts in a haze as Peggy-Ann makes her dream flight to New York; and, as the chorus accompanies her, it changes its costume from country to city dress. The impenetrable maze of New York traffic suddenly becomes unraveled as the police go quietly off for lunch. Peggy-Ann attends her own wedding dressed only in step-ins; during the ceremony a telephone book is used instead of a Bible. Disordered dances and undisciplined lights contribute to the planned chaos. Absurdities mount. Confusion is added to confusion. Peggy-Ann's ruthless sister appears as a devil with red horns; pills assume the size of golf balls; fish speak with an English accent; policemen sport pink mustaches; Cuban race horses are interviewed. A yacht bearing Peggy-Ann and a lover on a cruise becomes the scene of a mutiny when the crew learns to its horror that the pair are not married. It was all like a chapter out of *Alice in Wonderland,* as Alexander Woollcott pointed out. And he added: "In singing Carroll's praises, I would fain suggest that here is something more of Lewis than Earl."

The authors had a field day in their freedom from accepted musical-comedy procedures. Peggy-Ann's love affair in New York is not the satin-and-lace, perfumed kind of romance expected on the traditional musical-comedy stage, but earthy and real. There is no opening chorus; actually there is no singing or dancing whatsoever for the first fifteen minutes. The end of the play takes place on a darkened stage, consisting only of a slow comedy dance. That dance, and those that preceded it, were not typical musical-comedy routines, but suggested the ballet—a forewarning of the bold direction Rodgers and Hart would later take.

Rodgers' music was also at times unconventional, though it did contain such good tunes as "A Tree in the Park," "Where's That Rainbow?", and "Maybe It's Me," the last taken out of the *Fifth Avenue Follies.* He achieved fantasy by means of nebulous chords that follow Peggy Ann in her dreams. Through delicate harmonizations (particularly in the verse), "A Tree in the Park" becomes a rhapsody of love. The Cuban scene ("Havana") has a rich dash of Spanish color in its rhythms.

After a two-week out-of-town tryout, *Peggy-Ann* opened at the Vanderbilt on December 27. The cast represented a veritable alumni association of earlier Rodgers and Hart shows. Helen Ford, who played the title role, came from *Dearest Enemy;* Lulu McConnell, who handled the comedy sequences so admirably that many said she stole the show, was from *Poor Little Ritz Girl;* Edith Meiser and Betty Starbuck were graduates from *The Garrick Gaieties.*

The critics were unanimously enthusiastic, using such accolades as "unique," "bright and fantastic," "fruity, frisky, frolicsome, festive, funny, fantastic, and fascinating," and "a chipper entertainment." Nevertheless, the show started lamely at the box-office. It had to meet the opposition of four other new shows opening the same night; and the word had spread that this was too original and arty for public consumption. But the production found an enthusiast in Alison Smith, critic of the New York *World* and a member of New York's intellectual elite which met regularly at the Hotel Algonquin. She transferred her excitement to the Algonquin set. One of them, Alexander Woollcott, raved over the show in a feature first-page story in the Sunday section of the *World.* Others—notably Robert Benchley, Frank Sullivan, and Dorothy Parker—said that this was the best musical they had seen, and their influence was soon felt at the box office. *Peggy-Ann* ran almost a year before proceeding to London, where it opened at Daly's Theatre on July 29, 1927.

Almost as if to demonstrate that they were human after all, Rodgers and Hart ended their first year of triumph with a fiasco.

Florenz Ziegfeld had committed himself to starring Belle Baker, the popular vaudevillian, in a musical. He asked Irving Caesar and David Freedman to write a play tailor-made for her personality and talent. After their script had been revised by Anthony Maguire, Ziegfeld asked Rodgers and Hart to write the songs. Both men were reluctant to undertake the assignment, for it meant their separation from Herbert Fields, with whom they had been working so fruitfully; but they also recognized the value and importance of being associated with a showman like Ziegfeld.

It was an unhappy adventure from the start. The play itself was hardly calculated to bring out the best efforts of a composer. Set in New York's East Side, it revolved around the ludicrous efforts of a mother and a sister to get the heroine, Betsy, married to a bird fancier. As if a bad book were not hardship enough, Rodgers intensely disliked working for Ziegfeld. The great showman knew nothing about music, yet was dictatorial in his demands on composers.

Betsy came to the New Amsterdam on December 28, one day after *Peggy-Ann* had its Broadway opening. Despite an excellent cast and beautiful settings by Joseph Urban, it proved a dismal failure. Nor were the songs of Rodgers and Hart much of an asset. The best number came not from their pens but from that of Irving Berlin. Berlin had written a ballad, "Blue Skies," for Belle Baker, and it was interpolated for her into the second act. *Betsy* lasted only five weeks and cost Ziegfeld a fortune.

On January 26, 1927, Rodgers and Hart sailed for London to a catch glimpse of *Lido Lady*. There they met Charles B. Cochran, the famous London producer of musicals, who engaged them to write music for a London revue. Renting their old apartment on Saint James's Street, they renewed old acquaintances and made many new ones. All in all, this was a pleasant experience for both of them, in contrast to their first visit to London. Working with a sympathetic producer like Cochran was a joy, just as associating with him and his wife on friendly terms was an undiluted pleasure.

The Cochran revue was called *One Dam Thing after Another*. Starring Jessie Matthews and Sonny Hale, it began a moderately successful run at the Pavilion on May 20. It would hardly deserve even passing mention but for the fact that among the eleven new numbers contributed by Rodgers and Hart was one of their most beautiful songs, "My Heart Stood Still." The idea for the lyric had come to Hart a few weeks earlier in Paris during a taxi ride with Rodgers and two girls. In one of those perilous episodes for which Parisian taxis are so notorious, their car avoided collision by a hair's breadth. "My heart stood still," gasped one of the girls. Completely oblivious of the near-accident, Hart remarked calmly, "That would make a nice title for a song." Rodgers, in turn, made a note of the song idea. During their first evening in London, while Larry was asleep, Rodgers came upon the title in his notebook and proceeded to write a melody for it. When he turned it over to Hart for the lyric, the latter confessed he had completely forgotten about the Paris taxi ride and the remark that had inspired their song.

It was the Prince of Wales who helped make the song not only the big success of the revue but also popular throughout London; he had been taught the song by Rodgers himself. One evening at the Café de Paris, in London, the Prince of Wales asked Teddy Brown, the American heavyweight orchestra leader who had a band there, to play "My Heart Stood Still." When Brown confessed he did not know it, the Prince sang the entire number, verse and chorus. The band picked up the strains from the Prince and finally struck up the melody. This incident was widely publicized and proved the making of the song.

Rodgers and Hart recognized its value, for they purchased it back from Cochran for $5,000.00, so that they might use it for their next American production. Rumor had it that they made this purchase after Ziegfeld had wired them offering to buy it at any reasonable price, but this is apocryphal.

"My Heart Stood Still" crossed the ocean in 1927 and appeared in the most successful musical written by Rodgers, Hart and Fields up to this time—*A Connecticut Yankee.*

A Connecticut Yankee had taken a long time to jell. As far back as 1921, Rodgers and Hart had seen a motion picture based on the famous Mark Twain story. They became so convinced of its value for the musical-comedy stage that they walked from the theater straight into the law office of Charles Tressler Lark, which handled the affairs of the Mark Twain estate. They explained that they wanted an option on the musical-comedy rights to the story—and, much to their amazement, received it free. Unfortunately, unable to make any headway with Broadway producers with any of their projects, they were compelled to allow this option to lapse.

Six years later, the three young men (now the authors of seven produced musicals) decided to return to their abandoned project, and once again secured an option from Lark —this time for a price. As Lew Fields was departing for England to help stage the London production of *Peggy-Ann,* they gave him a copy of the story, explaining their intention to make it a musical. Fields wired back from the boat that the story did not lend itself to popular treatment and that he was not interested in their venture. The trio, nevertheless, continued working on it. When Lew Fields returned from Europe they presented him with a completed script in which the Yankee becomes "Sir Boss" in sixth-century Camelot "on a percentage basis." He creates a one-man revolution

by introducing radio, telephone, efficiency experts, and other
refinements of twentieth-century culture. Suddenly Camelot
resembles a modern American town. King Arthur begins to
talk suspiciously like Calvin Coolidge; Merlin likes to spice
his conversation with Broadway slang ("methinks yon damsel
is a lovely broad"); advertising signs dot the countryside ("I
would fain walk a furlong for a Camel" and "Ye Hibernian
Rose of Abie").

Now enthusiastic over the book, Lew Fields enlisted Lyle
D. Andrews as coproducer and assembled a cast that starred
William Gaxton and Nana Bryant. The critics liked everything about the show when it made its triumphant appearance at the Vanderbilt Theatre on November 3, 1927, but
best of all they liked the songs. "It was Richard Rodgers,"
wrote Alexander Woollcott, "with his head full of tunes who
made the most valuable contribution . . . [with] so many
fetching songs." Brooks Atkinson said: "Set to as fresh and
lilting songs as we may hope to find with well turned lyrics
. . . it makes for novel amusement in the best of taste."

Such enthusiasm is understandable. *A Connecticut Yankee*
contained some of the best song writing to be encountered in
the musical theater of the 1920's. Hart had never before
been wittier, more dexterous in his technique, happier in his
choice of the *mot juste.*

> Our minds are featherweight
> Their together weight
> Can't amount to much;
> You use no better words
> Than three-letter words:
> "Dog" and "Cat" and such.
> You have no head at all.
> Something like your knob
> Is used as a door knob;
> That's why I feel at home with you.

So runs the tongue-in-cheek love song of Sir Galahad to Mistress Evelyn La Belle-Ans. And "On a Desert Island with Thee" boasted some of the finest lyrics of the day, lines like these being characteristic:

> Let the prudish people quarrel
> We'll forget them for the nonce,
> If they think our love immoral,
> *Honi soit qui mal y pense.*

The melodies were no less distinguished. The aristocracy of their style and the freshness of their lyricism placed Rodgers solidly in the front rank of all those writing music for the stage.

The song "Thou Swell" (second only in popularity to "My Heart Stood Still") was almost withdrawn before *A Connecticut Yankee* reached Broadway. The audience in Philadelphia was so cold to it—possibly they were puzzled by Hart's rapid and nimble alternation between Arthurian phraseology and modern-day slang—that the producers asked Rodgers to delete it. Rodgers balked because he was convinced it was an asset. The song was kept, but only on the condition that if the New York first-night audience was as indifferent to it as that in Philadelphia, it would be removed the following morning. Fortunately that first-night audience—and the critics the next morning—were enthusiastic, and "Thou Swell" stayed in permanently.

A Connecticut Yankee was a major success not only on Broadway (418 performances) but also on the road, where it remained a year and four months. Other presentations were less fortunate. In London, renamed *A Yankee at the Court of King Arthur,* it survived only 43 performances at Daly's Theatre in 1929. A first attempt to revive it in the United States—in St. Louis in 1936—received only a half-hearted welcome, while a second revival in New York in 1943 (in a revised and modernized version) was a failure.

8

"AND A SOURCE OF PERMANENT IRRITATION"

Rodgers would have been less than human if the wine of success had not proved somewhat heady. In 1925 his prospects for the future had been bleak; he was in debt and ready to abandon music for the children's underwear business. One year later he was the white-haired boy of show business, earning about a thousand dollars a week.

He left his parents' home for a terrace apartment at the Hotel Lombardy on East 56th Street. (The only other apartment on his floor was then occupied by Edna Ferber.) He also purchased a flashy La Salle coupé with a red body and black hood. His social life expanded as he found attractive and desirable show girls in his various productions not altogether indifferent to his personal charm and to his now impressive position in the theater. And, for a while, as his income kept mounting, he became free with his money.

His father did not fail to notice all this, nor did he stand by passively. As soon as Rodgers had saved his first thousand dollars from *The Garrick Gaieties,* his father presented him with a gift: a safe deposit box at the Chase National Bank on 86th Street, rental paid up for one year. "Buy a government bond with your money," he advised Dick, "and put it into the vault. Those bonds will work for you when you no longer can work for yourself." His father also now took over the keeping of Dick's financial accounts, as a deterrent to further reckless and uncalculated spending.

Rodgers' friends reveal that this is the one period in his life that success affected him adversely. He became brash, cocksure, somewhat snobbish. But this period was of brief duration. As the intoxication of his first victories began to wear off, and as he grew accustomed to them, he reverted to type. Success—even the resounding triumphs of his later years—was never again to turn his head.

Though he was having things his own way (and enjoying the experience to the full) he was not without problems. Working with Hart was a constant irritation, a perpetual trial to test a saint's patience. Hart's leave-it-to-chance, irresponsible, undisciplined and impractical nature—his tendency to leave for tomorrow what should be done today— was a source of deep annoyance to Rodgers, who thrived on work and needed set schedules and discipline. Rodgers continually had to badger, cajole, order, plead, and trick Larry into working; had to connive to get him to keep schedules and appointments; had to be a scold to get Larry to behave himself. If he wanted to keep his collaborator he had to assume the roles of father and older brother, even though he was many years Hart's junior. "Only one thing remained constant in Larry's approach to his job," says Rodgers. "He hated doing it and loved when it was done."

As a friend and companion Hart was charm itself. Quick of tongue and brain, a perpetual geyser of enthusiasm and gaiety, he provided endless fun and entertainment for all those around him. He was also soft, generous, and lovable—"the sweetest little guy in the world," as Rodgers once described him. For all the heartache Hart caused him in their work, Rodgers was always deeply attached to him; and for all of Rodgers' tyrannical drive to get him to work, there never was a time when Hart did not have both the highest regard and the warmest affection for his collaborator.

Hart was Puck, the eternal sophomore, the boy who would not grow older. He had such an extraordinary capacity for good times that the enjoyment of life became the be-all and end-all of his existence. He liked playing poker, and pinochle with George S. Kaufman, Marc Connolly and Groucho Marx. His idea of heaven was a gathering (improvised at a moment's whim by telephone) turned into a noisy and disorderly all-night affair—the living room filled with guests, heavy with smoke and the smell of liquor, loud with conversation and laughter. A party that broke up before dawn was to Larry a "bust." He loved those parties because he needed gaiety, people (particularly *young* people), liquor, girls; most of all he liked parties because he hated being alone. He always surrounded himself with people. Some were close friends, but most were just hangers-on who saw their chance to get a free meal or drink, a loan, and a possible "in" among important theatrical people.

He was all nerves—jumpy, quick of gesture, continually active and on the move. "He was always skipping and bouncing," Oscar Hammerstein II recalls. "In all the times I knew him, I never saw him walk slowly. I never saw his face in repose. I never heard him chuckle quietly. He laughed loudly and easily at other people's jokes, and at his own, too. His large eyes danced and his head would wag. He was alert and dynamic." In his favorite bar or restaurant he never sat long in any one place but would hop from table to table, saying hello at one, telling a joke at another. At home he would pace his living room for hours at a time. On opening nights he never sat in his seat but walked frantically up and down the lobby, rubbing his hands together (a favorite gesture) when he felt things were going well in the theater. In his travels, he preferred being "on the go," impatient for what lay beyond the horizon even while ignoring what could be seen nearby. Each of his three trips to Europe with his friend Milton Bender was a mad whirl of all-night revels, champagne, girls—and laughter. He needed laughter the way some men need praise. A carefully timed wisecrack, a well-told joke, a neatly turned pun, a skillfully perpetrated prank —these were the meat and the drink of his soul.

He never seemed to know or care for the price or value of anything material. The way he handled his money was characteristic. He would carry an uncounted wad of cash in his pocket, sometimes as much as a thousand dollars. Coming home late at night he would shake his head incredulously when he saw how much he had spent that day. He never seemed to learn that always grabbing the check, making indiscriminate loans, hopping in a taxi even when his destination was a hundred miles away, or buying expensive clothes that momentarily attracted his eye—that all this was destructive even to the healthiest bankroll. He never gave much concern to how much he spent, however, just as he never really knew how much he earned. (He was probably the only man in show business who habitually signed contracts without reading them.) At one time Rodgers consulted his father on the most efficacious method of curbing Larry's wild extravagance. They finally evolved an effective strategy. Each week Rodgers would collect Larry's check and cash it, translating a part into securities which were then placed in a vault at the

86th Street branch of the Chase National Bank. Though
Hart had access to the vault, the transfer of securities into
cash was for him a much too involved process, and he laz-
ily permitted them to accumulate in the vault. After a while,
Rodgers prevailed on Hart to hire a business manager to
handle his finances. That manager, William Kron, doled out
to Larry a specific sum each week. "What he doesn't know,"
Larry confided to a friend with the undisguised glee of one
who has just put over a fast deal, "is that I have sources of income he knows *nothing* about!"

Until 1928, Hart lived in the brownstone house on 119th
Street where Rodgers had first met him, with his parents, his
brother Teddy, and their maid, Mary Campbell, nicknamed
"Big Mary." One writer has described this place as a "happy
pandemonium." It was always in a state of confusion to which
Hart's own shiftless habits generously contributed. He always
got up late and went to bed late. He ate at irregular hours;
lounged about sloppily for most of the day; left books and
newspapers and magazines in scattered heaps all over the
place; smoked about twenty cigars a day. He thought nothing
of improvising a party at which a hundred people would
have to be fed; at one of these affairs Paul Whiteman dropped
in casually with his entire orchestra. "Big Mary" would
stalk about the apartment swearing under her breath, making pointed remarks about each member of the family, and
even speaking her mind freely about the various guests. Her
simple directness was as celebrated as her profanity. One evening, when Fanny Brice brought Josephine Baker to dinner,
Baker innocently asked Mary for a "cup of coffee *au lait, s'il
vous plaît.*" Mary barked back, "Use your mouth like the day
you was born!" "Big Mary" was a personality and an institution. It is no secret she was the prototype for Rheba in the
Moss Hart comedy *You Can't Take It With You.* When in
1928 Larry moved to his own apartment at the Beresford, he

took with him not only his family but also Mary, who remained in his employ as long as he lived.

To his work Larry brought all the careless habits, all the charming irresponsibility of his daily life. He detested the grind and routine of writing. The very thought of sitting down and working could raise his body temperature by several degrees.

Rodgers and Herbert Fields soon learned not to ask Larry down to their apartments for their conferences. Larry rarely came; and when he did he was always several hours late. Instead, Rodgers and Fields would go up to Larry's place, to snare him in his own lair before he could escape. Before taking the subway at 86th Street they would always telephone him that they were on their way, hoping he might be out of bed by the time they arrived. But he was always still in bed. They had to wait patiently while he went through a dilatory breakfast, took a leisurely smoke, glanced through his mail and the morning paper, tried to sabotage work by engaging them in a discussion. Each time they attempted to hurry him along, he would snap at them: "I'm not a machine!" It usually took several hours before Rodgers and Fields could finally get him to concentrate on the day's creative problems.

On those rare occasions when Hart did manage to come down to Rodgers' place for some work, he became a will-o'-the-wisp. Suddenly he would remember he did not have a cigar, go downstairs, and disappear for the rest of the day. If Rodgers happened to have a cigar handy, he would have to go to the bathroom. Then, when Rodgers' attention was diverted, he would vanish. "It was never wise to leave him alone," Rodgers recalls, "because he would simply disappear and would have to be found all over again." Sometimes even when he walked in the street with Rodgers he would make a sudden and unexpected getaway. "You would suddenly find you were talking to yourself."

If he was reluctant about doing any writing, and irresponsible about appointments, he was no less erratic in his work habits. He wrote only when the mood struck him—putting down a random thought, a pleasing rhyme scheme, or an ingenious song idea on slips of paper, which he would stuff into his pockets. When he joined Rodgers to plan songs, he would take out these disorderly and sloppy bits of paper from his various pockets and try to find something usable. When this method did not serve him, he would have to submit to the torture of sitting down in one place and developing a tentative idea into a lyric.

He managed to write as much as he did, and as well as he did, because he did not usually have to sweat out his lyrics. Fortunately for him they came easily, effortlessly; he could produce a gem in a remarkably short time and in spite of any distractions at hand. "I saw him write a sparkling stanza to 'The Girl Friend' in a hot, smelly rehearsal hall," writes Rodgers, "with chorus girls pounding out jazz time, and principals shouting out their lines. In half an hour he fashioned something with so many interior rhymes, so many tricky phrases, and so many healthy chuckles in it that I just couldn't believe he had written it in one evening."

Yet when revision or editing were required, it was always difficult to get him to extend himself. "He loathed changing any word once it was written down," says Rodgers. This was the case, Rodgers might have added, not because Hart felt each word had become too precious for handling, but simply because he was lazy. "When the immovable object of his unwillingness to change came up against the irresistible force of my own drive for perfection, the noise could be heard all over the city. Our fights over words were furious, blasphemous, and frequent, but even in our hottest moments we both knew that we were arguing academically and not personally. I think I am quite safe in saying that Larry and I never had a single argument with each other."

Yet Hart had the creator's pride in his work, would chortle with glee when he came upon a happy line or a tricky rhyme, and knew well how much he had accomplished in bringing an adult intelligence to the song lyric. To quote Rodgers once more: "He didn't care where he lived, how much he earned, what the social or financial status of his friends was, or what row he sat in at opening nights. He did care tremendously however about the turn of a phrase and the mathematical exactness of an interior rhyme."

Most of the time the melody was written first and the lyric was fitted to it. In writing words to Rodgers' music, Hart often allowed himself to be guided by the musical materials at hand. Hart has given us a clue to his method by explaining how he wrote "Here in My Arms": "I take the most distinctive melodic phrase in the tune and work on that. What I choose is not necessarily the theme or the first line but the phrase which stands out. Next I try to find the meaning of that phrase and to develop a euphonic set of words to fit it. . . . The first line runs like this: 'Here in my arms, it's adorable.' The distinct melodic phrase comes on the word 'adorable,' and the word 'adorable' is the first word that occurred to me, so I used it as my pivotal idea. And as the melodic phrase recurs so often in the chorus it determines my rhyme scheme. Of course, in a song of this sort the melody and euphonics of the words themselves are really more important than the sense." In "The Blue Room" the most important note in the chorus is a half-note on which the ascending melodic phrase comes to rest; Hart used that half-note on which to fix not only the term "blue room" but also all of its varied rhymes.

As a team they worked together wonderfully—in spite of Rodgers' anguish in getting Hart to work, meet commitments, come to rehearsals, and in general conform to some kind of routine; in spite of Hart's fierce resistance to Rodgers' incessant and irresistible drive. Each respected the other's ability and opinions. Hart had a sound critical sense for music, an intuitive feeling for a good melody, which made it possible for him to respond to and work within the framework of Rodgers' musical thinking. Rodgers admired and appreciated good writing; he was able to understand the subtlest demands of his collaborator. Besides, they were exceedingly fond of each other; it is doubtful if there was any man for whom Hart had a greater affection and admiration than for Rodgers. Thus discords arising from the often passionate, the often turbulent exchange of ideas were always resolved when they finally put on paper the songs they had previously discussed.

9

AN INTERLUDE BETWEEN SUCCESSES

Between January, 1928 and February, 1930, six Rodgers and Hart musicals were produced on Broadway. None of these was either as good or as successful as *Peggy-Ann* or *The Connecticut Yankee*. Four did passingly well, with runs averaging 125 performances; two were flops. If these musicals had any value in further solidifying the place of Rodgers and Hart in the theater of the 1920's it was mainly through the quantity of their output rather than the quality; through the persistence with which they reappeared on the stage rather than through the consistent brilliance of any single production.

She's My Baby on January 3, 1928—book by Bolton, Kalmar and Ruby—had nothing to recommend it, even with a cast headed by Beatrice Lillie, Jack Whiting, Irene Dunne, and Clifton Webb. A silly plot failed to stimulate these distinguished performers, or for that matter to evoke from Rodgers and Hart a single creditable song. *Present Arms,* on April 26, was a good deal better. This was an attempt by Herbert Fields to repeat a success he had achieved a year earlier for Vincent Youmans with *Hit the Deck.* Having profitably exploited the navy in the Youmans musical, he now used the marines and stationed them in Honolulu. A high point in the production was achieved by the staging of a shipwreck, but it was Rodgers and Hart who made the major entry on the credit side of the ledger. The importance of the chorus and dancing provided Rodgers with an opportunity to bring a new spaciousness to his writing; and, for the first time, he used transitional passages to provide the play with greater cohesion. Two songs were also noteworthy. "You Took Advantage of Me," which had intriguing chromaticisms in the chorus, was a bright and lively melody which Alison Smith of the *World* (now a self-appointed missionary spreading the gospel of Rodgers and Hart) prophesied would "alone . . . keep the music of *Present Arms* echoing over the roof gardens far into the summer." "A Kiss for Cinderella," sung by four males, was a parody on the Cinderella theme.

No sooner did *Present Arms* depart from the Mansfield than *Chee-Chee* sprang up there to replace it. *Chee-Chee* had the shortest run of any Rodgers and Hart production— 31 performances. Nevertheless it was in many respects one of the most interesting of their musicals of this period: a courageous attempt on their part to endow the musical stage with new dimensions and materials. "It was a brave thing to attempt," Rodgers explains, "but so is a swim across the Atlantic. And it was just as foolish."

Herbert Fields was the first of the trio to become excited over a project to make Charles Petit's novel, *The Son of the Grand Eunuch,* into a musical. He infected Hart with his own enthusiasms. Rodgers, however, remained a skeptic. He was not sure that, creatively, he could respond to a play with an

Oriental setting. But he was even more disturbed by the story itself. Li-Pi Tchou and his wife, Chee-Chee, escape from their realm since the young man—about to succeed his father as Grand Eunuch—must submit to castration. On their journey they encounter varied adventures, some of them extremely risqué. There were many comical allusions to the plight of a young man deprived of his masculinity. "You just can't talk about castration all evening," Rodgers argued with his partners. "It's not only embarrassing. It's downright dull." But Fields was excited, Hart insistent—and Rodgers finally succumbed. He joined his collaborators at Valley View Farm, in New York, for a period of concentrated work. Once he started writing, Rodgers fell in completely with the adopted purpose of making this as exotic, novel, and unusual a play as had yet hit Broadway.

Chee-Chee received a lavish production. The Chinese settings, costumes and curtains were a riot of arresting colors. The Oriental dances were eye-filling. With Helen Ford playing Chee-Chee, William Williams as Li-Pi Tchou, George Hassell (a graduate of Gilbert and Sullivan productions) bringing a touch of Savoyard absurdity and an amusing falsetto to the part of the Grand Eunuch, and Betty Starbuck as a delightful comic ingenue, the play was well cast. Yet it proved a bore, as Rodgers had feared it would, and as virtually every critic remarked. One or two of the more squeamish critics suggested that there simply was no laughter in a sexually mutilated man.

In their pained boredom, most of the critics failed to single out the element that gave *Chee-Chee* its distinction. This was the first time that Rodgers and Hart made a conscious effort to make music an inextricable part of the play's design. So basic were the various musical numbers to the action that Rodgers and Hart refused to list all the principal numbers in the program, as was then and is still the custom.

"The musical numbers," a note in the program stated, "some of them very short, are so interwoven with the story that it would be confusion for the audience to peruse a complete list." And the score was more than a collation of some appealing and other functional numbers. There were, however, tender, wistful, and attractive songs such as "Moon of My Delight" and "I Must Love You," and a rousing male chorus, "The Tartar Song." But the score was also made up of many little fragments, recurrent motives, brief transitional passages which at times were suggestive of the opera. These musical interludes helped to identify characters, point up situations, heighten emotions, accentuate a piece of stage business.

Gilbert Gabriel was one of the few critics to recognize and point to the importance of the score as a whole, while others liked only one or two individual numbers. He wrote: "Mr. Rodgers has, to my way of listening, done far the prettiest share of the collaboration. The music is truly ingratiating, often lovely. Much of it comes in short, seemingly spontaneous spurts, as in the old English ballad operas; and, having come, is content to depart without plugging at a dozen reprises. But there are definitely popular numbers, too . . . and these have no less of a bouquet."

The year 1929 brought two new Rodgers and Hart musicals—*Spring Is Here* and *Heads Up*—in neither of which Herbert Fields participated. *Spring Is Here* was the first Rodgers and Hart show produced by Alex A. Aarons. Aarons was an astute and discerning musician who, a decade earlier, had been responsible for getting George Gershwin to write his first musical-comedy score. Aarons could appreciate fully a creative gift as forceful and original as Rodgers', and he could always work harmoniously with him. On a lesser level of compatability, Aarons was something of a playboy whose company Rodgers enjoyed as keenly outside the theater as in it. Indeed, together with the play's musical director, Alfred Newman, they were a happy trio enjoying fully the blessings of Broadway's night life.

With his partner, Vinton Freedley, Aarons brought *Spring Is Here* to their theater, the Alvin, on March 11. This was a mild little comedy by Owen Davis about two people the course of whose true love refuses to run smoothly. But *Spring Is Here* will always be remembered for one reason alone—a single song that has since become a Rodgers and Hart classic, "With a Song in My Heart." Jules Glaenzer, vice president of Cartier's and one of Rodgers' friends, insists it was written one Sunday morning at his Long Island estate at West Hampton. But this was not strictly the case. Rodgers was a week-end guest at Glaenzer's in Long Island on the Sunday he wrote the song; but he did not write it there but at his own apartment at the Hotel Lombardy a few hours after returning from this week-end visit. However, he did introduce it at a small gathering at Jules Glaenzer's New York apartment that evening.

Once again there was an involvement with Glaenzer and "With a Song in My Heart" six weeks after the opening of *Spring Is Here*—and in Paris. Rodgers came to Paris on April 22 and the next day was invited to dinner by Glaenzer and his wife at Laurent, a fashionable restaurant on the Champs Élysées. They were having a drink at the bar when Rodgers grew increasingly suspicious over the fact that the dining room was slowly being filled by so many people who seemed to know Glaenzer well, and some whom Rodgers knew too, including Noel Coward and Elsa Maxwell. Not until everybody had sat down to dinner did Rodgers discover the true purpose of that evening. When the orchestra struck up "With a Song in My Heart," Rodgers looked at the menu and discovered that he was the guest of honor. The music for the remainder of that evening consisted mainly of Rodgers songs, many played by the composer himself at the piano, some by a New Orleans jazz band. When the dinner party broke up toward dawn, Rodgers, the Glaenzers, and a few others went off to a small bistro in Montmartre for breakfast. A few days later Rodgers departed for a holiday in Cannes, but when he came back to Paris—the day before he sailed home—he returned Glaenzer's compliment by giving a dinner for him and his wife at the Astoria Hotel, attended by many who had been Glaenzer's guests at Laurent and several others then in Paris, including Grace Moore, Walter Wanger, and Jesse Lasky.

In *Spring Is Here,* "With a Song in My Heart" was introduced by the two principals, Lillian Taiz and Glenn Hunter. A year later, Alexander Gray and Bernice Claire sang it in the motion-picture adaptation of the musical; and in the same year it enchanted London audiences in *Cochran's Revue of 1930.* But subsequently the song has been most closely identified with Jane Froman, so much so that it was used as the title of her screen biography in 1952.

Aarons and Freedley were also the producers of *Heads Up* at the Alvin on November 11. The subject of rum-running— with which the book by John McGowan and Paul Gerard Smith was concerned—was neither fresh nor exciting in 1929; nor, for that matter, was the complication in which beautiful Mary Trumbell is accused by her lover of being involved in this illicit business. But a well-assembled cast headed by Jack Whiting, Victor Moore, Ray Bolger and Barbara Newberry contributed considerable effervescence to a hackneyed story. Victor Moore, as the sad-faced, broken-voiced hapless inventor of strange concoctions and gadgets, stole the show. The best song was "A Ship Without a Sail," distinguished for an expansive twelve-bar melody instead of the traditional eight.

Simple Simon was a production created in 1930 for Ed Wynn, who appeared as a simpleminded newsdealer delighting in dreams that carried him into the world of nursery rhymes and Mother Goose fairy tales. This was a Florenz Ziegfeld production, given at the Ziegfeld Theatre on February 18, with book by Guy Bolton and Ed Wynn himself.

Despite their past unhappy relations with Ziegfeld, Rodgers and Hart were willing to write the songs for *Simple Simon*. An assignment from the great Ziegfeld was not to be easily dismissed. But this second association with Ziegfeld proved no happier for Rodgers than the first. Ziegfeld had not abandoned his habit of dictating to composers the kind of music he wanted. A song to which Rodgers and Hart were especially partial, "Dancing on the Ceiling," was summarily turned down by Ziegfeld as unsuitable for his show; it was to become a tremendous hit elsewhere. Another song, "I Can Do Wonders with You," was withdrawn by Ziegfeld during the out-of-town tryouts. Besides being highhandedly decisive as to what songs should or should not go into the production, Ziegfeld was also inflexible about the way the music should be presented; his ideas frequently did not coincide with those of the composer.

In *Simple Simon* Ziegfeld had trouble not only with his composer but also with his leading lady. It was no secret that she was partial to the bottle—frequently just before a rehearsal. When at a final tryout in the Colonial Theatre in Boston she almost fell off the stage, Ziegfeld decided he had had enough of her. He telephoned to New York, asking Ruth Etting to take over the feminine lead. Ruth Etting flew into Boston and, though the New York première was only a few days off, learned her role to the letter. In New York, she scored so decisively in the Rodgers and Hart song "Ten Cents a Dance" that it is sometimes said it was written for her; but the song had been in the show before Etting stepped in.

10

LITTLE GIRL BLUE

On March 5, 1930, Richard Rodgers married Dorothy Feiner.

In choosing a bride, Rodgers returned to his own back yard. He had known Dorothy since he was seven years old; and there had never been a time in Dorothy's life when she had not known Dick. Dorothy's father—Ben Feiner, Sr., a successful corporation lawyer—and Dr. William Rodgers had known each other over a long period; Dr. Rodgers was the Feiner family physician from time to time. And Dorothy's brother, Ben Feiner, Jr., was for many years Dick's friend.

In 1909 both families were spending the summer in Long Island when Ben Feiner, Jr., aged five, contracted typhoid fever. During his convalescence, he often played with Richard Rodgers, and one afternoon, as they were playing, Dorothy Feiner, an infant of two months, was wheeled through the room out to the porch. This was the first glimpse Dick had of his future wife, but, as he remarks, "It wasn't a case of love at first sight."

Although they saw each other intermittently after that, she was his friend's kid sister and consequently for a long time he regarded her condescendingly. But a change of attitude came when Dorothy reached sixteen. One day in 1926, Dick dropped in at the Feiner apartment at the Hotel Chatham to pick up Ben for a movie date. It happened that on the same day Dorothy had a date to see the Kern musical *Sunny* with a young beau, Andy Goodman (now of Bergdorf Goodman, the smart women's shop on Fifth Avenue) and as Dick was waiting for Ben, Dorothy came into the living room. She was wearing a light blue dress that accentuated the color of her hair. The glow of her gentle brown eyes and her radiant and delicate face took Rodgers by storm. "That was the minute I knew—this was it. She was the girl I would someday marry." Dorothy also confesses that it was from this day on that she began to think romantically of Dick, even though as a successful theater man surrounded by bevies of glamorous girls he seemed hopelessly out of reach.

Between 1926 and 1929 Dorothy went to Europe with her parents for a few weeks each summer to study sculpture in Paris, one time at the Grand Chaumière. After her visit abroad in the summer of 1926, the Feiners sailed home from Cherbourg on the *Majestic*. Once aboard they discovered— much to Dorothy's delight—that Richard Rodgers, following his first visit to London, had boarded the boat at Southampton. Before the *Majestic* was out at sea twenty-four hours, Dick and Dorothy were inseparable companions; by the time the boat docked in New York they knew they were in love.

Back from Europe, Dorothy studied at Wellesley College, waiting for each week end impatiently, hoping it would bring a "date" with Dick. It often did. Sometimes Dick would spend the week end with the Feiners at their summer home in Tarrytown. Sometimes he would pick her up at the Hotel Chatham and take her for a drive in his La Salle. She confessed to her brother that she was "crazy" about Dick, and he told her as gently as he could, "You'll get over it, Dot. All the other girls do."

Despite her attachment for Rodgers, she was at the time going out with other men, too, one of whom was Bennett Cerf. "She was indescribably lovely, and a pleasure to be with," he recalls, "but I don't think I was ever in love with her. I guess I could never fall in love with anybody who had such an eye for exactitude as Dorothy had and has. I remember taking her to see a musical. From the first row balcony she was able to detect that the third chorus girl on the left was wearing shoes slightly different from those worn by the other chorus girls. She was also then—as she is now—a fusspot over order and symmetry. Nothing tickles me more than to visit the Rodgerses, disarrange one of the ash trays in the living room, then watch out of the corner of my eye for Dorothy to try putting the ash tray back in its place without being noticed."

It was during a date with Bennett Cerf that she had the first hint that she was more to Rodgers than just another passing fancy. She and Cerf, in the company of Mortimer Rodgers and his date, went one evening in 1927 to a Theatre Guild production. When the two couples first met, Mortimer growled at Cerf, "Say, what are you doing—going out with my kid brother's girl?"

By 1928 Dorothy and Dick were seeing each other steadily, but the subject of their marriage had not yet come up. Dorothy lost interest in school and left Wellesley after her sophomore year. It was over a year before Dick proposed, but they had long tacitly accepted the fact that they belonged with each other.

She went to Philadelphia with Cerf and several others of

Rodgers' friends for the opening there of *Spring Is Here* on February 25, 1929. "It was then that I came to know how serious it was between Dorothy and Dick," says Cerf. "Sunday morning, while Dick was still sleeping, Dorothy and I went downstairs in the hotel for breakfast. I started looking through the Sunday paper and in the way I invariably have with Sunday papers it soon became a disheveled and disorganized mess. Dorothy then started straightening it out carefully and putting each section and page in the proper place, explaining that Dick always wanted his newspaper neat and in order when he came down for breakfast. When a girl becomes so concerned over a young man's newspaper, you don't have to be warned how serious she is about him."

The engagement of Dick and Dorothy was announced on December 7, 1929, and about five weeks later, on January 12, a reception was held at the Park Lane Hotel. The marriage ceremony took place at the Feiner apartment on 270 Park Avenue, with Rabbi Stephen S. Wise officiating. Mortimer was Dick's best man; Dorothy's maid of honor was Rosemary Klee, her college roomate; Larry Hart and Herbert Fields were ushers. Escorted by her father, Dorothy walked down the aisle dressed in an ivory white satin gown, cut in medieval fashion, with long white sleeves made of old family lace, and veil of tulle; she carried a bouquet of white calla lilies. "All brides are beautiful," says Rodgers. "Mine was the most beautiful of all."

After the wedding ceremony, the Richard Rodgerses left on a European honeymoon aboard the *Roma*. "We just couldn't stand the idea of spending our first night of marriage at the Hotel Plaza or some such place," explains Rodgers, "and then have Dorothy's mother call the next morning and make coy inquiries."

They spent their first days in Europe in Taormina. Then

they went north to Italy, where they were squired around
Rome by Elsa Maxwell, to France, and finally to London.
Since Rodgers was now scheduled to write the music for a
new Cochran musical, they rented a house at 10 York Terrace and invited Larry Hart to stay with them.

In London, Rodgers became absorbed not only in his
work but also with a whirlwind social life. He was eager to
introduce his bride to friends old and new. There were, of
course, the Charles B. Cochrans, who welcomed Dorothy
warmly into their circle and soon became her devoted
friends. There were Lord and Lady Louis Mountbatten, at
whose festive dinner party Dick and Dorothy were the honor
guests. At that party, Lady Edwina slyly told Dick she had
just received a recording of what at the moment was the big-
gest song hit in New York. Taking him into an adjoining
room she played "Ten Cents a Dance"—the first hint Rodgers had had that his song from *Simple Simon* was doing so
well.

There was Noel Coward, who a year earlier had expressed
to an American interviewer his enthusiasm for Rodgers'
music. "Rodgers," he said, "has melody, romance, glamour,
rhythm—in short everything."

There was the Duke of Kent, with whom Rodgers struck up
an acquaintanceship for the first time and who from now on
remained a close friend. When at a party Rodgers sat down
at the piano to play some of his songs, the Duke sat near him
and began asking him to play his favorite Rodgers numbers,
some of them little known or long forgotten. When Rodgers
complied, the Duke started singing the songs, revealing that
he knew not only all the lyrics of the choruses but even
those of the verses. "As you see," he explained, "I have been
your admirer for several years now."

There was Baron Robin d'Erlanger, a banker and art pa-
tron, and his wife Myrtle. Rodgers had met them before in

London but during the present visit became more intimate with them. Myrtle had just given birth to a daughter, Zoe, whose godfather was the Duke of Kent. During the years of World War II, Zoe would come to live with the Rodgerses in America.

But the early spring of 1930 meant work as well as play for Rodgers, his immediate chore being to write music for *Evergreen,* starring Jessie Matthews and Sonny Hale. The first number he wrote was also his first love song since his marriage—"Dear, Dear"—and, of course, he wrote it with Dorothy in mind. Another song, which became the principal hit of the show, was "Dancing on the Ceiling," meant originally for *Simple Simon.* Cochran gave *Evergreen* a handsome production at the Adelphi on December 3. Particularly effective was the way "Dancing on the Ceiling" was presented. Jessie Matthews sang and danced to its strains against a set made to look like a ceiling, with a huge crystal chandelier rising from the middle of the stage.

But several months before *Evergreen* opened, and as soon as Rodgers had finished writing its music, Rodgers and his wife returned to New York. They set up house in Rodgers' apartment at the Hotel Lombardy. They were still living there when, on January 11, 1931, their first child, Mary, was born at Lenox Hill Hospital, delivered by Mortimer Rodgers.

11

TO HOLLYWOOD—AND BACK

In 1926 a revolution had taken place in motion pictures: the screen had acquired sound. Two years later, the first singing and talking picture, *The Broadway Melody,* inaugurated a vogue for screen musicals which caused imitations to sprout like mushrooms. Even some pictures not intended as musicals had to have interpolated songs. The demand for music was now insatiable. Hollywood began combing Broadway and Tin Pan Alley, luring their leading composers and lyricists with fabulous offers.

Rodgers, Hart and Fields were among the first to be called. First National Pictures paid them $50,000.00 each to come to Hollywood and write the music for two pictures.

Rodgers and Hart had had some personal and some impersonal experiences with motion pictures before this. They had appeared in a twenty-minute short subject called *Makers*

of Melody in which a synthetic story enabled them to explain
how they wrote some of their songs. These songs were then
performed by various artists and dancers. Released the same
year in local theaters, this "short" was described by *Variety*
as "a novel try that failed." Association with motion pictures
of quite a different character took place in 1929 and early
in 1930 through the sale of two of their musicals: *Spring Is
Here* to Warner Brothers and *Heads Up* to Paramount.

But the First National contract was their first offer to write
original music for the screen. Rodgers, Hart, and Fields left
in July of 1930, a few weeks after Rodgers had returned from
London. Since Dorothy, who was now pregnant, was not feeling well, she had to remain behind in New York, but she
joined Dick in Hollywood a few weeks later.

A few days after Rodgers and Hart arrived in Hollywood
they were given an official welcome and an opportunity to
meet the elite of the movie industry at an extravagant garden
party in their honor at Jules Glaenzer's Beverly Hills home.
Among the eighty or so guests were Charles Chaplin, Louis
Bromfield, David Selznick, Louella Parsons, Dolores Del
Rio, Frederick Londsdale, Jesse Lasky, Joan Bennett, Bebe
Daniels, and Ben Lyons.

At the First National studios, they were also given a regal
welcome and luxurious offices. All they were expected to
do was to write three songs to Herbert Fields' screen play
The Hot Heiress, starring Ona Munson, Walter Pidgeon and
Ben Lyons. The job was supposed to take Rodgers and Hart
a few weeks, but they completed the songs in a few days.
When they had finished the first song, they brought it to one
of the executives, who was delighted. "Take your time in
writing the others," he advised them.

After the delivery of the three songs, Rodgers and Hart
left Hollywood for a hurried visit to London to help with the
production of *Evergreen.* Early in 1931 they returned with

Fields to Hollywood to write their second picture for First
National. But the executives there informed them that
since *The Hot Heiress* had proved a flop, and since musical
films were now a drug on the market, the studio stood ready
to buy back the contract and abandon the second production.

That first adventure in Hollywood provided Fields, Rodgers, and Hart with grist for their creative mill. Back in New
York they completed a new musical, *America's Sweetheart,* a
satire on Hollywood which Schwab and Mandel produced at
the Broadhurst on February 10, 1931. Practically the entire
play, except for a brief sequence in the Tennessee hills, was
set on the movie lot of "Premier Pictures." With their impressions of Hollywood still fresh, Rodgers and Hart allowed
their natural bent for wit and satire full freedom. They wrote
a delightful satire on movie magazines in a hillbilly style in
"Sweet Geraldine"; presented a naughty commentary on sex
mania in Hollywood in "I Want a Man"; lamented has-been
stars in "Innocent Chorus Girls of Yesterday." They also
wrote a song that made no allusions to Hollywood—"I've Got
Five Dollars," which had the town humming even before the
show opened. "It is the songs," said Gilbert Gabriel, "which
must be the standbys . . . excellent songs, happily phrased,
insinuatingly clever and memorable." Brooks Atkinson also
had kind words for the songs. "There is a rush about the
music and mocking touch in the lyrics that makes the score
more deftly satirical than the production."

The heroine of *America's Sweetheart* was played by a
young actress, Harriet Lake, whom one critic described as "a
veritable find." Like the character she portrayed she was
soon destined to reach the summits in Hollywood—under
the name of Ann Sothern.

The cast also included the three Forman Sisters, who had
come fresh from the Tennessee hills. They sang nicely and

made a good appearance; but they were somewhat naïve. When the show tried out in Washington, D.C., Rodgers recommended them as entertainers for a party. The following day, one of the sisters told Rodgers how much they had enjoyed the party and how well they had been paid. She then slipped into Rodgers' hand a carefully folded ten-dollar bill. "That's your commission, Mr. Rodgers," she told him.

In the spring of 1931, Rodgers and Hart were back in Hollywood. This time they came to work for Paramount on a one-picture deal, but they stayed in Hollywood almost three years, writing songs not only for Paramount pictures but also for the productions of several other studios.

When in the fall of 1931 Rodgers was joined by his wife and daughter—as well as his parents, now that his father had retired as a physician—he rented a house owned by Elsie Janis, the first of several rented Hollywood homes, and Hart came to live with them. After 1932 Hart lived by himself in a magnificent home on North Bedford Drive, where each Sunday he would entertain about a hundred guests in "brunch" and swimming parties at his enormous swimming pool; on one occasion he had as guests most of the Olympic swimming team.

Rodgers and Hart did some good—and at times original—work for the screen. They spent many hours at the studio, in cutting rooms and sound laboratories, trying to learn something of the inner mechanism of the motion-picture business; trying to get a better understanding of the techniques of picture making which they might adapt to their own work. And they made a conscious attempt to evolve new methods. For their first Paramount picture, *Love Me Tonight,* in which Maurice Chevalier was starred with Jeanette MacDonald, they conceived the technique of "rhythmic dialogue": spoken dialogue in verse against a musical background. This and a few effective songs added considerably to the Gallic verve and sparkle of the picture. Of the songs the best was "Lover," the first of the celebrated Rodgers waltzes (a style in which he was to create some of his most magical tonal moods). No less delightful were "Mimi" and "Isn't It Romantic?", in the latter of which a change of rhythmic sequence in the first bars of the chorus produces a charming effect.

The use of rhythmic dialogue is even more extended in *Hallelujah, I'm a Bum,* starring Al Jolson—though little else in this picture is of any consequence. In several scenes, Jolson spoke lines in rhyme against a subtle musical background. Rodgers and Hart also made a deliberate attempt here to allow songs to evolve naturally from the story material. In one scene Jolson finds a gold watch and puts it to his ear. "Tick, tick, tick," he says, "ain't it slick." As he speaks, the orchestra simulates the ticking of the watch, which then serves as a prelude to a song. But this and other songs in this picture were undistinguished and are deservedly forgotten, with the single exception of "You Are Too Beautiful."

Between *Love Me Tonight* and *Hallelujah, I'm a Bum,* Rodgers and Hart worked on a score for a second Paramount picture, *The Phantom President,* in which George M. Cohan made his first appearance in talking pictures, filling a dual role: as President of the United States, a cold, forbidding, humorless person; and as a colorful, lovable carnival man who so closely resembles the President that he is recruited to impersonate him to win the favor of the people. Making this picture was one of the sorriest experiences of Cohan's life. Many of those who worked with him at the studio refused to give him the deference he felt he deserved. All his ideas were summarily dismissed. Only one of his songs was used, "She's a Grand Old Flag," but—crowning humiliation —the director insisted on trying to teach him how to do the flag routine—Cohan, who had spent a quarter of a century on the Broadway stage doing flag routines! "If I had my choice between Hollywood and Atlanta," Cohan said after returning from California, "I'd take Leavenworth." It was in all probability because of his miserable experience on the movie lot that he reacted so frigidly to both Rodgers and Hart, whom he regarded as young upstarts. He either avoided them completely or cut them off with sharp remarks. His relationship with them was no more cordial when, a few years later, he was starred in a Rodgers and Hart musical.

The three songs Rodgers and Hart wrote for *The Phantom President* added little of value to the picture. And the individual numbers they contributed to several other unimportant pictures between 1932 and 1933 are hardly more impressive.

Ironically, the one important song they did manage to write in Hollywood was never used on the screen. While working at the Metro-Goldwyn-Mayer studios in 1933 they were assigned to a picture starring Jean Harlow. One of the songs they wrote for it was "Make Me a Star." When Jean Harlow was dropped from the picture, so was the song. Hart then prepared a new lyric for the same melody, called it "The Bad in Every Man," and resubmitted it to M.G.M. for another picture, *Manhattan Melodrama*. Once again it was left out. After Rodgers and Hart returned to New York, Jack Robbins, a music publisher affiliated with M.G.M., called them suggesting they write a new lyric and title for the beautiful melody. The next day Rodgers and Hart rewrote their song as "Blue Moon." Published by Robbins as an independent song, without any relation to a motion picture or play, it enjoyed the largest sheet-music sale of any Rodgers and Hart song up to that time—about a million copies—and is one of the dozen or so of their songs by which they are most often remembered.

By 1934 Rodgers was growing increasingly restive. For over a year both he and Hart had been unhappy over living in Hollywood and working for motion pictures. When in a later song they remarked, "Hate California, it's cold and it's damp," they were not merely pronouncing the credo of a lady who's a tramp but uttering a conviction born out of personal experience. To Hart, to whom any kind of timetable or system represented mental cruelty, punching a clock regularly at the studio was a detestable procedure against which he continually rebelled. He disliked intensely the kind of pictures with which he was associated. Besides, he deeply resented the anonymity surrounding anyone in the industry who was neither a star nor a producer—particularly song and scenario writers. "Writers, who ever heard about them out here?" he would grumble. "The movie fans think the actors make up the dialogue as they go along."

To Rodgers the most annoying aspect of life in Hollywood was his comparative inactivity. Up to now he had been highly productive. He functioned best, and was happiest, when absorbed by more commitments than he could handle, when he was continually pressed by deadlines and opening nights. But in Hollywood, notwithstanding his fat weekly check, he was kept idle most of the time. The songs he had to write for the various movies were done quickly; in New York all of these would have been completed in about two or three weeks. "I was completely disconnected from my work and leading the life of a retired banker. That's no way for a thirty-two-year-old fellow to live." Creatively, too, the Hollywood period had been sterile. He was proud of the score he had written for *Love Me Tonight,* and deservedly so; but almost everything else he wrote for the screen during this period was of inferior quality, and he knew it. And the song of which he was most proud had twice been rejected.

A casual item—one single sentence—in a newspaper col-

umn galvanized him into action. It appeared in O. O. Mc-
Intyre's column in the Los Angeles *Examiner* and inquired,
"Whatever became of Rodgers and Hart?" "That really made
my head jerk," Rodgers recalls. "I sat right down and wrote
him a letter thanking him and telling him we were getting out
of Hollywood as fast as we could. The day our contract was
up, we climbed aboard the Chief and came back to the United
States. I felt as if I had just been given my pardon—a few
short years ahead of Mooney."

Back in New York, Rodgers returned to the ten-room apartment at 50 East 77th Street which he had rented in the fall
of 1931 and then subleased during his stay in Hollywood.
With a household retinue comprising a maid, nurse, and
cook, Rodgers was still living in the grand manner to which
his past prosperity on Broadway and his recent affluence in
Hollywood had accustomed him but which his present financial position did not warrant. The money he had earned in
Hollywood went quickly. (He did have a paid-up annuity
but he refused to touch it since it represented the only measure of security he could provide his family.) The birth of
his second child, Linda, on March 5, 1935—delivered like her
sister by her Uncle Mortimer at Lenox Hill Hospital—further aggravated Rodgers' financial difficulties. With very little
coming in, and a great deal flowing out, he even had to resort
to borrowing from the bank.

The sorry truth was, as Rodgers discovered to his horror,
that Broadway producers had either forgotten Rodgers and
Hart or now considered them has-beens. Suddenly the team
which had headed the league only a short time before was no
longer even in the running. The ideas they brought to producers were received coldly and then rejected. Only one of
these was optioned—by Lee Shubert—but at the moment
production seemed a distant prospect.

For this was a new era, no longer the frenetic and pleasure-

loving 1920's of which their musicals had been such an appropriate voice. This was the grim depression era of Roosevelt's first administration. Broadway producers had to be
doubly wary about financing musicals, doubly certain of
the marketability of their product. The often fresh and
original projects Rodgers and Hart were trying to sell represented a serious risk. Besides, the names of Rodgers and Hart
were no longer assets at the box office. And the two motion
pictures released in 1935 with which they had been associated—*Evergreen* and *Mississippi*—did nothing to restore
their lost popularity.

In the year and a half following their return to New
York only one new Rodgers and Hart song was heard on the
Broadway stage: "You're So Lovely and I'm So Lonely" in
Something Gay, a play starring Tallulah Bankhead and
Walter Pidgeon. As if to underscore their present failure, the
play lasted only 72 performances and the song passed into
quick oblivion.

Rodgers had sunk to an emotional nadir when Billy Rose
suddenly brought him the promise of a change of fortune.
Rose had known both Rodgers and Hart for many years. As
far back as 1918 or 1919 he was a friend of Hart's, and when
Rose began writing song lyrics, Hart is said to have given
him a helping hand. In 1926, when he opened his Fifth
Avenue night club, Rose asked Rodgers and Hart to write
special numbers for his show, promising them a royalty
which, however, was never paid. Since 1926 Rose had become the successful producer of several Broadway shows and
the wealthy proprietor of the first theater-restaurant, the
Casino de Paree. In that time he often came across Rodgers
or Hart, both of whom he liked and admired.

Rose was one of the few who had not forgotten them. Now
planning a grandiose production for the Hippodrome Theatre which he hoped would restore to that historical show-

place some of the splendor it had known at the turn of the century, he turned to Rodgers and Hart for the songs. The show Rose had in mind was not the kind that Rodgers and Hart were partial to. But after the recent rejections from other producers, this assignment represented manna from heaven.

The spectacular that Rose was producing was *Jumbo*, which combined the most attractive features of musical extravaganza and circus. The book, by Ben Hecht and Charles MacArthur, was a routine saga about two circus proprietors whose lifelong feud and rivalry is finally ended when the son of one falls in love with and marries the daughter of the other. The story provided a convenient hook on which to hang big-top attractions: clowns, jugglers, wirewalkers, animals. It also provided fat roles for Jimmy Durante as a circus press-agent and for an elephant named Big Rosie, sometimes known as Jumbo.

Financed by Jock Whitney, Rose took over the Hippodrome and tore out its innards to accommodate a huge circus ring in the middle of the stage. The rehearsals, not only at the Hippodrome but also in units at the Manhattan Opera House and in Brooklyn, consumed so much more time than had been anticipated that the première had to be postponed five times. During this three-month rehearsal period, Rose kept alive the growing curiosity in his production by posting huge billboards outside the theater announcing: "Sh-h! *Jumbo* Rehearsing." He also ran ads in the papers saying, "I'll be a dirty name if I'll open *Jumbo* before it's ready."

When it was finally ready—and presented on November 16—it fulfilled its promises by providing more novelty, thrills, surprise, and spectacle than any musical in the memory of most critics. Percy Hammond described it as an "exciting compound of opera, animal show, folk drama, harlequinade, carnival, circus, extravaganza, and spectacle." There were acrobats who did aerial stunts dangling by their toes from moving planes; tightrope performers who balanced themselves over an open cage of roaring lions; a clown who played the violin while bananas were being tossed into his pocket. Paul Whiteman made his entrance on a big white horse; Jimmy Durante, by hanging on to the neck of Big Rosie. Jimmy and his elephant provided the best laugh of the show. In one scene he is caught red-handed trying to steal an elephant. As he is leading it away he is stopped by the sheriff, who barks, "What are you doing with that elephant?" Jimmy answers innocently, "What elephant?"

For this mammoth production Rodgers tapped a rich vein of melodic beauty he had long neglected; this was the best song writing he had done in several years. In line with the circus setting of the play, "The Most Beautiful Girl in the World" was sung while the hero and heroine were riding horseback around the ring. But this unorthodox presentation could not rob the song of its musical appeal, which lay in an intoxicating waltz melody that swept expansively through seventy-two bars. "Little Girl Blue," its trio a delicate waltz in smaller dimension, and "My Romance" were also in a happy lyrical vein. Apparently, Rodgers' return to Broadway had had a salutary effort on his inspiration. He had recovered his happy touch.

12

TOWARD NEW HORIZONS

Their four-year absence from Broadway between *America's Sweetheart* and *Jumbo* had given Rodgers and Hart a new perspective on both the musical comedy and their own work. They had always been restless with the *status quo* in the musical theater, had always chafed under the limitations it imposed upon them, even when first they began writing for it. Now that they had been away from the theater for several years they were determined to open up new horizons.

Through the years there had been several attempts by courageous writers to break down the established boundaries that hemmed in the musical stage. Rodgers and Hart knew of those attempts and respected them. The "Princess Theatre Shows" of Guy Bolton, P. G. Wodehouse, and Jerome Kern had succeeded in stripping the musical comedy of the late 1910's of some of its superficiality and decoration, in reducing the musical comedy to essentials. Thus a new note of informality and intimacy was introduced. In 1927, *Show Boat,* by Oscar Hammerstein II and Jerome Kern, based on Edna Ferber's novel (about which more will be said in a later chapter) was a historic achievement. It brought about a greater cohesion between play and music and at the same time introduced to the musical-comedy stage characters and subject matter which it had up to now ignored. *Of Thee I Sing* (1931) by George S. Kaufman, Morrie Ryskind and George and Ira Gershwin, injected the realities of American politics into the musical theater and treated it with withering satire. To do this successfully old procedures had to be abandoned—and an altogether new spaciousness had to be brought to the musical writing. *Rainbow,* a romantic play by Laurence Stallings and Oscar Hammerstein II, with music by Vincent Youmans, also brought artistic validity and dramatic truth to a musical production, even though it was a failure when introduced in 1928. The adjustment of music to the play, and vice-versa, was almost operatic in *Rainbow;* atmosphere, characterization, and local color were in the best traditions of the legitimate theater.

From the beginning of their career on Broadway, Rodgers and Hart had experimented with unusual texts as well as fresh musical-comedy techniques and approaches. By 1935 they knew what they wanted to do, and it was a departure from what they had done in the past. They had lost all interest in "musical comedy" and were now talking only about a "musical play" in which all the elements were to be integrated into a single artistic entity.

Hart now told an interviewer that he and Rodgers envisioned "a new form of musical show for Broadway. It will not be a musical comedy and it will not be operetta. The songs are going to be part of the progress of the piece, not extraneous interludes without rhyme or reason." And Rodgers also said for publication: "I should like to free myself for broader motifs, more extended designs—but within the framework of the theater, for that is where I belong."

When Rodgers and Hart sought to re-establish themselves on Broadway after their return from Hollywood, they tried to do so with musicals embodying their new aesthetics. *Jumbo* was a temporary digression from those aesthetics—but a necessary one to bring them back to Broadway. Once they were back, they had no intention of reverting any longer to old procedures.

One of the projects Rodgers and Hart brought back with them from Hollywood was a musical built around the backstage life of a ballet company. In Hollywood they heard that Pandro Berman, head of R.K.O., was looking for a story for Fred Astaire. Within a few hours they developed a two page synopsis about a vaudeville hoofer who gets involved with the Russian ballet. Berman liked the idea, but when he presented it to his associates they turned it down.

A few weeks after coming to New York, Rodgers and Hart met Lee Shubert on 45th Street and Broadway. Shubert revealed that he was grooming Ray Bolger for stardom and was searching frantically for a musical for him. Rodgers and Hart rapidly summarized for Shubert the plot of the story they had written for Astaire. Shubert was sufficiently impressed to conclude a deal then and there.

Rodgers and Hart now began to work on the first draft of their text. It turned out to be so heavy in its timing and so complicated in its plot structure that they decided to enlist the help of George Abbott, whose skillful direction of fast-paced Broadway comedies like *Three Men on a Horse* and *Room Service* had won their admiration. "George straightened out the story line," says Rodgers, "and kept it straight through the turmoil and upheaval of rehearsals and out-of-town tryouts."

After they had finished writing their play, Shubert found that after all he had too many commitments to produce it in the near future. He turned the entire enterprise over to Dwight Deere Wiman, who scheduled it for immediate production.

The musical was named *On Your Toes,* and its principal character was Philip Dolan III, the son of a vaudeville hoofer, who turns to the ballet. He succeeds only in making a ridiculous spectacle of himself in a classic work, *Princess Zenobia.* One of his pupils, Frankie Frayne, creates a bailet in a modern jazz style and tempo which Philip brings to the attention of the noted ballerina Vera Barnova. Largely out of her romantic interest in Philip, Vera introduces it with Philip as her dancing partner. The ballet, "Slaughter on Tenth Avenue," is a triumph, a development that convinces Philip he loves Frankie more than he does Vera.

"Slaughter on Tenth Avenue" and "Princess Zenobia" were both large ballet sequences. Such a strong accent on ballet called for an experienced choreographer. Hart found him one day in a 54th Street theater where he dropped in to watch a ballet rehearsal. He was George Balanchine, one-time ballet master for the Diaghilev troupe and for the Ballet Russe de Monte Carlo. The rehearsal Hart saw convinced him Balanchine was the man to work out the ballet episodes for *On Your Toes.* Balanchine, in turn, was intrigued by the idea of working for a musical comedy and creating dances in a more popular vein than had been customary for him up to now.

With George Balanchine as choreographer, Wiman gathered other suitable collaborators: Worthington Miner for the staging, Jo Mielziner for the sets, Irene Sharaff for the costuming. Ray Bolger was to be the male lead; Doris Carson was chosen for Frankie and Tamara Geva for Vera Barnova.

On Your Toes began a one-year run at the Imperial Theatre in New York on April 11, 1936. All the critics voiced approval, calling it "one of the seven wonders of 1936," "a dancing show that is witty as it is nimble," and "a smart, amusing, debonair entertainment."

On Your Toes was the first of their musicals in which Rodgers and Hart helped to write the book—a practice they would now continue from time to time in an effort to achieve a better fusion between text and music. Another "first" was also significant. This was the first popular musical play in which dancing was used as an integral part of the story, and in which ballet episodes were utilized. In the first act, in "Princess Zenobia," ballet was lampooned through a satirical treatment of a classical dance based on the Scheherazade theme. But ballet was also treated with seriousness of artistic purpose in "Slaughter on Tenth Avenue," which carried the play to its exciting climax. This was a satire on gangster stories. A hoofer and his girl, fleeing from murderous gangsters, take refuge in a Tenth Avenue café, where the gangsters catch up with them and shoot the girl. The hoofer himself is finally saved by the police.

For his music to "Slaughter on Tenth Avenue," Rodgers borrowed none of the material previously used in the play. This, then, became his first sustained piece of orchestral writing, though in earlier plays he had written smaller interludes; and to it he brought both a technical facility in developing musical materials and a feeling for architectonics. There is sound craftsmanship in the way the basic melodic subjects are given, and in the injection of fragmentary ideas to change the mood and pace. (One of these minor ideas is an amusing adaptation of "Three Blind Mice.") There is also a fresh and winning charm in his choice of principal themes.

The most significant is a broad lament, first foreshadowed in the opening grim bars, then, somewhat later, erupting opulently in the strings; a secondary theme is a saucy jazz melody now given by the full orchestra, now presented by a rakish trumpet.

When Rodgers first played this ballet music for Balanchine, the choreographer sat throughout with an expressionless face. Rodgers became convinced his music was a failure. Suddenly Balanchine exclaimed: "But it's vunderful, simply vunderful."

"Slaughter on Tenth Avenue," which Percy Hammond found to be "full of theatrical color and cadence," always brought down the house. It became the single outstanding feature of the motion-picture adaptation of the play, with Vera Zorina and Eddie Albert, released by Warner Brothers in 1939. And, once again, it became the one cause for rejoicing in the Broadway revival of *On Your Toes* in 1954. On that occasion Richard Watts, Jr. said, "A sizable number of jazz ballets have passed this way since it first appeared, but it still is something of a classic in its field, and the music Mr. Rodgers wrote for it continues to seem one of the major achievements of his career."

There was another little treasure in the *On Your Toes* score—one of the most lovable of the Rodgers and Hart songs, "There's a Small Hotel." Meant to be sung in the play by two innocents—Philip and Frankie—the song manages to catch the ingenuousness of these people through the simplicity of melody, harmony, and rhythm and through the lack of sophistication in the lyrics. This unaffected directness in the writing, particularly in the delightful release of the chorus, leads to an altogether irresistible charm.

Before writing a new musical play, Rodgers and Hart had a few lesser jobs to complete. As soon as *On Your Toes* became an established hit, they went to Hollywood for a screen assignment for R.K.O., resulting in two songs for *Dancing Pirate.* (About the only distinction this film had was that it was the first feature picture in the three-process Technicolor now in general use.) Later the same year, they contributed a special number, "Rhythm," for Beatrice Lillie and Reginald Gardiner for their Winter Garden revue *The Show Is On.*

But another commitment took them completely off the well-beaten track. Paul Whiteman, impressed by the new dimensions in Rodgers' writing in "Slaughter on Tenth Avenue," called on him for a composition. The writing of abstract music never appealed to Rodgers, whose musical thinking had to be sparked into flame by a play, scenario, or lyric. He discussed the problem with Hart, who solved it by writing *All Points West,* a long narrative to be set for voice and orchestra. It begins with the announcement of the departure of the Great Lakes Express on Track 33 for Albany, Syracuse, and "all points west." There follows a description of the farewell of a wife to her salesman husband and of a mother to her son going west for a job; the departure of rookie soldiers for Plattsburg, young girls for college, a honeymoon couple for Niagara Falls, and a prisoner for Ossining. The narrative ends tragically. The train announcer is accidentally killed by a policeman pursuing an escaped prisoner. The announcer is able to make a journey of his own—to celestial spheres.

This text gave Rodgers elastic scope for his natural gift at varied lyricism. Deems Taylor described the composition as a combination of orchestral tone poem, song cycle, and dramatic recitation—but it is actually simpler than that: structurally it is a cantata. Rodgers combines accompanied spoken words and recitatives with fully developed melodies in a cohesive and fluid composition. Abrupt changes of mood

and feeling are achieved effortlessly through skillful modulations. Contrast of recitatives (both *secco* and *stromentato*)
with song, and of one song with the next, provides continual
interest.

If there are some passages that are too literal in translating
text to music (as in some of the background music for the
spoken word) Rodgers compensates for this naïveté by the
flexibility of his melodic writing: by the folk-song character
of the young man's hymn to the west *(cantando)*; by the
feminine charm of the passage about the college girls *(con
leggierezza)*; the affecting tenderness of the music for the
honeymooners *(con amore)*.

All Points West, orchestrated by Adolph Deutsch, was introduced by Paul Whiteman when he appeared as guest conductor of the Philadelphia Orchestra on November 27 and
28, 1936. Ray Middleton was the soloist. "The orchestral
and vocal music," wrote Linton Martin in the *Inquirer,*
"takes on real musical beauty, if with musical-comedy learn-
ings." A few days later, on December 1, Whiteman and his
orchestra, with Middleton, introduced it to New York at the
Hippodrome Theatre; and the following January the same
performers broadcast it over radio station WEAF. On March
16, 1937, the famous American baritone Reinald Werren-
rath concluded his New York song recital with this composition, accompanied on the piano. *All Points West* was made
by Russell Markert and Nat Karson into a production number for the Radio City Music Hall in June, 1939; and Rudy
Vallee used it as a feature of his floor show at the Hotel
Astor Roof in New York.

A little over two years after he introduced *All Points West,*
Paul Whiteman and his orchestra presented another new
Rodgers work, a little three-movement suite, *Nursery Ballet,*
orchestrated by Roy Bargy. This première took place at

Carnegie Hall on December 25, 1938, after which it was heard over radio station WEAF. This is the only Rodgers composition which has no poetic text or which was not rooted in some play, movie, or ballet scenario. Nevertheless, it is still descriptive music, the titles of the respective movements providing the clue to the programmatic content: "March of the Clowns," "A Doll Gets Broken," and "Little Girls Don't Fight." This work, which Rodgers wrote for his daughter Mary, makes no pretense at doing anything more than the composer intended: to evoke for adults the enchantment of a child's world while providing children with musical entertainment, much in the way Bizet did in *Jeux d'Enfants* and Debussy in *Children's Corner.*

Rodgers' most ambitious musical score outside the theater during the 1930's was *Ghost Town,* an American folk ballet commissioned by the Ballet Russe de Monte Carlo and orchestrated by Hans Spialek. It was first given by the Ballet Russe at the Metropolitan Opera House on November 12, 1939. Mia Slavenska and Frederic Franklin were the principal dancers, and Rodgers conducted. After receiving seven performances in New York, *Ghost Town* was taken on tour, after which it returned to New York for one more performance.

The libretto (by Marc Platoff and Richard Rodgers) recreated the background of the gold country of the 1860's. The prologue presents two hitchhikers on the main street of a ghost town in the Sierras. They meet an old mining prospector who tells them the strange history of the town. In the ensuing scene, a busy, roaring mining town is recreated. Ralston, a young prospector, strikes it rich and celebrates by buying a red coat with gold buttons. He loses the papers confirming his rights to his strike and is accused of having jumped the claim. The vigilantes are about to lynch him when the papers are found by Eilley Orrum, the town heiress, who is interested in him. A celebration follows in which Jenny Lind sings "The Last Rose of Summer" (this old favorite presented against interesting chromatic harmonizations). An interruption comes with the news that the gold ore is petering out. Panic sets in. The people, faced by ruin, flee. Eilley entreats Ralston to come with her, but he insists upon remaining behind. The scene fades into the epilogue, in which Ghost Town reappears stark and grim and barren. The two hitchhikers go on their way. The old prospector is left alone again; he is wearing a faded red coat with gold buttons.

Rodgers' score is made up of many delightful melodies and fragments of melodies, many of them rich with American folk flavor. Particularly inviting are a gay polkalike tune and a theme that is a rephrasing of his own song, "Spring Is Here." But integration is absent; so is the driving power to bring force and distinction to the writing. The music remains more interesting as occasional passages than as an artistic entity.

John Martin wrote in the *New York Times,* "It is really not so much a ballet as a musical comedy without singing. As such, it is as cute as Punch, but in certain ways a mite surprising to find at the Metropolitan. Mr. Rodgers' score might be tops a little farther uptown, where he ranks quite legitimately among the crowned heads of Broadway, but as the musical setting for an American folk ballet . . . it is a styleless anachronism." However in *Modern Music* Edward Denby said of the music: "It is catchy and unpretentious and keeps going, and I enjoyed the clarity of it. . . . It does say something of its own." And in his little book *Ballet,* George Amberg felt that the ballet as a whole was "a charming and entertaining piece with many delightful moments of genuine humor and good fun."

13

AT THE SUMMIT

The accolade of critics to *On Your Toes*, the brisk business at the Imperial Theatre, and the healthy sheet-music sale of "There's a Small Hotel" all combined to carry Rodgers and Hart to the top of their profession after their temporary eclipse. Once again they were eagerly sought after by producers, and once again each of their new shows was an event eagerly anticipated by the critics and theater audiences. Except for one week, there was no time between 1935 and 1938 when they did not have at least one smash success running on Broadway.

Strengthened in their purpose by the restoration of both their popularity and prosperity, they were now able to inject their fresh ideas into the musical theater with renewed vigor. *Babes in Arms* came on April 14, 1937. For this musical, Rodgers and Hart wrote the entire book without outside assistance. Their aim in *On Your Toes* to make songs and dance basic to the plot was now fortified. For the first time they exerted a deliberate effort to make every number a "plot number," to include no element in the production that was not germane to the story they were unfolding. Nevertheless, though each song had its specific function, many of them have retained their interest and appeal even when divorced from their context. This score abounds with musical riches. Of the eleven numbers, five may be said to be among the best by Rodgers and Hart. Not one but several are in Rodgers' most infectious melodic manner—that bitter sweetness of lyricism that is passionless yet endearing: "Where or When?", "All at Once," "You Are So Fair," and "My Funny Valentine." The last particularly has musical distinction. The harmonic writing in the release of the chorus is daring in its originality. On the other hand, the personalized melody of the verse achieves individuality through the absence of all harmonic accompaniment: only a simple line in the treble retraces the melody of the voice.

There are also some gay, flippant numbers such as "I Wish I Were in Love Again" and "Imagine"; a hard-boiled, sophisticated number like "The Lady Is a Tramp" (which for Rodgers has unusual rhythmic vitality); a second dynamic number, "Johnny One Note." Rodgers' versatility was never greater; never before was his touch surer in so many different styles and manners. And Hart's brilliant lyrics followed the demands of the music with agility.

Babes in Arms was about the children of touring vaudevillians who are left behind by their parents in Eastport, Long Island. Throughout the production the accent was on youth. Though it boasted a beautiful ballet in "Peter's Journey" (once again with choreography by Balanchine), the interest was not centered on large numbers or impressive sets and costumes. Since much of the play consisted of an amateur show by the youngsters, elaborate trimmings were unnecessary; for example, all the costuming called for in an Egyptian scene was a few towels.

It was the vitality of young people that charged the play with its electricity. Youth had a holiday. The stage was so crowded with youngsters running around with sleeveless sweaters or gay-colored skirts, full of animal energy, that the production brought back to Robert Benchley nostalgic memories of the first *Garrick Gaieties*. The two principals, Mitzi Green and Wynn Murray, were only sixteen years old. Other teenagers in the cast—each of whom was in a later day to achieve a considerable measure of fame in show business—were Alfred Drake, Dan Dailey, Ray Heatherton, and Robert Rounseville. As Brooks Atkinson remarked, Rodgers and Hart succeeded in writing a "genial and buoyant" show for these youngsters without "condescending from the sublime heights of maturity"; a show which, in the words of Robert Coleman, "thrust aside the conventional musical-comedy formula in favor of novelty, surprise, and freshness."

A few months later, in *I'd Rather Be Right* (title conceived by Dorothy Rodgers), Rodgers and Hart temporarily dispensed with the writing of their book. This play was a political satire in the style of Gershwin's *Of Thee I Sing*. Its text was by George S. Kaufman and Moss Hart, two incomparable satirists, one of whom (Kaufman) had had a considerable share in the making of the Gershwin Pulitzer Prize musical comedy. Where *Of Thee I Sing* reduced the Washington scene to absurdity through exaggeration and burlesque, *I'd Rather Be Right* stuck closer to political realities by naming actual names and focusing its wit and irony boldly on specific timely issues.

But, as had previously been the case with the Gershwin musical, a highly improbable situation sets into motion all ensuing developments. Peggy and Phil find they cannot get married until he gets a raise, and a raise will not be forthcoming until the national budget is balanced. Phil dreams that he and Peggy meet President Franklin D. Roosevelt on a bench in Central Park. When they confide their problem, the President promises to do all he can to balance the budget. But the political forces inside Washington—and the social and economic forces outside—nullify his every effort. When, in a fireside chat, he suggests to the women of America that they give up cosmetics for a year to donate the money to the budget, they arise in vociferous protest. An effort to use the gold in Fort Knox results in the threat of a stock-market crash and panic in the business world. The budget remains unbalanced. Nevertheless the President urges the young people to have faith in themselves and their country by getting married without the raise. Phil awakens and finds through his dream the courage to face the future.

It was in the details rather than in the overall theme that *I'd Rather Be Right* was most incisive in its satire. Through the sharp-edged dialogue of Kaufman and Moss Hart, though Larry Hart's equally keen lyric writing, *I'd Rather Be Right* became a scalpel which cut deeply into the body of American politics. A passing remark, a fleeting suggestion, an amusing aside brought sharply into focus some national foible. "Cummings—take a law," dictates F. D. R. . . . When the Secretary of the Treasury complains he has no more money in the national till, F. D. R. inquires peevishly: "What did you do with all the money I gave you? Three hundred millions ought to last a week." . . . The Postmaster General, James A. Farley, informs the President that the chairman of the fourth Assembly district in Seattle wants to be Collector of the Port of New York. "But we have a Collector of the Port of New York," exclaims F. D. R. "Not

Richard Rodgers' grandparents, Rachel and Jacob Levy.

(left) His mother, Mamie Rodgers. *(right)* His father, Dr. William A. Rodgers.

Dick, aged one.

Dick, aged three.

The family of Dr. Rodgers, 1905.
Mortimer at left, Dick at right.

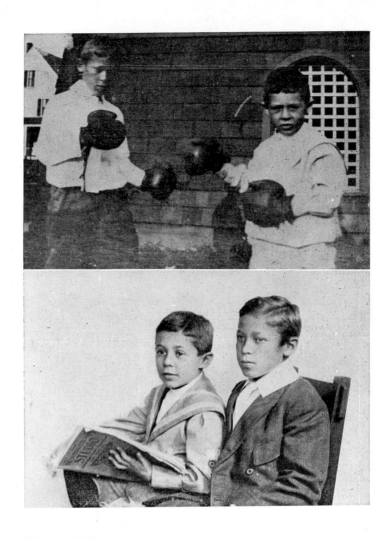

Dick and Morty.

Auto Show Girl

Words by David Dyrenforth

Music by Richard C. Rodgers

The first song.

Rodgers and Hart.

Photograph by Melbourne Spurr

THE TRIUMVIRATE
Fields, Rodgers, and Hart.

Photograph by Florence Vandamm

(*top*) Dick's first musical comedy, *Poor Little Ritz Girl*, 1920.

(*above*) Dick's first success, *The Garrick Gaieties*, 1925.

Dick and his wife, Dorothy, in Hollywood.

Dorothy and their first child, Mary.

On Your Toes, 1936

THREE
RODGERS AND HART
TRIUMPHS

Babes in Arms, 1937

I Married an Angel, 1938

Photographs by John Swope

Rodgers and Hammerstein.

Oklahoma! 1943

BY
RODGERS
AND
HAMMERSTEIN

Carousel, 1945

Allegro, 1947

Photograph by Cosmo-Sileo

A birthday party for *Oklahoma!* and *Carousel.*

The Hammersteins and the Rodgerses.

South Pacific, 1949,
with Ezio Pinza
and Mary Martin.

Photograph by John Swope

The King and I, 1951,
with Yul Brynner
and Gertrude Lawrence.

Life Photos by Leonard McCombe

Dick at work.

Dr. Mortimer Rodgers.

Mrs. Dorothy Rodgers.

Mary and Linda Rodgers.

Dorothy and Dick Rodgers at Rockmeadow.

in Seattle," replies Mr. Farley quickly. . . . A national theater, mounting taxes, Walter Lippmann are some other victims of this devastating wit—even the President himself, when he speaks "off the record":

> My messages to Congress
> Are a lot of boola-boola.
> I'm not so fond of Bankhead
> But I'd love to meet Tallulah.
> But that's strictly off the record.
> If I'm not re-elected
> And worst comes to worst
> I won't die of hunger
> I won't die of thirst.
> I've got one son with du Pont
> And another one with Hearst
> But that's off the record.

Rodgers wrote his complete score in three weeks—even for him, always a fast worker, a record time. Some of the composition was done on the Superchief en route to Hollywood. Other parts were written in Hollywood, in Larry Hart's apartment on Central Park West, at the homes of friends in Long Island, and in a booth in Sardi's restaurant in New York.

Of all of Rodgers' scores up to this time, this is the one which is best integrated with the text—so completely, in fact, that, unlike the best musical moments of *Babes in Arms*, to separate any of the numbers from the play is to rob them of their relevance. There are no big single songs here with a strong enough individuality to enable them to stand on their feet. (A possible exception is "Have You Met Miss Jones?", whose chorus has a middle section striking for its modulatory changes; but even this number, away from the play, is second-rate Rodgers and Hart.) Other numbers—"A Homogeneous Cabinet," "A Little Bit of Constitutional Fun," "We're Going to Balance the Budget," "Labor Is the Thing," and so forth—are, as their titles tell us, completely functional. They derive their interest only from the stage situations they illuminate. John Mason Brown was most certainly correct when he said that Rodgers' music here "seems to be more serviceable than catchy."

I'd Rather Be Right came to the Alvin on November 2, 1937, with an advance sale of $247,000—one of the largest for a Broadway musical up to that time. Burns Mantle considered it one of the most important plays of this generation. Other critics, while less effusive, were in general agreement with Robert Coleman when he described the play as "an exhilarating cocktail." A 290-performance run on Broadway, supplemented by an extensive out-of-town tour, placed it in the hit class. Since this was the first of their shows in which Rodgers and Hart invested their own money, its success brought them an income far in excess of their royalties.

The principal role of President Roosevelt was played by George M. Cohan, the grand old man of the American stage, who at the dusk of a fruitful career was here giving one of his warmest and most winning performances. It had not been easy to get Cohan to appear in the play; but to work with him after that proved more difficult still.

At first, Cohan had not been enthusiastic about taking over the part because he felt that neither the play nor the role was his kind. But the enthusiasm of the producer, Sam H. Harris (who many years earlier had been Cohan's producing partner), and that of Kaufman and Moss Hart—both of whom called at Cohan's apartment to convince him to change his mind—proved infectious.

Two months before the show opened, an audition of the complete score took place at Jules Glaenzer's apartment.

Kaufman, Moss Hart and Larry Hart were there, together with Cohan, who sat in a far corner of the room slumped in his chair. As Rodgers went through the score at the piano, Cohan sat in his seat, his face a frozen mask of indifference. When Rodgers finished, Cohan remained seated momentarily without a change of either posture or facial expression. Suddenly he rose, walked across the room, pulled his hat over his right eye and patted Rodgers patronizingly on the shoulder. "Don't take any bad money, kid," he said. Then he was gone, without a single word about the music.

He never did warm up to the songs. Now (as a few years earlier in Hollywood) he considered Rodgers and Hart young smart alecks who were not in his league. Their kind of brilliance and versatility never appealed to him any more than his own kind of homespun sentimentality and clichés appealed to them. Throughout the rehearsals he refused to call them by their names, usually preferring to designate them as "Gilbert and Sullivan." He did not keep it a secret that he thought their songs were not much of an asset.

There was almost an explosion in Boston. When the show opened there at the Colonial Theatre, Cohan, in one of the songs, spontaneously omitted a few lines about Alfred E. Smith and improvised some of his own. (Governor Smith, he said was a friend; and Cohan would not think of insulting him with satirical allusions.) Lorenz Hart, standing in the rear of the theater, was so infuriated that he wanted to leave the show for good and take his lyrics with him. George S. Kaufman assumed the unpleasant duty of going to Cohan and telling him firmly that in the future he was never again to tamper with any of the lines. Strangely, Cohan took Kaufman's command in good spirit and actually never disobeyed it. But his resentment against the composer and lyricist had not been alleviated by this experience.

"Our association with Cohan remained disagreeable," says

Rodgers. "He was never happy with the success of the show. I really don't know what it was, I never knew. Perhaps he never really liked Larry or me or our tunes. We made every effort to be friendly and cooperative, but we never had a meal with him. Never, in fact, any conversation whatsoever."

Rodgers went out to Hollywood in 1937 to write songs and incidental music for a Warner Brothers picture, *Fools for Scandal*. He stayed in California three months and collected $25,000. But when *Fools for Scandal* was released early in 1938, the songs were used as the incidental music.

The Hollywood wonderland in which such episodes were daily occurrences involved Rodgers once again in 1938. He and Hart had read a play by John Vaszary, *I Married an Angel*, which they liked so well that, for a fee, they adapted it as a movie-scenario synopsis for M.G.M., who owned the rights. When the studio shelved the synopsis as unsuitable screen material, Rodgers and Hart acquired the musical-comedy rights and themselves made a stage adaptation.

On May 11, 1938, Dwight Deere Wiman produced *I Married an Angel* at the Shubert Theatre. On that night Rodgers was sure his play was a failure. Only the reviews the following morning, which hailed it as "an imaginative, opulent and tuneful frolic," and "a Forty-fourth Street miracle," convinced him he had been wrong. With *I Married an Angel* a major success, M.G.M. meekly returned to buy the screen rights which they could have had originally for a fraction of what they were now willing to pay.

I Married an Angel hovered delicately between fantasy and reality, creating a half-real world in which Count Willy Palaffi, disillusioned with women, marries an angel who comes flying through his window. The angel was played by Vera Zorina, a Norwegian-born ballerina who had been a member of the Ballet Russe de Monte Carlo. She had previously been in the London company of *On Your Toes,* where Wiman had seen her and recommended her to Rodgers for a minor part in his new play. Rodgers said there was just no part for Zorina in *I Married an Angel.* A few months later, he met Vera Zorina at a party. The following day he wired Wiman, SMALL PART NOTHING. ZORINA PLAYS THE ANGEL. (She was also chosen for the female lead in the film adaptation of *On Your Toes.*)

With a trained ballerina in the cast, George Balanchine could permit his choreography greater scope than heretofore. The "Honeymoon Ballet" was the most ambitious he had thus far devised for Rodgers and Hart, and he himself considers it his best.

The ballet music, the title song, and "Spring Is Here" stood out prominently in a score distinguished for several other reasons. There were two excellent musical interludes, entitled "The Modiste" and "Angel Without Wings," which once again provided testimony to Rodgers' skill to think in forms larger than the song. Rhythmic dialogue, with which they had experimented in Hollywood, now became a salient technique: the conversation was allowed to proceed naturally against a musical accompaniment before slipping easily and gracefully into a song.

The production of *I Married an Angel* marked the first time that Joshua Logan, who staged the play, worked with Rodgers. He would work with him again in the future and, in one or two instances, have a significant part in the making of some of Rodgers' later stage triumphs.

En route to Atlantic City, New Jersey, to work on *I Married an Angel,* Rodgers asked Hart what he thought of adapting some Shakespeare comedy into a Broadway musical. Any bold and unorthodox project was certain to entice Hart; besides, he had always been a passionate Shakespeare enthusiast. He was delighted. As he began exploring the subject further, he suddenly remembered that his brother Teddy had often been annoyed by being confused with Jimmy Savo, the beloved comedian and pantomimist, to whom he bore a striking resemblance. Before their train reached Atlantic City, Rodgers and Hart had decided to work on the *Comedy of Errors* and to use Teddy Hart and Jimmy Savo as the two Dromios.

Back in New York, Hart asked George Abbott to prepare a tentative script. When he did so, calling it *The Boys from Syracuse,* it was so completely in line with the thinking of Rodgers and Hart, and so completely fulfilled their aims, that they had no need to change it. Abbott used only one line from Shakespeare: "The venom clamours of a jealous woman poison more deadly than a mad dog's tooth." Otherwise he borrowed only the setting of ancient Greece and the principal characters of the Antipholus and the Dromio twins. He retained Shakespeare's device of mistaken identity to involve them in all kinds of amusing and at times bawdy situations.

The two Antipholuses were played by Ronald Graham and Eddie Albert. Wynn Murray, who had done so well as a "babe in arms," was Luce; Burl Ives, whose career as a folk singer was still to come, appeared in a minor role as a tailor's apprentice. But the happiest piece of casting was that of Teddy Hart and Jimmy Savo as the two Dromios, "the outstanding highlight of the whole production," according to *Variety.* Teddy Hart had already become successful in fast-moving Broadway comedies; his wide-eyed, pathetic air and high-pitched voice became his trademark. And Jimmy Savo was a pantomimist with a Chaplinesque flair for portraying a pathetic soul. In gesture, voice, and appearance they were Dromios to the manner born. For Teddy Hart, this was his first appearance in a play by his brother; he consented to break precedent only because he was now famous in his own right and could not possibly be suspected of capitalizing on his brother's influence. Teddy looked so much like Jimmy Savo—the built-up heels of Teddy's shoes now gave them identical heights—that after the play became a success, he often as a gag sent Savo's photographs to his admirers with his own autograph.

The comedy of Teddy Hart and Jimmy Savo, the breathless excitement of George Abbott's swiftly paced direction, brought to *The Boys from Syracuse* an ebullience which was also found in many of the songs. To numbers like "Ladies of the Evening," "He and She," "What Can You Do with a Man?" and "This Can't Be Love," Rodgers brought a feathery touch which was matched by the brillant iridescence of Hart's lyrics. But Rodgers and Hart were equally adept in purple moods, in music and words filled with poetic feeling and romantic sentiment. The beguiling waltz "Falling in Love With Love" has become famous, but the ballads "The Shortest Day of the Year" and "You Have Cast Your Shadow" have not and deserve to be.

The Boys from Syracuse, at the Alvin on November 23, 1938, was the twenty-fifth Rodgers and Hart production and the second in which they were investors. Aware that Rodgers and Hart had here written their sixth successive hit in three years (since their return from Hollywood they had not had a single box-office failure), Garson Kanin wrote Rodgers that he was liable to prosecution for violation of the anti-trust law.

After six successive triumphs that began with *Jumbo* and ended with *The Boys from Syracuse,* Rodgers and Hart took a temporary breathing spell with two productions of lesser significance. To change the figure, it almost seemed that they were assuming an attitude which the French call *recouler pour mieux sauter,* taking a temporary step or two backward before making a leap forward.

Too Many Girls, presented by George Abbott at the Imperial on October 18, 1939, was neither as provocative nor as sustained in its flashes of brilliance as any one of the six musicals that preceded it. It benefited from an outstanding song, "I Didn't Know What Time It Was," and an arresting dance routine, "Give It Back to the Indians," starring Hal LeRoy, coming as a climax of the production.

Besides Hal LeRoy, the cast included Desi Arnaz and a young unknown named Van Johnson, completely ignored in a bit part. For Desi Arnaz, the role of Manuelito, a Cuban football player, marked his graduation from rhumba bands to the Broadway stage. When one year later *Too Many Girls* was made into a motion picture by R.K.O., and Desi Arnaz reassumed his stage role, he was co-starred with Lucille Ball, now in her first important screen role. Their partnership became permanent when before the end of 1940 they were married. The screen adaptation, therefore, was responsible for bringing together a team that would a decade or so later make television history.

Higher and Higher, at the Shubert on April 4, 1940, was even less impressive. Vera Zorina had been intended for the part of Minnie, a maid decked out as a debutante by her fellow servants to ensnare a wealthy playboy. But Zorina found other commitments in Hollywood more pressing, and a replacement had to be hurriedly recruited. The book now had to be completely revamped to meet the talent and personality of the new star, Marta Eggert. Unfortunately, the patches showed. "A bad book is contagious," says Rodgers about this disaster. "The failure of the piece was wholly logical and proceeded neatly in mathematical steps from our original blunder." The real star of the show turned out to be a seal found in an animal fair in Woodstock, New

York, and for which a part was hastily interpolated. "When a trained seal steals the show," comments Rodgers further, "you know how bad that show really is."

The leap forward—and it was a giant one—came in the form of what is undoubtedly the best of all the Rodgers and Hart musicals, possibly the only one that is likely to endure in our theater, *Pal Joey*.

Pal Joey originated as a series of sketches in letter form by John O'Hara and published in the *New Yorker* in 1939. One night, at a dinner in Brentwood Heights, California, O'Hara was asked by his host if he ever thought of making *Pal Joey* into a play. For the moment the suggestion seemed silly to O'Hara, but it dogged him for days until he decided to communicate with Rodgers about it. "I don't know whether you happened to see any of a series of pieces I've done for the *New Yorker* in the past year or so. They're about a guy who is a master of ceremonies in a cheap night club, and the pieces are in the form of letters from him to a successful bandleader. Anyway, I got the idea that the pieces, or at least the character and the life in general, could be made into a book for a show, and I wonder if you and Larry would be interested in working on it with me."

The letter reached Rodgers in Boston, where he and Hart had gone for the opening of *Higher and Higher*. Hart was delighted with O'Hara's letter. He had read the *Pal Joey* pieces and enjoyed every one of them. Joey was a night-club hoofer, a cheap opportunist who stood ready to give up the girl he loved, Linda, for a wealthy, hard-boiled, pleasure-loving matron, Vera Simpson. Since Vera never believed in the rewards of virtue and was ready to pay cash for her love, she set up Joey in his own swanky night club. But Joey soon tired of Vera and looked for sexual adventure elsewhere. Eventually, both Vera and Linda washed their hands clean of him; and Joey, a victim of blackmailers, was as broke as he had been when he had first met Vera.

The seamy side of Chicago's South Side, which was the background for most of the story, and the blackmail, hypocrisy, double-dealing, illicit love making and downright skullduggery that goes on—all this was exciting to Hart. And the characters (everyone except Linda being a disreputable individual) were the kind Hart liked to associate with, whom he understood, and who for some strange reason had a strong appeal for him. As Rodgers says, "He knew what O'Hara knew—that Joey was not a disreputable character because he was mean, but because he had too much imagination to behave himself, and because he was a little weak."

They wired O'Hara of their interest, urging him at the same time to come East as soon as possible and start work. They had hardly sent out the wire when Rodgers knew with lightning intuition who it was that simply had to play the part of Joey. There was a young dancer he had seen perform in William Saroyan's *The Time of Your Life*. His name was Gene Kelly. Hart had an equally valuable suggestion regarding the part of Vera. When Vivienne Segal had played the part of Countess Peggy Palaffi in *I Married an Angel* she had told Hart how happy she was at last to be able to play a comedy role; for up to then she had appeared only in sickly, sentimental operetta parts. Hart promised her he would find a *wicked* comedy part in one of his future plays. Vera Simpson, said Hart, was that role, and Vivienne Segal would be a "natural." Thus even before O'Hara reached the East, in early spring of 1940, the two principal parts were cast. Rodgers and Hart still had no producer but, says Rodgers, "George Abbott wasn't too hard to convince."

Nobody connected with *Pal Joey*—not even Rodgers or Hart—doubted that translating the O'Hara story into musical-comedy terms presented formidable obstacles. The world of musical comedy had never before been populated by such an assortment of immoralists as these O'Hara characters, and certainly it never before had for its hero a "heel" like Joey. The story called for a realism and a cynicism which were certainly far from the material out of which musicals were generally fabricated. George Abbott was certain *Pal Joey* would be a commercial failure; a play on a disagreeable subject with disagreeable people, he said, could never be escapist theater. "The only reason we kept on with the production," he confesses, "is that we were all caught in a whirlwind and couldn't get away. It was easier going with the wind than against it." When the show tried out in Philadelphia, Abbott's worst fears seemed realized when the story editor of a leading movie company, whose judgment was always respected, advised him to allow the show to die out of town rather than tempt disaster with it in New York.

Yet to both Rodgers and Hart, *Pal Joey* was something they felt was worth doing—the consequences notwithstanding. "It seemed to us," says Rodgers, "that musical comedy had to get out of its cradle and start standing on its own feet, looking at the facts of life." Later, when *Pal Joey* was revived, Rodgers said again: "While Joey himself may have been fairly adolescent in his thinking and morality, the show bearing his name certainly wore long pants and in many respects forced the musical-comedy theater to wear long pants for the first time."

Rodgers and Hart made no concessions in their writing. For Larry Hart to write lyrics as suggestive, callous, and cynical as the characters for which they were meant was easy. Many of his smartest lyrics in the past had been in that vein. He had merely to let himself go, and he could write with mockery and frivolity about the musings of an intellectual strip-tease artist in "Zip"; allow Joey and Vera to express their personal credos without inhibitions—the former in "Happy Hunting Horn" and the latter in "What Is a Man?";

and, most felicitously of all, describe Vera's earthy reactions to Joey in "Bewitched, Bothered and Bewildered."

> Couldn't sleep
> And wouldn't sleep
> Until I could sleep where I shouldn't sleep.
> Bewitched, bothered and bewildered am I.
>
> I'll sing to him,
> Each spring to him,
> And worship the trousers that cling to him.
> Bewitched, bothered and bewildered am I.
>
> Vexed again,
> Perplexed again,
> Thank God, I can be oversexed again!
> Bewitched, bothered and bewildered am I.

But for Rodgers, *Pal Joey* was in some respects a departure from earlier ways. One of the scenes in the play called for a "performance number" on the floor of the night club. Such a setting needed a hot-jazz piece, for which Rodgers provided "That Terrific Rainbow," the solitary occasion when he employed this torrid style. In this and other numbers he had to abandon temporarily that tenderness and poetry which so often brought enchantment to his love songs. The one with which Joey tries to woo Linda—"I Could Write a Book"—is not actually a love song, but a song with which Joey *thinks* he can ingratiate himself with a girl like Linda. Vera, speaking of her love for Joey in "Bewitched, Bothered and Bewildered" and Vera and Joey describing their "little den of iniquity" are not primarily concerned with their hearts but with their insistent sex urges; and Rodgers' melodies for both numbers had to be abandoned and voluptuous.

Neither "I Could Write a Book" nor "Bewitched, Bothered and Bewildered" was at first popular. At the time *Pal Joey* was first produced, the radio networks were knee-deep in a life-and-death struggle with ASCAP (the American Society of Composers, Authors and Publishers), which resulted in the banning from the air of all music by ASCAP members. The score of *Pal Joey* thus lost the most powerful medium for the dissemination of music; it remained familiar only to those few to whom the play was a particular favorite. However, some time after *Pal Joey* closed, "Bewitched" turned up as a feature number in a plush cabaret on the Champs Élysées in Paris. Renamed *"Perdu dans un rêve immense d'amour"* ("Lost in a Deep Dream of Love") and recast into a dreamy and haunting *chanson parisienne,* it became a hit. In America, "Bewitched" returned suddenly and inexplicably in 1950 to become so popular over the radio that in a short period it climbed to the top rung of the Hit Parade. This newly aroused enthusiasm in a ten-year-old song did much to revive an interest in *Pal Joey.* A recording of the complete score was now made by Columbia Records, produced by Goddard Lieberson; and three years after that came a revival of the play on Broadway that made stage history.

A musical so completely off the beaten track as *Pal Joey* inevitably inspired sharply divided reactions. At the opening-night performance—at the Ethel Barrymore on December 25, 1940—the audience was either extravagantly enthusiastic or completely apathetic. The same division was found among the critics. Louis Kronenberger said it was the most unhackneyed musical show he had seen since *Of Thee I Sing,* and Richard Watts, Jr., described it as an outstanding triumph. On the other hand, Brooks Atkinson said: "If it is possible to make an entertaining musical comedy out of an odious story, *Pal Joey* is it. . . . Although *Pal Joey* is expertly done, can you draw sweet water from a foul well?" Some loved the show, others hated it. *Pal Joey* was too positive and compelling to reduce anyone to indifference.

In spite of its many highly articulate supporters (these included not only some of the critics but also people like Sally Benson, Robert Benchley, John Hay Whitney, and Ludwig Bemelmans), *Pal Joey* did not do particularly well at the box office, despite a respectable performance run. The public could not be completely won over to a musical on an unsavory subject with unsavory characters; and, owing to the radio ban, it had little opportunity to become acquainted with its excellent songs.

But Rodgers and Hart remained proud of their play. Hart was particularly fond of it—to none other of his musicals was he so partial. In the next decade, *Pal Joey* returned to Broadway to become the most successful musical revival in Broadway history. But by that time Hart was no longer alive to enjoy the fruits of this belated victory, or to witness the full vindication of his faith in his play.

14

A MAN BOTHERED AND BEWILDERED

The gulf that had separated the personalities of Rodgers and Hart grew wider as the years passed. Fame and prosperity only accentuated the ingrained personal attributes of each, sharpened the edges of their strength and weaknesses, until the two men, always dissimilar, became antipodes.

Rodgers grew increasingly sober and disciplined in his habits. He had never been patient with intemperance of any kind and was much less so now that he was making such progress in the theater. Life had by now assumed for him a regulated pattern to which he willingly conformed. Work was an essential element to the good life: he thrived on being busy. An ambitious man, he enjoyed his success completely.

He was now the careful planner who tried to build his life on a foundation of financial security so firm that it could henceforth withstand any storms. In his family and social life he created around him an atmosphere of emotional stability.

While Rodgers continually radiated contentment and well-being, Hart had become a sad and forlorn figure. As he grew richer and more famous he began losing his onetime incomparable zest for living and became restive and moody. The pleasures he once derived from all-night parties, pranks, dissipation, and wisecracks had finally begun to pall; if he continued to indulge in these things now it was more out of habit than relish.

After 1940 his physical and moral disintegration became complete. It came quickly and stayed permanently. Though there had been warnings of the coming disaster in his past continual drinking, his free and easy way of life, and his consistently erratic behavior, the collapse when it came was unexpected by his friends, and they were shocked. No longer was he able to find the joy he once did in their society but started going around with shabby characters of all kinds, whose company seemed to provide him with the excitement he found lacking elsewhere. He seemed to understand these people and to find delight in their colorful speech and sordid experiences. At the same time he became less concerned about his personal appearance. There were times when he was so disheveled that many acquaintances of the theater, seeing him, would cross the street to avoid him. He became something of a Broadway Toulouse-Lautrec frequenting local bars and drowning himself in drink. (His favorite hangout was Ralph's on 45th Street, which he sometimes described as the "poor man's Sardi's.") When his periods of alcoholic stupor began to increase, his close friends would compel him to enter Doctors Hospital in New York City for a rest cure. He usually emerged with pious resolutions never again to lose control of himself. But within a few weeks he was back again at the bars, back again at the bottle, back again in a dizzy round of uncontrolled drinking.

What was destroying him? From what was he escaping in drink? Various friends give different explanations. Probably there is some truth to all of them, if no complete truth to any one. He was, despite the crowds around him, a lonely man. By the end of the 1930's most of his best friends were married, and so was his brother Teddy. This domesticity pointed up for him the emptiness of his own way of life. Rodgers, to whom he was closest at all times, stood out as a pattern of man Hart really wanted to be and never could become: emotionally stable and of sober habits; surrounded by a loving family; serious of purpose and with a deep concern for his artistic development; passing from one day to the next with peace of mind and heart.

Besides his loneliness Hart was troubled about his size, about which he had always been extremely sensitive. Probably nothing ever infuriated him more than when he was called "Shorty" or some such epithet; and he flew into a rage when someone thoughtlessly made some wisecrack like "the shortest distance between two points is Larry Hart." He wore custom shoes with elevated heels to give him a few additional inches in height. His size-consciousness made him smoke the largest cigars he could find and usually go out with the tallest girls. He suffered continually and poignantly during the early years of World War II when the playing of the National Anthem was habitual in the theaters. Invariably someone was near him to upbraid him for not standing up, which, of course, he was doing.

Probably the greatest single torment in his life was his conviction that no woman would ever come to love him or want him. Why he should have felt this way when women—and usually very beautiful women—loved him and were attracted to his wit and charm, it is hard to say. It is possible, as some have suggested, that he was sexually inadequate or that his maladjustment to women was due to latent homosexual leanings. Whatever his physical inadequacy may have been —and Rodgers strongly denies he suffered from it—it could not be said that he avoided women. On the contrary, he was always pursuing them, always carrying on some sort of an affair.

He loved one woman above all others through the years, and up to the time of his death: Vivienne Segal. It is believed he asked her to marry him and she turned him down. "He was a sweetheart," she once said, "but he was never *my* sweetheart." Less intense but no less sincere was his love for Nanette Guilford, the lovely young soprano of the Metropolitan Opera in the early 1920's, and, somewhat later, for the attractive widow of the songwriter Anatole Friedlander. Both of these women also rejected him when he suggested marriage.

Hart's irresponsibility—possibly because he was so unhappy and frustrated—became chronic. In the early days Rodgers had been obliged to hound him to get a job started, and, once started, to see that he finished it. But as time went on, Rodgers not only had to play watchdog to Hart's working habits but also to his daily behavior. Rodgers had to look after his partner with the solicitude of a parent, to protect him from major indiscretions, to save him from their consequences. (On one occasion Hart was the victim of attempted blackmail.) Rodgers might fume and rage and curse at the role into which he was placed—and often he did so. But he never thought of breaking up the partnership, nor did he ever waver in his admiration and affection for Hart.

Hart no longer made any pretense at keeping appointments. Once he had been merely lackadaisical about the hour at which he would arrive at rehearsals; after 1940 he would stay away for days at a time. On several occasions his absences proved serious. In *Too Many Girls,* for example, Rodgers had to make all the changes in the lyrics and, in one case (the opening number, "Heroes in the Fall") even had to write the complete lyric for Hart, who was nowhere to be found.

In 1940, the Rodgerses' London friend, Myrtle d'Erlanger, sent her daughter Zoe and a nurse to America to save Zoe from the ravages of war in Europe. The apartment on East 77th Street was now too cramped, so the Rodgerses bought an old rambling house on six and a half acres in Fairfield, Connecticut, and went to live there. But Pearl Harbor produced shortages in fuel, gas, oil, and servants, making living in Connecticut extremely difficult, and a return to the city seemed the only practical solution. After three years in a residential hotel, the Rodgerses bought the duplex apartment in the East 70's which is their present city residence. In 1945 they also sold their Fairfield house and acquired another in Southport, which from then on became their summer and week-end home.

One major tragedy, and one or two disappointments, struck Rodgers in the early years of the war. The tragedy was the sudden death of his mother. Dr. William Rodgers and his wife had gone for a brief holiday to the Traymore Hotel in Atlantic City, New Jersey, where on September 3, 1940, Mamie died of a ruptured aneurism. Her body was brought back to New York, and she was buried near her own parents in Mount Hope Cemetery.

This quiet and gentle little woman had never assumed the dynamic place in Rodgers' career that his father had. She preferred hovering in the background, always surrounding her son with the reassurance and warmth of her overwhelming love. The loss of that love created an emptiness that affected Rodgers poignantly for some time.

The failure of the public and some of the critics to respond to *Pal Joey* was only one of several distressing experiences at this time. Another was the release in May, 1941, of a motion picture, *They Met in Argentina,* produced by R.K.O., for which he and Hart had written seven songs. A critic of the *Herald Tribune* called it "American musical at its worst," which caused no surprise to either Rodgers or Hart, who on frequent occasions had referred to it as a "real stinker," and felt revulsion for having been associated with it.

What probably upset Rodgers most during this period was his failure to get a commission in the Air Force, for which he applied immediately after Pearl Harbor. Both he and his father keenly felt the need of participating not only in a war involving their country but also a war waged against the Nazi barbarians. Both of them met frustration. Dr. William Rodgers was rejected because of his age; Richard because early in June, 1942, there was a sudden crackdown in Washington, D.C., on commissions to civilians. His only contribution to the war effort had to be made through his music.

In April, 1942, he wrote with Hart "The Bombardier Song," dedicated to the bomber crews of the U. S. Army Air Force—all rights and royalties accruing to the Army Air Force's Aid Society Trust Fund. For the Navy Relief Society he and Oscar Hammerstein II wrote in 1943 "The P.T. Boat Song" ("Steady As You Go"), dedicated to the officers and men of the motor torpedo boats. And in 1944, once again with Hammerstein, he wrote a song for the infantry, "We're On Our Way" and for the Treasury Department, "Dear Friend." He also helped raise the morale of the fighting troops in the Pacific by organizing and sending there a special company of *Oklahoma!*

But these difficult years also brought some compensations. During most of 1941 Rodgers was deriving considerable satisfaction from studying the piano for the first time since his boyhood. (His courses at the Institute of Musical Art had not included the piano.) Since the end of 1939, and until Pearl Harbor, he worked with Herman Wasserman, applying himself several hours a day to formal practice with the diligence of a prodigy. Rodgers feels that this intensive immersion in music study at this time had a profound influence on his subsequent composition. It brought him, by way of Debussy and Ravel, a new conception of writing melody; and, by way of Brahms, a deeper appreciation of the importance of the left hand. Rodgers also believes that his own application to the piano helped arouse in his little daughters a profound respect for and interest in music study, becoming a significant factor in making them as musical as they are.

During these early years of the war, Rodgers also made his bow as a producer. He made this debut—and a highly successful one—with *By Jupiter,* whose run of a year and ten days was the longest of any Rodgers and Hart musical. The book, also by Rodgers and Hart, was based on *The Warrior's Husband,* originally a one-act play by Julian F. Thompson, produced in 1921 and eleven years later expanded by him into a three-act comedy in which Katherine Hepburn achieved her first Broadway success. The setting was Asia Minor in mythological times. In the land of Pontus, the sexes were reversed: the Amazon men stayed at home to primp and cook while the women were the warriors. In a war between the Amazon women and the invading Greeks, the former discovered that their sex was a more potent weapon against their enemy than their weapons.

As a producer (a role he shared with Wiman), Rodgers was beset by problems from the day rehearsals began virtually up to the moment of the first curtain in New York. First of all, radical rewriting became necessary to introduce some badly needed comedy, and the working title of *All's Fair* (retained up to the Boston opening) needed replacement. At one of the rehearsals, Constance Moore appeared showing severe bruises she had sustained at dueling practice, and for a while it seemed that she would not to able to play the role of Antiope. She recovered sufficiently to be able to play the part. But at this point the actor performing Theseus had to be replaced, since he was now found unsatisfactory.

These difficulties were ironed out, but World War II brought still others no less pressing. Joshua Logan, who staged the play, and Jo Mielziner, the scenic designer, both faced imminent induction into the army; miraculously both were just about able to complete their respective chores before leaving. A few hours before opening night in New York, Benay Venuta, who was cast as Hippolyta, said she would not appear that evening unless a nurse was found for her eleven-month-old baby; her own nurse had suddenly eloped with a sailor.

Nevertheless, *By Jupiter* opened on schedule at the Shubert Theatre on June 2, 1942. It was an amusing and beautifully produced harlequinade with four particularly effective songs: two romantic numbers, "Nobody's Heart Belongs to Me" and "Careless Rhapsody"; a good comedy piece in "Ev'rything I've Got"; and a timely production sequence in "Jupiter Forbid." After receiving a handsome send-off from the critics, it settled down comfortably for a long run. It was still enjoying capacity houses—and gave every indication of being able to extend its run of over 400 performances to twice that figure—when the star of the show, Ray Bolger, who played Sapiens, withdrew because of poor health and the play was forced to close down while it was still doing capacity business. At the time Bolger was subjected to severe criticism since he looked remarkably well and fit. It was felt he was using the pretext of ill health as an excuse for stopping work. Only much later was it discovered he had left the show to make a secret flight to the South Seas to entertain the American troops there.

Hart was sick—physically, mentally, morally. His nerves were at the breaking point; his will to live seemed completely depleted. His behavior was more than ever unpredictable, and the depression into which he was sinking grew deeper. The periods between his binges became shorter, just as the sprees themselves lengthened. When *By Jupiter* was being written, he was in such a continual state of alcoholic depression that he had to be hospitalized. Rodgers took a guest room at Doctors Hospital, moved in a piano, and there continued to work on the play. Hart left the hospital weary and penitent, and for a while was able to keep his drinking under sufficient control to be able to work by fits and starts. But when his work was finished and *By Jupiter* opened in Boston, he disappeared in that city for three days. He turned up from his escapade without any explanations—a sorrier sight than ever.

By the middle of 1941 Rodgers knew that his days as Hart's collaborator were numbered. At that time he was one of the producers (though his name did not appear on the billing) of the musical comedy *Best Foot Forward,* which began a one-year run on October I. When *Best Foot Forward* tried out in Philadelphia, Rodgers went to Doylestown to pay a visit to his lifelong friend, Oscar Hammerstein II. He confided to Hammerstein the troubles he had been having with Larry, and his suspicion that the collaboration was about over. Rodgers further explained that he and Hart had been planning a musical based on a book by Ludwig Bemelmans but that it was impossible to get Hart to work. Rodgers finally asked if Hammerstein would consider becoming his collaborator. Hammerstein was delighted with this suggestion, not only because he admired Rodgers but also because he himself had recently had bad luck with his plays. But he was reluctant to displace Hart. "But I'll tell you what I will do, if you wish," Hammerstein suggested. "You get Hart to work with you on the Bemelmans thing, and if he falls by the wayside, I'll gladly step in and finish the job for him without anybody being the wiser."

The Bemelmans musical never materialized. Soon after *By Jupiter* opened in New York, the Theatre Guild called on Rodgers with still another project: the musical adaptation of Lynn Riggs' folk play *Green Grow the Lilacs*. When Rodgers discussed this idea with Hart, the latter dismissed it wearily. Finishing *By Jupiter* had completely sapped his energy. He could not think of starting work again so soon. Besides he did not like the Riggs play and did not think it could become a satisfying musical. When Rodgers insisted that he wanted to go ahead with this play and added that he was thinking of asking Oscar Hammerstein II to work with him, Larry said softly: "Sure, you ought to get Hammerstein as your collaborator. I don't know why you put up with me all these years. I'm going to Mexico for a long holiday." A few days later, in Chappell's office, Hart once again told Rodgers he did not want to work on *Green Grow the Lilacs* and would soon be off for Mexico. After Larry left, Rodgers remarked sadly to Dreyfus: "A long and wonderful partnership just went out of that door."

With Hart in Mexico, Rodgers and Hammerstein finally decided to settle down to their job. When this project finally materialized as *Oklahoma!*—and was unveiled on the evening of March 31, 1943, as one of the monuments of the American theater—Hart was already back from Mexico. He came to the première with his mother and after the performance came upon Rodgers in Sardi's. "You have at least another *Blossom Time*," Hart told him enthusiastically. "This thing of yours will run forever."

It might well be said that the first day Rodgers began working with Hammerstein was the day Hart's life was over. After that he went through the motions of living. He did speak of doing a musical with another composer. His friend Milton Bender had interested him in a musical based on a Nazi story by Paul Gallico and had lined up Vivienne Segal for a starring role and the Viennese composer Emerich Kálmán for the music. Hart said yes and began putting down some lines on paper. But he was only shadow-boxing, and he knew it. Throughout the years Rodgers had been the dynamo providing him with the energy he needed for creation. Once the dynamo was removed, Hart could no longer function.

For one brief period Hart seemed to come back to life. In the weeks following *Oklahoma!* Hart appeared to take hold of himself. He was sober most of the time, behaved well, and talking of getting down to work. Rodgers felt that Hart's recovery could be hastened, and perhaps made permanent, if the lyricist could now get himself absorbed with a new project. He discussed this problem with Herbert Fields. It was then that they decided to revive *A Connecticut Yankee* with timely revisions. Hart seized upon this idea zestfully and went to work with a will, producing the lyrics for four new songs. One of the last was particularly dear to him—"To Keep My Love Alive," which he wrote expressly for Vivienne Segal, who was starred in the revival.

But his spirit gave out. He attended the opening in Philadelphia and the party that followed, but later the same night he went on an alcoholic binge that made it necessary to send him back to New York early the following morning for another rest cure at Doctors Hospital.

He left the hospital to appear at the New York première, at the Martin Beck Theatre, on November 17, 1943. Instead of sitting in the audience, he kept pacing up and down in the back of the theater mumbling to himself. Rodgers looked for him after the final curtain, but he was nowhere to be found. He did not return to his apartment at the Delmonico Hotel that night or the next two days. He was finally found Friday evening in his apartment, sprawled out in bed, unconscious.

An ambulance rushed Hart to Doctors Hospital, where his condition was diagnosed as an advanced case of pneumonia, probably first contracted in Philadelphia, where he had stayed out all night in the rain and sleet. Penicillin, then a recently discovered drug, offered the only possible hope of saving him. Although it was still rare and, because of the war, virtually unavailable, some was found, but it was useless against Hart's advanced condition.

He never regained consciousness. Richard and Dorothy Rodgers kept visiting the hospital hoping to see him. On Monday, November 22, they were seated outside Hart's hospital room. Suddenly the air-raid sirens shrieked for a blackout. Almost as if in a reflex action the hospital lights were extinguished. Dick and Dorothy remained seated in the darkened corridor. Soon they heard the movement of footsteps in and out of the corridor. Hart's physician had come to tell them that Hart was dead. Even as the physician spoke, the all-clear sounded and the hospital once again became flooded with light.

15

RODGERS AND HART—A POSTSCRIPT AND A RÉSUMÉ

Hart was dead. But the fruits of his collaboration with Rodgers remained fresh. The best songs of Rodgers and Hart have lost none of their onetime popularity. These songs are still heard so often and through so many media today that they still keep Hart on the top level of ASCAP ratings—in the select company of Richard Rodgers, Irving Berlin, Oscar Hammerstein II, George Gershwin, Ira Gershwin, Otto Harbach, Jerome Kern, and Cole Porter. (The Hart estate receives from ASCAP about fifty thousand dollars a year.)

But through the years there have been other reminders—although not always happy ones—of the era of Rodgers and Hart. About two months after Hart's death, the motion-picture adaptation of *Higher and Higher* was released. This was an R.K.O. production with Michele Morgan, Jack Haley and Frank Sinatra, and with Victor Borge (not yet celebrated as

music's buffoon) in a small part. Rodgers and Hart frequently suffered abuses in the motion-picture versions of
their plays, and *Higher and Higher* was no exception. Some
of the music they had written for the play was now used only
as an incidental background, while just one of their songs—
"So Disgustingly Rich"—was retained intact. All the other
songs in the picture were by Harold Adamson and Jimmy
McHugh.

A little over five years after Hart's death, Hollywood paid
Rodgers and Hart the supreme gesture of honor—a screen
dramatization of their career. *Words and Music* was a
Metro-Goldwyn-Mayer production directed by Norman Taurog and produced by Arthur Freed. Tom Drake portrayed
Rodgers; Janet Leigh, his wife, Dorothy; Mickey Rooney,
Larry Hart; Marshall Thompson, Herbert Fields, June Allyson, Judy Garland, Lena Horne, Gene Kelly, Cyd Charisse,
Mel Tormé, and Vera-Ellen played themselves. The picture
did well in contrasting the personalities of the two men,
even if it often played fast and loose with biographical truth.
But Larry Hart's precipitous decline was oversimplified,
here caused solely by his rejection by a girl who objected to
his size; and the portrayal of his last days was sheer bathos.
Nevertheless, *Words and Music* provided eloquent testimony
why Rodgers and Hart had occupied a unique place in popular music. The picture was a mighty cavalcade of their
greatest songs, beginning with their first hit, "Manhattan."
Betty Garrett sang "There's a Small Hotel"; Perry Como,
"With a Song in My Heart" and "The Blue Room"; Lena
Horne, "The Lady Is a Tramp" and "Where or When?";
Judy Garland, "Johnny One Note" and "I Wish I Were in
Love Again"; Ann Sothern, "Where's That Rainbow?". Gene
Kelly and Vera-Ellen danced in "Slaughter on Tenth Ave-
nue." Cyd Charisse appeared in two other extravagantly
mounted ballets inspired by songs. "When you hear almost

two dozen of [Rodgers and Hart's] best tunes in one sitting," said Lee Mortimer, "sold by some of the most talented . . . stars in Hollywood, you realize how great they really were."

The greatness of Rodgers and Hart was reaffirmed when *Pal Joey* was revived on January 3, 1952, at the Broadhurst. Vivienne Segal returned to her old part of Vera, but the other principals were new, with Harold Lang playing Joey. There were some changes in the play. A few topical references that had lost their meaning were deleted and a new production number was introduced in the second act. Otherwise *Pal Joey* was the same in 1952 as it had been in 1940. What had changed, however, was the audiences. In the interim—and probably through the influence of Rodgers and Hammerstein—they had acquired a new orientation to the musical theater and were now able to find *Pal Joey* exciting and stimulating in background, story, and characterization. "There were people eleven years ago who were confused by *Pal Joey*," explained John Lardner. "When *Pal Joey* returned to the wars . . . it was perhaps easier to see that it is and always was a fine piece of work." Brooks Atkinson, who had once described the play as a foul well, now had a complete change of heart. "No one is likely to be impervious to the tight organization of the production, the terseness of the writing, the liveliness and versatility of the score, the easy perfection of the lyrics. Brimming over with good music and fast on its toes, it renews confidence in the professionalism of the theater." Richard Watts, Jr., now called it an authentic work of art, while Robert Coleman did not hesitate to label it a masterpiece.

The 542-performance run was the longest of any musical revival in the history of our theater. *Pal Joey* earned other distinctions as well. It was selected by the New York Drama Critics Circle as the best musical of the year. It also received eleven out of sixteen Donaldson Awards sponsored by *Bill-*

board—including one as the best musical—the first time in the then nine-year history of these awards that one play had captured so many honors. In 1957 *Pal Joey* was made into an ambitious motion picture by Columbia Pictures, starring Rita Hayworth, Kim Novak and Frank Sinatra.

A revival of *On Your Toes* in the fall of 1954 was a much less happy occasion. George Abbott was the one who first suggested that it be brought back to Broadway. When Rodgers expressed approval, Abbott planned a newly designed production. The revival, however, was delayed for failure to find a suitable performer for the principal role of Philip Dolan III. When Bobby Van, a George Abbott discovery, finally filled this gap, there was no trouble in casting the other parts. Vera Zorina was engaged for Vera Barnova; Kay Coulter for Frankie Frayne; and Elaine Stritch for a lesser role. A few minor changes were made in the play itself. The song "You Took Advantage of Me" was lifted from *Present Arms* for Elaine Stritch and brought into the second act just before "Slaughter on Tenth Avenue"; and, immediately after the New York première, the roles of Philip Dolan II and Lil Dolan were eliminated.

On Your Toes opened on October 11, 1954. Everything about it—except some of the wonderful songs and the "Slaughter on Tenth Avenue" ballet, still the *pièce de résistance*—showed the lines and wrinkles of premature old age. Brooks Atkinson, formerly so enthusiastic, now regarded it "labored, mechanical, and verbose." Walter F. Kerr said it drifted "across the stage like an autumn ghost," and Walter Terry described it as "more of an exhumation than a revival."

Such a funereal chorus inevitably spelled doom. *On Your Toes* closed after only 64 performances. "There's no use talking," said Robert Coleman, "times have changed." They had, indeed! The musical comedy had moved so rapidly since 1936 that it had succeeded in leaving far behind even

shows like *On Your Toes,* which—paradoxically enough—
had actually helped to bring about this change.

The collaboration of Rodgers and Hart, begun professionally in 1918 with "Any Old Place with You" in *A Lonely
Romeo,* ended a quarter of a century later with its greatest
box-office attraction, *By Jupiter,* and the revival of *A Connecticut Yankee.* There can be little question but that this
words-and-music partnership was one of the most fruitful
and significant that Broadway and American popular music
knew at the time. In twenty-five years the team wrote twenty-
seven stage musicals and eight motion-picture scores, not
counting the film adaptations of nine of their stage shows.
Between the *Garrick Gaieties* and *America's Sweetheart,*
Rodgers and Hart averaged three shows a season. With seven
major successes, and ten failures in varying proportions,
these shows averaged a run of five months each. But beginning with *Jumbo*—as they grew less prolific, gave greater attention to each production, sometimes even took a hand in
preparing the book—their batting average shows a remarkable advance. Their output of three shows now required two
seasons instead of one; and the average run of each show
was now nine months at a time when a nine-month run was
a healthy one. In this period eight out of ten of their productions were highly profitable ventures, seven of them coming
in succession.

These figures tell us how successful these plays were in
bringing gaiety and enchantment to the stage for twenty-
five years. They do not even hint at the influence they had—
individually and collectively—both on song writing and
musical comedy. It is this influence, rather than the quantity
of their output and the success it brought them, that
placed Rodgers and Hart in the vanguard of all those writing
for the popular stage.

Among the thousand or so songs Rodgers and Hart wrote for their various productions, at least twelve are classics whose survival in the popular-song repertory seems assured: "The Blue Room," "My Heart Stood Still," "With a Song in My Heart," "A Ship Without a Sail," "Blue Moon," "The Most Beautiful Girl in the World," "There's a Small Hotel," "Where or When?", "I Didn't Know What Time It Was," "My Romance," "My Funny Valentine," and "Falling in Love with Love." There are many others which have a sophistication and spontaneity that time cannot wither, and among these are "The Lady Is a Tramp," "Ten Cents a Dance," "Johnny One Note," "I've Got Five Dollars," and "Bewitched, Bothered and Bewildered."

In all these and many other gay numbers, Hart's verses created a one-man revolution in the art of writing lyrics. "His work," says Ira Gershwin, himself one of our most distinguished lyricists, "sings for itself, and we listen to one of the wittiest and most original lyricists of our time or any other." When Hart started writing, the commercial song lyric in Tin Pan Alley on Broadway was a neglected stepchild of the song family. At its best it was only a functional commodity, serving the melody with unimaginative phrases, cloying sentiments, an impoverished vocabulary, and inadequate poetic techniques. At its worst it was a sad mixture of shopworn clichés, bad grammar and prosody, and trite sentiment. But from the beginning Hart brought to his lyrics not only an adroit technique at versification, but also wit and charm and the courage always to be his own disarming and informal self. His use of exterior and interior rhymes, male and female rhymes—and all the other devices of excellent light verse—had all the agility of a Heifetz negotiating a Paganini caprice. His writing was always seemingly spontaneous and effortless. He had a way with a line that was entirely his own; an instinctive feeling for a figure of speech that avoided the obvious; an instinct for saying the unexpected when it could create the greatest shock. His irreverent poses and impudent attitudes, his excursions into esoterica and erotica, his frequent allusions to cultural matters, his interpolations of foreignisms—all this was like a gust of fresh wind in a musty corridor. It cleared the musical air of all its existing stuffiness and maliferous odors and created a healthy climate in which it was henceforth possible for other inventive and original lyricists to function and thrive.

"The great thing about Hart's work," writes P. G. Wodehouse, who may well be considered the first distinguished lyricist of our time, "was its consistency, even more than its brilliance. Larry Hart was always good. If there is a bad lyric of his in existence, I have not come across it. It seems to me he had everything. He could be ultrasophisticated and simple and sincere. He could handle humor and sentiment. And his rhyming, of course, was impeccable. But the great thing about his work was that, as somebody once wrote, he was the first to make any real assault on the intelligence of the song-listening public. He brought something quite new into a rather tired business."

In Rodgers, Hart found a composer able to understand what he was trying to do, to be completely sympathetic to him; a composer able to write music with such a wide gamut of mood and such a willingness to avoid the standard formulas of song writing that it could meet every demand made by Hart's nimble words. An unexpected chromaticism or modulation neatly coincided with an unusual turn of phrase or rhyming scheme; a fleet, light-hearted tune reflected perfectly the sparkle of Hart's smartness; a poignant melody would follow Hart in some of his gentler moods. The singleness of expression of words and music in every major Rodgers and Hart song is one of its salient strong points.*

No less significant than the value of their song writing is the contribution that Rodgers and Hart made to the musical theater. They were not the only ones to revolutionize the musical comedy, but they were certainly in the forefront of those trying to effect this change in the 1920's and 1930's. Rodgers and Hart achieved this not only through the creative strength of their songs but through a trenchant understanding of what the American musical theater could become if freed from old behavior patterns and habits that so long stultified its growth. With dynamic understanding of the role music should perform in the theater, they consciously sought an integration of song and text, at first tentatively, later uncompromisingly. They continually tried out new formats and techniques, never lost their excitement in experimentation. In their later musicals they injected a new vitality into the production of musicals, just as through the introduction of ballet they were pioneers in introducing a new esthetic dimension to them.

It should be added that, like Moses, Rodgers and Hart pointed out a promised land without ever actually getting there. They suggested, rather than realized, the kind of art our musical theater could become. Much that was dynamic and courageous and advanced of its times in their musicals is decidedly old hat today; only *Pal Joey* is an exception. Compared to *Oklahoma!*—which came only one year after *By Jupiter*—the musicals of Rodgers and Hart are for the most part as much of an obsolete world as the musical comedies of George M. Cohan and many of the early musicals of Berlin, Gershwin and Kern became when Rodgers and Hart

* A more detailed discussion of Rodgers' music will be found in the concluding chapter.

appeared on the scene. The failure of the revivals of *A Connecticut Yankee* and *On Your Toes* stresses this fact.

It is more than probable that the awareness, subconscious or otherwise, that *Oklahoma!* had finally accomplished what he had been reaching for all his life and had never quite attained, proved more deadly to Larry Hart than pneumonia.

Part Two

RODGERS AND HAMMERSTEIN

"The most profound change in forty years of musical comedy has been—Rodgers and Hammerstein."

—COLE PORTER

1

THE SECOND OSCAR HAMMERSTEIN

So many similarities and coincidences have linked Rodgers and Hammerstein throughout their lives that one is tempted to entertain a superstitious belief that their ultimate collaboration had been preordained. Both of them spent their boyhoods in the same district near 125th Street, their summers at the camp of Weingart's Institute in Highmount; both attended Columbia College, though at different times, where they became involved in varsity shows. In both instances a grandfather became a significant early influence; both had fathers named William; both have wives named Dorothy, who were interior decorators. Both have strikingly similar tastes. Neither one smokes or drinks excessively or favors night life. Each has the same kind of placid temperament and leads the same kind of orderly existence.

To compound coincidence, Hammerstein's first wife was

related to Dr. William Rodgers, who delivered the two children of that first marriage. Both Rodgers and Hammerstein fell in love (and in the same year!) with the women they married—Hammerstein for the second time—aboard a transatlantic liner; both women became pregnant at the same time. More curious still, the bridesmaid at the Rodgers wedding later married the former husband of Hammerstein's second wife.

Rodgers was only thirteen when he first met Hammerstein; at the time Hammerstein was about twenty—Hart's age. It was Rodgers' brother Mortimer who came to know Hammerstein first. They both attended Columbia, where Mortimer was Hammerstein's fraternity brother in Pi Lambda Phi Fraternity. Even in those days Mortimer had a profound admiration for Hammerstein: first because Hammerstein was a senior, whereas Mortimer was only a freshman; then because Hammerstein was "the kindest person I had ever met"; and finally because Hammerstein played leading roles in the varsity shows. "He was, truthfully speaking, a pretty awful comedian," says Mortimer, "but in those days I used to think he was just about the greatest actor in the world."

The circumstance of the first meeting of Rodgers and Hammerstein—after a performance of the Columbia Varsity Show, *On Your Way*—has already been described. It will also be recalled that Hammerstein was on the committee which accepted Rodgers' score for the varsity show, *Fly with Me*. Though most of its lyrics were by Larry Hart, one of them— "Room for One More"—was by Hammerstein himself. But this was not the first time that Rodgers and Hammerstein teamed up. A year earlier, in 1919, in the Akron Club presentation of *Up Stage and Down*, two of Rodgers' songs also had Hammerstein's lyrics: "Can It" and "Weaknesses."

They did not work together for another quarter of a century. But their paths crossed frequently, both on Broadway

and in Hollywood. Hammerstein attended the first performance of the *Garrick Gaieties* and subsequently was a first-
night spectator at virtually every outstanding Rodgers and
Hart musical. Rodgers had also been present at many of the
significant musicals and operettas in which Hammerstein
collaborated. But though they knew each other well, often
moved in the same social circles, and respected each other's
talent, the question of their collaborating did not come up
until Rodgers paid his visit to Hammerstein's farm in Doylestown, Pennsylvania, in 1941.

In 1942, when he began working with Rodgers on *Oklahoma!,* Hammerstein was already a person of considerable
consequence in the musical theater: the author of books and
lyrics for about twenty-five stage productions, and words
to several hundred songs; the partner in the creation of several operettas, musical comedies and songs that were formidable successes.

Oscar Hammerstein II was born in New York City on July
12, 1895, in an apartment house near 135th Street on the
upper West Side. The elder Oscar Hammerstein, his grandfather, had acquired wealth through various inventions including suspenders for men's trousers, several devices for
making cigars, a new kind of inkwell, and a nursing bottle
for babies. In the 1890's he built theaters and apartment
houses in New York; and in the 1900's, after having put on
some opera performances in his theaters, he became one of
the most celebrated opera impresarios in the world. With his
shining top hat, Prince Albert jacket, striped trousers, Van-
dyke beard, and the inevitable cigar in his mouth, he entered the opera arena with all the dash and drama of a
matador entering the bull ring. After building the Manhattan Opera House in New York, he produced there for four
years, beginning with 1906, such brilliant performances—

and introduced to America so many dazzling personalities of the opera stage—that the competitive Metropolitan Opera Company was thrown completely into the shade. From this the Metropolitan was able to emerge again only after it had bought out Hammerstein for a million dollars and had him agree contractually not to produce opera in America for a decade.

The impresario was not the only one to bring the glamour of the theater world into the Hammerstein household. William Hammerstein, son of the impresario and father of the lyricist, was the manager of New York's cathedral of vaudeville, the Victoria, on 42nd Street. This house had been built by his father. Arthur Hammerstein, young Oscar's uncle, was a Broadway producer.

When Oscar was four, his family moved a few streets downtown to 125th Street near Madison Avenue, only a few blocks away from where Rodgers would later spend his boyhood. Since Oscar's mother was of delicate health and had to care for Oscar's infant brother, Reginald, Oscar lived for three years with his grandfather, James Nimmo, one floor below his own apartment, while sharing meals with his own family. Oscar still remembers the frequent walks he took early in the morning with the old man to Mount Morris Park. There they would climb to the top of the hill at the foot of the bell tower and spend several hours exchanging confidences. The more celebrated grandfather—the fabulous Oscar I—hovered only nebulously in the family background. The grandson saw him only about half a dozen times in his life, and even then only briefly. The four or five minutes young Oscar spent at his grandfather's deathbed in Lenox Hill Hospital was, as he has confessed, "the longest time I had ever spent with him."

The most vivid experience of young Oscar's early boyhood, like that of Richard Rodgers, came from his first visit to a theater. He was only four when his father took him to the Victoria. Seated alone in a box overlooking the stage, Oscar was so affected by the lights, colors and music—and especially by the performances of Irene Franklin, Ed Blondell (father of the motion-picture star, Joan), and Frank Fogarty as he sang "You Can't Bunko Me"—that he broke out in a cold sweat and felt faint. When he came home he was so sick he had to be put to bed. He recovered fully the following day, but only from his physical disturbances. The theater remained forever after a fever which was to last for life. "The theater at its best," he has said, "is a nightly miracle. . . . The fact is that I am almost foolishly in love with the stage. The mere sight of a bare stage sends pains up and down my back."

Before going to Columbia, he attended P.S. 9 in Manhattan and after that a private school on Central Park West, the Hamilton Institute. His first story, "The Adventures of a Penny," was published in the *Hamilton Echo* when he was twelve. Three years later, at Weingart's camp in Highmount, New York, where he spent his summers, he was able to indulge not only his overwhelming love for the country but also his literary proclivities by editing *The Weingart Review*.

In his seventeenth year he matriculated at Columbia College. There his classmates included Larry Hart, Howard Dietz, Morrie Ryskind, Bennett Cerf, M. Lincoln Schuster, and Mortimer Rodgers. Oscar was a good but not sensational student, his marks hovering between "B" and "B+". Only in his English classes was he outstanding; one of his professors was Carl Van Doren, who encouraged him to become a writer.

Beginning with his junior year in 1915, Hammerstein appeared in the annual Varsity Show at Columbia. His initiation took place with *On Your Way* and was noticed by a reporter for the New York *World*, who commented facetiously:

"Oscar was funny without trying to be. He had some original steps and faces of his own, and danced like Al Jolson." A year later Hammerstein wrote some lyrics for *Peace Pirates* (a travesty on the Ford Peace Ship by Herman Mankiewicz, later a distinguished Hollywood screen writer and producer). Here Hammerstein did a few routines, including one in blackface, and a comedy dance while wearing a leopard skin. In 1917, after he had transferred to Columbia Law School, he helped write *Home James* and in one sequence appeared as a French waiter called Dubonnet. The music of *Home James* was by Robert Lippmann, who one year earlier had been the music counselor at Camp Wigwam, where Rodgers had spent the summer; most of the text was by Herman Axelrod, father of the author of *The Seven Year Itch* and *Will Success Spoil Rock Hunter?*.

In 1917, while still at law school, Hammerstein began working part time, first as a process server for, then in the office itself of, a New York law firm. His salary was $5.00 a week, but fortunately this was supplemented by an income of about fifty dollars a week from securities left him by his father. However, when Hammerstein fell in love with Myra Finn, cousin of Dr. William Rodgers, he felt that $55.00 a week was not enough to support a wife. He asked his employer for a raise. "If they had given me twenty dollars a week, I would have stayed on—and probably become a lawyer. But they didn't. So I had to look for a job elsewhere."

He turned to his uncle, Arthur Hammerstein, who, in the same year of 1917, gave him the needed $20.00 a week in return for his services as assistant stage manager for the Broadway show *You're In Love*. For about a year, Hammerstein shifted the scenery, switched the lights on and off, gave actors their cues, and performed any other job that needed doing backstage. He learned a good deal that was to serve him well in later years about the mechanics of putting on a play. "I may write bad scenes, but I never write impractical ones," he says now. During this period he wrote a song lyric which was used as the opening chorus of one of the musicals produced by his uncle. The verse went:

> Make yourself at home,
> 'Neath this spacious dome.
> Do just as you please,
> In twos and threes,
> If you'd rather—
> But rest assured it is no bother.

This was Hammerstein's debut as a lyricist for the musical theater.

Hammerstein married Myra in the summer of 1917. A year later he was promoted to full stage manager for *Sometime,* a musical comedy by Rida Johnson Young based on Young's own scenario. Mae West, who starred with Ed Wynn, took Hammerstein aside one day to advise him, "Get out of the theater, kid, and go back to law. You've got too much class to hang around the stage."

At his uncle's suggestion, Hammerstein resigned as stage manager to write a play of his own. He completed a four-act tragedy of small-town girls called *The Light,* which his uncle promised to bring to New York. But *The Light* was extinguished during its New Haven tryout after only five performances. There were only about twenty in the audience for its last performance on Saturday, but they were provided a treat not called for by the script. As the ingenue moaned, "Everything is falling around me," her petticoat sank to her ankles. Hammerstein fled out of the theater and found refuge on a park bench. As he sat there cursing the fate that had brought him to the theater, an idea for a new musical occurred to him. He later wrote both the book and the lyrics, and Herbert Stothart provided the music. As *Al-*

ways You it was produced on Broadway by Arthur Hammerstein on January 5, 1920. Hammerstein's bow as a writer of
book and lyrics for the Broadway musical stage had a
meager run of sixty-six performances, but it did receive some
good notices, including one in the *New York Times* that took
note of the fact that "the lyrics are more clever than those of
the average musical comedy." *Always You* did much better
on the road, where it stayed six months. A few days after
this tour ended, Hammerstein had another musical on
Broadway, *Tickle Me,* for which Otto Harbach and Frank
Mandel helped him write the book and lyrics while Stothart
once again contributed the score. *Tickle Me* gave Hammerstein his first taste of success. Described by the critics as "a
joyous romping absurdity," and "a riot of fun," it stayed on
Broadway seven months before going on a successful tour.
One of its songs, "If a Wish Could Make It So," sold a million phonograph records—but it is necessary to explain that
the reverse side happened to be "Whispering," one of the
great song hits of that period.

It took three years and four crushing failures before Hammerstein's luck turned. "I learned then what my grandfather
often told me, that there is just no limit to the number of people who stay away from a bad show." But when Hammerstein was a hit again, his reputation became established
permanently. In 1923 the team of Harbach and Hammerstein wrote book and lyrics for *Wildflower,* score by Vincent
Youmans and Herbert Stothart. A year later, Harbach and
Hammerstein wrote *Rose Marie* for Rudolf Friml. Both productions were triumphs, and *Rose Marie* has become a
classic.
    A first meeting with Jerome Kern, at Victor Herbert's
funeral in 1924, led to a fruitful collaboration. The first
was *Sunny* in 1925, which he wrote with Harbach for

Marilyn Miller in an effort to duplicate *Sally,* an earlier Marilyn Miller-Jerome Kern success. With its 517 Broadway performances, *Sunny* was in the hit class of *Wildflower* and *Rose Marie.*

But the greatest triumph of Hammerstein and Kern was *Show Boat* in 1927. Based on Edna Ferber's romantic novel of show-boat life along the Mississippi in the last two decades of the nineteenth century, and produced by Florenz Ziegfeld, it was not only a box-office attraction of the first magnitude but an epochal event in the history of our musical theater. It was musical comedy no longer, but an American folk play with music; and there are some who even consider it an opera. (Indeed it was presented by an opera company—the New York City Opera Company—in its regular repertory on April 18, 1954.) Up to now a skillful technician who could be counted upon to provide a composer with a functional book and lyrics (but hardly more), Hammerstein suddenly uncovered here deep, rich strains in his writing. He brought to his dialogue and verses simplicity, force, freshness, and eloquence. With Jerome Kern's score an inexhaustible cache of melodic riches, *Show Boat* well deserved the encomiums heaped upon it by critics like Robert Garland, who called it "an American masterpiece," and John Chapman, who said it was "immortal . . . what every musical comedy should be—and no other has been." Already in 1927, *Show Boat* gave Broadway audiences a foretaste of what the musical theater would become in a later era—once again with Hammerstein, but this time with Richard Rodgers' music.

He had other stage triumphs to his credit before 1943. Among these were *The Desert Song* in 1926 and *New Moon* in 1928, both with music by Sigmund Romberg, and Jerome Kern's *Music in the Air* in 1932. In 1938 he was associated with a motion picture that was a box-office smash, *The Story of Vernon and Irene Castle,* starring Fred Astaire and Ginger Rogers. And in 1941 he wrote the lyrics for a song by Jerome Kern, "The Last Time I Saw Paris," which won him for the first time the Motion Picture Academy Award.

But he also had more than a normal quota of reverses. In 1930 he went to Hollywood on a four-picture deal at Warner's earning him $100,000 a picture. After the failure of the first two of these he was paid $100,000 on condition that he tear up the contract. A motion-picture executive said of him at the time, "He is a dear friend of mine, but he can't write his hat." His ventures on Broadway immediately after his return from California offered little solace. *Free for All* and *East Wind,* both in 1931, lasted respectively fifteen and twenty-three performances. Since his own money was invested in each, he lost about eighty-five thousand dollars in five weeks.

Music in the Air and *May Wine* (the latter with Romberg's music) were oases in the desert. Except for these two productions—and *The Story of Vernon and Irene Castle*—he met failure after failure on both coasts. There was one period in Hollywood, in the middle and late 1930's, when four of his pictures were junked before they even reached the screen; two others were fiascos at the box office; and two just broke even. His record on Broadway and in London was not much better. Just before he joined up with Richard Rodgers he suffered three Broadway disasters in succession, not to mention a few similar calamities in London. Most of his friends in the theater were whispering privately that "Hammerstein is through, only he hasn't discovered it yet." "I kept going only through inner conceit," he explains. When at long last he recovered his winning stride with *Oklahoma!,* he published an advertisement in *Variety* with the following headline: I'VE DONE IT BEFORE AND I CAN DO IT AGAIN. Under this heading came not the succession of his triumphs but the procession of his recent failures: *Very Warm for May* (7 weeks); *Ball at the Savoy* (5 weeks); *Sunny River* (6 weeks); *Three Sisters* (6 weeks); *Free for All* (3 weeks); *The Gang's All Here* (3 weeks); *East Wind* (3 weeks); *Gentleman Unafraid* (1 week).

2

OH, WHAT A BEAUTIFUL MORNIN'

One day in 1942 Rodgers telephoned Oscar Hammerstein II to invite him for lunch at the Barberry Room on 52nd Street and Madison Avenue. There he explained to Hammerstein that he wanted him as a collaborator for the musical adaptation of *Green Grow the Lilacs,* about which the Theatre Guild had recently called him.

Rodgers told Hammerstein everything he knew about the Guild's interest in the project. The Guild had recently suffered a series of box-office failures which had brought it to the brink of insolvency. This critical financial situation dictated a drastic change in its production policy. The directors, Theresa Helburn and Lawrence Langner, felt a musical might be the answer they were looking for. Since 1935, when the Guild had put on Gershwin's *Porgy and Bess,* Theresa Helburn had wanted to do another musical; and she had been convinced that the Lynn Riggs folk play, which the Guild had produced in 1931, would make a fascinating text. In 1942, Helburn called Rodgers to inquire if he and Hart were available for this assignment. Rodgers was interested, but Hart could not be controlled. It was then that Rodgers asked Hammerstein to become his collaborator.

Hammerstein was familiar with *Green Grow the Lilacs* and had been aware of its possibilities as a musical. He had actually once tried to get Jerome Kern to write the music. When Hammerstein read the play to Kern one day at his pool in Beverly Hills the composer liked it, though he felt that the third act was weak. However his final judgment was that it posed too many problems for a composer, and he rejected it. But Hammerstein himself was so enchanted with its lyric quality that he refused to lose faith in it. He asked the Guild for permission to write a new libretto based on the play and was informed that since it was considering Rodgers and Hart for it, such permission could not be granted.

Rodgers and Hammerstein decided to go ahead. They bought from M.G.M. an option for the motion-picture rights, which they could pick up for $50,000 two weeks after the première of the play. (They took over these rights in four days.) They also signed a contract with the Theatre Guild. As far as they knew at the moment they might never earn anything more than the few hundred dollars they received from the Guild as an advance on signing the contract. The Guild was broke. It was a moot question if it could raise the money needed for the production.

"What happened between Oscar and me was almost chemical," explains Rodgers about their coalition. "Put the right components together and an explosion takes place. Oscar and I hit it off from the day we began discussing the show."

Before a single line of verse, dialogue, or music was put down on paper they discussed in detail all the problems facing them. These were considerable. They came to an early conclusion: the play would always dictate the techniques employed; never would the techniques influence the way the play would be adapted. Musical-comedy tradition might insist that the first-act curtain rise on a large, crowded and eye-catching scene. Their version of *Green Grow the Lilacs* would have to start simply and unpretentiously to maintain the spirit of the play: only one character would be seen—a woman churning butter; the only sound to be heard would be the off-stage singing of the hero, Curly. Musical-comedy tradition might demand the early use of chorus girls; the Riggs text made no provision for girls for half of the first act, and that was the way it would have to be in the musical adaptation. Musical comedy might never be partial to a character as villainous as Jud, nor would it tolerate a murder scene. But Jud and murder were basic to the play and would have to stay in. Rodgers and Hammerstein also agreed early that every song, every bit of humor, every dance, every production number must be germane to their text—otherwise it would not go in, no matter how sure-fire it might be in winning audience enthusiasm. "We realized," wrote Hammerstein, "that such a course was experimental, amounting almost to the breach of an implied contract with a musical comedy audience. I cannot say truthfully that we were worried by the risk. Once we had made the decision everything seemed to work right and we had the inner confidence people feel when they have adopted the direct and honest approach to a problem."

They made still another major decision. In order to achieve a complete integration of book and music they would reverse the song-writing procedure widely prevalent on

Broadway and in Tin Pan Alley to which each of them had up to then conformed. Now the lyric would come before the music. Only in rare instances had Rodgers set a Larry Hart lyric to music; it was always the other way around. And it was invariably the music that came first when Hammerstein worked with Kern, Friml, Romberg, or Youmans. With Rodgers' sensitivity to a poetic text, his capacity always to find the exact musical equivalent for every mood and nuance of a given verse, this change of method would bring about a radical change in the nature and personality of his writing.

The first piece of actual writing completed by Hammerstein was the lyric of "Oh, What a Beautiful Mornin'." In the preface to his book *Lyrics,* Hammerstein recounts how these verses were written:

> Searching for a subject for Curly to sing about (in the opening scene), I recalled how deeply I had been impressed by Lynn Riggs' description at the start of his play. "It is a radiant summer morning several years ago, the kind of morning which, enveloping the shapes of earth—men, cattle in the meadow, blades of the young corn, streams—makes them seem to exist now for the first time, their images giving off a visible golden emanation that is partly true and partly a trick of the imagination, focusing to keep alive a loveliness that may pass away." On first reading these words, I had thought what a pity it was to waste them on stage directions. Only readers could enjoy them. An audience would never hear them. Yet, if they did, how quickly they would slip into the mood of the story. Remembering this reaction, I reread the description and determined to put it into song. "Oh, What a Beautiful Mornin' " opens the play and creates an atmosphere of relaxation and tenderness. It introduces the light-hearted young man who is the centre of the story. My indebtedness to Mr. Riggs' description is obvious. The cattle and the corn and the golden haze on the meadow are all there. I added some observations of my

own based on my experience with beautiful mornings, and I brought the words down to the more primitive level of Curly's character. He is, after all, just a cowboy, not a playwright.

"The corn is as high as an elephant's eye"—I first wrote "cow pony's eye." Then I walked over to my neighbor's cornfield and found that although it was only the end of August, the corn had grown much higher than that. "Cow pony" was more indigenous to the western background, but I had reservations about it even before I gauged the height of the corn. It reads better than it sounds. . . .

"All the cattle are standin' like statues." This picture had come into my brain several years before I wrote the song, and it had stayed there quietly waiting to be used. When I came to the second verse of "Oh, What a Beautiful Mornin'," I remembered it.

It took Hammerstein three weeks to write the lyric (he spent an entire week fussing over whether or not to insert the "Oh" in the first two lines). Then he went to Connecticut and read it to Rodgers. "I was a little sick with joy because it was so lovely and so right," Rodgers remembers. "When you're given words like 'the corn is as high as an elephant's eye,' you get something to say musically." Rodgers completed his waltz in less than ten minutes. It had all the charm and simplicity and sweetness of an authentic folk song; he had now begun to tap a poetic vein new even for him.

"Oh, What a Beautiful Mornin' " was characteristic of most of Hammerstein's lyric writing not only in *Oklahoma!* but also in the later plays. He uses the simplest possible vocabulary, and phrases that belong to everyday speech; he is partial to dialect and colloquialisms; his imagery is drawn from subjects indigenous to the play; he does not like unusual techniques. His verses are so direct and simple that at times they appear almost threadbare, yet they manage to retain the lyric quality of poetry. But Hammerstein is ready to confess that as he worked on *Oklahoma!* the shadow of Lorenz Hart hovered over him. He could not always free himself from an attempt to match Hart's skill where Hart had been strongest. Thus, in some of his verses, Hammerstein tried to be as witty, as sophisticated, and as pyrotechnical as Hart had been. Only when *Oklahoma!* was completely behind him—and when its overwhelming success gave him the reassurance he needed—was Hammerstein able to outgrow Hart completely and remain true to himself alone.

Most of the melodies were written after Hammerstein had passed on to Rodgers the completed lyrics. "People Will Say We're in Love" was an exception. In this instance, Rodgers and Hammerstein had agreed on the kind of love song required for the specific scene, and Rodgers was able to find the proper feeling and mood for his music without waiting for the words.

This song posed a knotty problem. It was to be the first-act love duet between Curly and Laurey—but it could not be a love song along familiar patterns. Although Curly and Laurey are highly attracted to each other, there is still at first some antagonism between them; and Laurey is much too shy to expose her inmost feelings. They can hardly speak of their love without lapsing into some sort of squabble. Rodgers and Hammerstein decided that the only kind of love song that would do was one in which Curly and Laurey cautioned each other against any outward demonstrations leading an outsider to believe they were in love. Yet beneath such warnings there must be a strong undercurrent of real tenderness. Once Rodgers knew that this was needed, his delightful and sensitive melody came quickly, and Hammerstein's lyric followed.

The proper presentation of the villainous Jud Fry raised

as great a difficulty for Rodgers and Hammerstein as did the love song. Jud was a despicable person, a pervert and a sadist, who had to be portrayed with bold realistic strokes. But before he could be acceptable to musical-comedy audiences he had to be explained to them. As Hammerstein explains in his preface to *Lyrics:*

We didn't want to resort to the boring device of having two other characters discuss him and give the audience a psychological analysis. Even if this were dramatically desirable, there are no characters in the story who are bright enough or well educated enough to do this. So we solve this problem with two songs, "Pore Jud" and "Lonely Room." They are both sung in the smokehouse set, the dingy hole where Jud lives with no companions but a mouse who nibbles on a book, and a gallery of Police Gazette pictures on the walls—a most unpromising background from a musical standpoint. In "Pore Jud," Curly, after suggesting to him how easy it would be for Jud to hang himself by a lasso from a rafter, goes on to describe what his funeral would be like. Unwelcome as the idea seems at first, Jud finds some features not unattractive to speculate on—the excitement he would cause by the gesture of the suicide, the people who would come from miles around to weep and moan. . . . He becomes, then, for a while, not just a wicked but a comic figure flattered by the attentions he might receive if he were dead. He becomes also a pathetic figure, pathetically lonely for attentions he has never received while alive. The audience begins to feel some sympathy for him, some understanding of him as a man.

In the second song, "Lonely Room," he paints a savage picture of his solitary life, his hatred of Curly and his mad desire for Laurey. This is a self-analysis, but it is emotional not cerebral. No dialogue could do this dramatic job as vividly and quickly as does the song.

It is no coincidence or accident that of all the songs Rodgers wrote for *Oklahoma!,* the only one that bears a family resemblance to the music he used to write with Hart was also the one in which the melody came before the lyric— "People Will Say We're in Love." All the others expose new grains in his writing. He caught the spirit and flavor of American folk character beautifully not only in "Oh, What a Beautiful Mornin'," but in three other songs that have the freshness and the personality of autochthonous Western music: "The Surrey with the Fringe on Top," "The Farmer and the Cowman," and "Kansas City." The bleak description of "Lonely Room," the mock tragedy of "Pore Jud," the virility of "Oklahoma!", the irresistible enchantment of "Out of My Dreams," and the beguiling seductiveness of the rippling triplets that begin each phrase of "Many a New Day" all demonstrate his rapidly growing creative powers.

The complete score has thirteen basic numbers. These are used in several different ways. They appear, of course, as self-sufficient numbers growing out of the text as naturally as a living organism out of rich soil. But they recur in the play, sometimes in fleeting quotations, sometimes in slightly altered shapes, sometimes as a background to the dialogue, thereby more closely knitting text and music. Six of these numbers provide the threads to make up the warp and woof of the dream-ballet music of the first act, "Laurey Makes Up Her Mind."

Oklahoma! was not easy to sell to potential backers. It carried on its shoulders the burden of too many failures. The straight play on which it had been based had had a run of only sixty-four performances. Rouben Mamoulian, selected as the stage director, had had only a single experience with a Broadway musical and that had been with *Porgy and Bess,* which had been a failure in 1935. Oscar Hammerstein II, author of book and lyrics, had not enjoyed a single Broadway success in ten years; his last appearance had been with a show that departed after only thirty-six performances. And while Rodgers was a highly successful composer, even his contribution was subject to question since he had never before worked with anyone but Hart and had still to prove that he could function successfully with somebody else.

Besides such deficits there were additional ones, no less serious. *Oklahoma!* as it was being planned by the Theatre Guild was hardly calculated to win public approval. Not only did it have little of the formal humor expected on the musical-comedy stage, but it also tried to bring both murder and an unpalatable character like Jud Fry into the musical theater. The show would have no chorus-girl sequences, no popular dance routines, no gay production numbers. Instead the emphasis was to be on American folk ballet— choreography by Agnes de Mille, who had been chosen because of her excellent work with and in *Rodeo*, a cowboy ballet recently presented by the Ballet Russe de Monte Carlo.

Perhaps most serious drawback of all—there were no stars in the cast. Alfred Drake and Joan Roberts were set in the leading roles of Curly and Laurey. The other important parts were filled by Howard da Silva (Jud Fry), Celeste Holm (Ado Annie), Joseph Buloff (Ali Hakim), Joan Mc-Cracken (Sylvie), Lee Dixon (Will Parker), Bambi Linn (Aggie) and Betty Garde (Aunt Eller). They were all competent performers, and a few were to become stars in the play. But to a backer in 1943 they were mostly little-known actors and actresses who could not be expected to lure box-office lines.

"Against all these odds," says Rodgers, "the Guild went into battle and came out with the money." But the money did not come easily. To raise the $83,000 needed for the production proved a Herculean task. Theresa Helburn at first tried to get M.G.M. to finance the whole production, since they had originally owned the *Green Grow the Lilacs* property. But the feeling in Hollywood was against "another Western," which had been the reason why M.G.M. had sold the rights to Rodgers and Hammerstein in the first place. A series of auditions was now held by the Guild to interest potential backers. Rodgers and Margot Hopkins played the score on two pianos; Hammerstein narrated the story, did the "Pore Jud" sequence and enacted Aunt Eller's role; Alfred Drake and Joan Roberts sang the leading songs. The results were discouraging, and at times completely depressing. At one point Hammerstein was tempted to withdraw from the project and accept a two-year Hollywood contract offered him by Arthur Freed, while Rodgers was hoping desperately to get his Air Force commission. But Hammerstein finally decided to continue to gamble on *Oklahoma!*, where his heart belonged, and Rodgers' commission did not come.

Two of these auditions—one at Jules Glaenzer's home, the other in a Park Avenue penthouse—drew an audience of bankers, influential movie people and some theater people. But at neither affair was a single dollar raised. Vivienne Spencer gave a party at her home off Fifth Avenue for her wealthy friends and acquaintances (including the Zeckendorffs and Tommy Manville), and had *Oklahoma!* run through for them. One of the guests commented he never did like plays about farmers. Only the Ewings responded, with $1000.

One evening, Rodgers and Theresa Helburn met the movie executive Harry Cohn in a French restaurant. They told him about their play and arranged a hearing for him in a studio in the Steinway Building. When Cohn learned about the Agnes de Mille ballet numbers, he inquired with astonishment, "You mean—one of *those* things?" And, delicately poising the tip of his forefinger on his head, he began to pirouet. After the audition Cohn tried to persuade the executives of his studio to finance the play, but they were not interested. However, he was induced by Max Gordon (who, Rodgers says, was one of the few rabid rooters of *Oklahoma!* from the very beginning) to invest $15,000 himself.

By dribs and drabs—through argument, pleading, coercion, prayer—the money started coming in for what by now was being derisively dubbed as "Helburn's Folly." Theresa Helburn managed to get S. N. Behrman, the playwright, to buy a $5000 interest. Various admirers of the Guild, or of the production, paid a thousand or two thousand dollars—not as an investment but mostly as a contribution to a worthy cause. By the time the production reached Boston, the entire $83,000 had been collected. At that time several others approached the Guild offering to buy a piece of the production and had to be turned down. M.G.M. was also firmly refused when after the New York opening it announced its readiness to buy back the screen rights from Rodgers and Hammerstein.

While the painful process of collecting the money was going on, the rehearsals were getting under way. These were also disturbing. Many of those associated with the production could not avoid feeling that they were involved in a potential flop—even many who knew that it would be a beautiful play and possibly an important one. The conviction was growing stronger all the time that the whole production was being poised on a level too high for Broadway audiences. In her autobiography, *Pay the Piper,* Agnes de Mille wrote that Rodgers was about the only one who maintained not only that the show would be a success but that it would be a sensation. ("He's got a kind of sixth sense," explains Dorothy Rodgers, "and seems to know what the people are ready to accept.")

The cast was finally rehearsed and the scenery and costuming finished. The first tryout was scheduled for the Shubert Theatre in New Haven for four evening performances beginning March 11, 1943, under the title of *Away We Go*. The audience reaction was excellent, and after the final curtain the show gave every appearance of being a potential hit, possibly a tremendous one. But unfavorable reports from New Haven came from the commercial bigwigs of Broadway, who insisted that the production was too static, that interest tended to lag, and that the need for more comedy was a sore one. "No Girls, No Gags, No Chance," was the word flashed back to New York.

After the New Haven tryout, the name of the show was changed to *Oklahoma!*. This was the title originally considered but discarded for fear it might mislead many into believing that this was a play about dust bowls and "Okies." After New Haven—where a rewriting session changed the "Oklahoma!" song into a big choral number—the first title was restored. Lawrence Langner suggested that an exclamation point might help avoid any confusion about the subject matter. However, since the posters and programs for the tryouts had already been printed, it was decided to keep *Away We Go* until the New York opening.

The next step was Boston, where a two-week engagement began at the Colonial Theatre on March 15. En route by drawing room, a feverish rewriting session began. More humor and action were introduced and a new three-minute dance sequence was outlined; the second act was tightened; "Oklahoma!," originally planned as a dance, became a rousing choral number.

The changes proved salutary. Despite inclement weather and the competition provided by a new Mary Martin musical, business in Boston was brisk. Sickness and accident threatened the first night. Some of the dancers and singers were afflicted with German measles and had to appear with thick layers of grease paint to conceal their spots. At the performance itself, Marc Platt sprained two toes in one of the dances, and one of the chorines fractured an arm in a vigorous routine. But these incidents apparently passed unnoticed. The critics and audiences were delighted with the music, and the message now began to wing back to New York: "No Girls, No Gags, No Tickets."

Oklahoma! came to the St. James Theatre in New York on March 31, 1943. Despite the good reports from Boston, the house was not sold out for the opening performance and there were some empty seats—the last time such a thing happened for several years. There was a sigh in the audience after "Oh, What a Beautiful Mornin'." From that moment on, the enthusiasm in the theater kept mounting, building up a crescendo which culminated in a vociferous ovation after the final curtain. This was something decidedly fresh and new in the theater, and everyone there that night seemed to sense that he was witness to a historic event.

While the audience reaction had been unmistakable, it was not yet certain that *Oklahoma!* was a success—not until the critics were heard from. That night, Jules Glaenzer gave a party at his home for Rodgers and Hammerstein, other leading collaborators in the production, and the principals in the cast. At midnight, the party tuned in to a radio theater critic whose opinions were regarded as the weather-vane pointing to the way the critical wind generally blew. They heard him say that the show would not last a week.

But the critics the next morning were of a different mind. One rivaled the other in the use of superlatives. Lewis Nichols did not hesitate to call it a "folk opera." Burns Mantle described it as "different—beautifully different" and Burton Rascoe said it was "fresh, lovely, colorful, one of the finest musical scores any musical play ever had." John Anderson called it "a beautiful and delightful show, fresh and imaginative, as enchanting to the eye as Richard Rodgers' music is to the ear." "My gratitude is practically boundless," wrote Wolcott Gibbs. Such accolades are not surprising. In its integration of music and text; in its effort to bring to a musical production dramatic truth, a logical story line, effective atmosphere and characterization; in its avoidance of all formal routines and sequences; in its simplicity and beauty and directness—this was musical comedy no more but a folk play with music.

With such a send-off, business at the St. James Theatre immediately became so brisk that within a short period capacity houses became the rule and it became difficult to beg, steal or borrow a ticket. *Oklahoma!* was a smash hit. But not even the most extravagant dreams of its most passionate enthusiast would have dared to suggest then how big a smash hit it would really become.

On March 31, 1953, *Oklahoma!* celebrated its tenth birthday at the National Theatre in Washington, D.C. The audience that night included political dignitaries and a contingent from New York comprising Rodgers and Hammerstein, Theresa Helburn and Lawrence Langner, Agnes de Mille, Alfred Drake, and Bambi Linn among others. Only one actor that night was a carryover from the première ten years ago—Owen Martin, in the minor part of Cord Elam. The evening presented the fortieth performer to play the part of Laurey, Florence Henderson, and the forty-fifth to do Curly, Ralph Lowe. After the final curtain a party was held on the stage. All those present sang "Happy Birthday," and Richard Rodgers played "Boys and Girls Like You and Me," which he had written for the show but had deleted during the New Haven tryouts.

There was good reason to celebrate. In New York, *Okla-*

homa! had run five years and nine weeks (2,248 performances)—the longest of any musical in Broadway history—
grossing over $7,000,000. In ten years, 28,000,000 people
had paid over $40,000,000 to see it. Two days after the New
York engagement ended, the company went on the road, to
cover seventy cities in fifty-one weeks. Meanwhile, in 1943, a
national company had been formed. Except for summer lay-
offs, it played during the entire ten-year period, appearing
in almost 250 cities and before an audience totaling about
10,000,000; the box-office return was about $20,000,000.
By the time the national company reached Cheyenne, Wyo-
ming, on December 23, 1950, it had played 3,000 times in
every state and had covered 250,000 miles. Many cities had
seen the show not once but several times.

When the play came to the state from which its name was
derived, on November 25, 1946, the governor decreed a
state holiday. The schools were closed. A mammoth celebration was planned to include the big oil and cattle men of the
state, and three thousand Indians in tribal ceremonies. A
special train was sent to New York to bring Rodgers and
Hammerstein and some other theatrical notables. Unfortunately, the elements refused to cooperate. Recalls Rodgers:

> The Governor of the State was waiting for us at the station.
> The parade was in readiness. The loudspeakers were all
> warmed up and waiting to play "Oh, What a Beautiful Morn-
> in'." Our train pulled into the station—and what happened?
> It rained. I have never seen a Governor cry but I came pretty
> close to it that morning. By noon the rain had turned to sleet,
> the pavement had turned to ice, three thousand horses were
> stalled in their stalls, forty-seven brass bands were disbanded,
> and all the loudspeakers were frozen in their sound tracks.
> Home went the children, back to their prairies went the In-
> dians, the horses stamped impatiently in their stalls, and the
> only happy natives were the members of the Street Cleaning

Department. There were a few other people in town, however, who managed to bear the ice and wind without sadness and perhaps my astute friend can figure out why those of us who came huddled in the discomfort of that private car were still able to sing in quiet and grateful tones, "Oh, What a Beautiful Mornin'."

Other companies brought *Oklahoma!* to Berlin, London, South Africa, Sweden, Denmark, Australia, and other distant places. In 1945, a special company was formed to tour the Pacific bases of the United States forces. This unit, the largest ever organized by U.S.O. Camp Shows, opened in Leyte, in the Philippines, on May 9 and subsequently played before 1,500,000 servicemen. In London, *Oklahoma!* had the longest run of any production in the 287-year history of the Drury Lane Theatre and the second longest run accumulated on the London stage—three and a half years (1511 performances); the gross was $4,300,000. In Berlin, at the Theatre Arts Festival on September 12, 1951, it received eleven curtain calls; the shouts of "Bravo, *Oklahoma!*" rang out from the audience, most of whom did not understand a single word that had been spoken on the stage. In South Africa, the production combined American principals with South African natives for the ensembles. In Denmark the play was given in a Danish translation by Holger Bech.

The original investment of $83,000 had brought in those ten years a profit of about $5,000,000. Each investor of $1500 (1 per cent share) earned in the neighborhood of $50,000. The Theatre Guild had profited about $4,000,000; Rodgers, about $1,000,000.

To this formidable performance history several interesting footnotes might be added. *Oklahoma!* received a special award from the Pulitzer Prize Committee in 1944. *Oklahoma!* helped launch a practice since become standard procedure in the record industry, the recording of the complete score with the original cast; Decca sold over one million such albums in the era before the long-playing record. Most significant of all, *Oklahoma!*—in its many and varied performances throughout the world—helped to incubate stars, many of them unknowns when they first appeared in this play. Among these were Celeste Holm, Shelley Winters, Pamela Britton, Alfred Drake, Joan McCracken, Joan Roberts, Bambi Linn, Howard Keel, Florence Henderson, Isabel Bigley, Iva Withers, Jane Watson, and Howard da Silva.

The history of *Oklahoma!* did not end with its tenth birthday.

On August 31, 1953, it was revived in New York City for a five-week engagement at the New York City Center, produced this time not by the Theatre Guild but by Rodgers and Hammerstein. This was the third visit paid the city by the play, the second having been a four-week stay by the national company in 1951. "There has been much fine work from them [Rodgers and Hammerstein] during the later years," wrote Brooks Atkinson at this time. "But none of it puts a tarnish on the golden score of *Oklahoma!* or the wonderful lyricism of the book and verses. The whole work retains the freshness of that opening."

The day on which a traveling company began a three-day stop in Bridgeport, Connecticut, before starting a tour of 140 towns under the auspices of Broadway Lights, Inc.— September 17, 1954—was proclaimed by the mayor as "Richard Rodgers Day."

On June 20, 1955, *Oklahoma!* was performed by an American company at the Théâtre des Champs Élysées as part of the "Salute to France" Festival sponsored by the International Exchange Program of the American National Theatre and Academy. This was the first opportunity France had to see the play and learn—as *Paris-Soir* commented—

"why the United States musicals are so famous." After weeks in Paris, the production was brought to Italy—to Rome, Naples, Milan, and Venice. *Il Tempo* of Rome said: "It was like a fresh shower. There isn't a grain of dust on the show, and not a grain of vulgarity. The music flows like a happy torrent." Only one tragic incident marred an otherwise triumphant tour. Just before the final performance in Milan, Jean Bradley, who was playing Laurey in that city, died suddenly.

As a tribute to Rodgers and Hammerstein, to the State of Oklahoma, and to the musical play, an "Oklahoma! Song-Fest" was given at the Central Park Mall on August 21, 1955. Fifteen thousand people attended, including Governor Harriman of New York, Governor Gary of Oklahoma, and Mayor Wagner of New York City. After the musical performances (mostly of numbers from the show) scrolls were presented to Rodgers and Hammerstein by Bernard F. Gimbel; Rodgers and Hammerstein, in turn, presented a score of their play to Governor Gary.

Also in 1955 came the screen adaptation of *Oklahoma!* in the then new Todd-AO process, produced by Arthur Hornblow, Jr., and distributed by Magna Theatre Corporation. Shirley Jones, who had previously appeared in the chorus of *South Pacific* and *Me and Juliet,* was starred as Laurey opposite Gordon MacRae's Curly; others in the cast included Rod Steiger, Eddie Albert, and Gloria Grahame. The dances, as in the original production, were created by Agnes de Mille, while the overall direction was by Fred Zinnemann.

The first public performance of this motion picture, on October 13 in New York City, was an occasion for some unusual fanfare. Governor Gary of Oklahoma rode a white horse at the head of a group of surreys which proceeded from the St. James Theatre, where the play had opened, to the Rivoli Theatre, scene of the motion-picture première.

There, after being welcomed by Rodgers and Hammerstein, the Governor announced the "annexation" of the theater to "Oklahoma territory." He then stepped on some Oklahoma soil, which had earlier been transplanted in front of the theater, and raised a flag of his state atop the building.

But the film version did not require such a pageant to attract notice. It was unquestionably one of the major motion-picture events of the year. Leading political figures, and representatives from the theatrical and social worlds, were on hand to witness a picture which, as Bosley Crowthers reported, "magnifies and strengthens all the charm that it [the play] had on the stage." *"Oklahoma!,"* said Alton Cook, "seems likely to become as much a box-office milestone in the movies as it was in stage annals." The validity of this last statement was proved after the screen version arrived at its sixth month on Broadway. Though the general national distribution had not yet begun, it had already been seen by almost 2,500,000 people and had brought in over $3,000,000 into the box office.

3

A THEATRICAL EMPIRE

From a highly successful composer who made an occasional foray into producing, Richard Rodgers now became the bulwark of a theatrical empire.

One part of that empire was a music publishing house. From 1926 to 1931, Rodgers' music was published by Harms, Inc., headed by Max Dreyfus. When sound came to the motion-picture screen, Warner Brothers bought out three major Broadway publishers, one of these being Harms. In this deal it took over the existing Rodgers and Hart catalogue, which it still owns and administers through the Music Publishers Holding Corporation. From 1931 on, Rodgers' music for Broadway was published first by Rodart, then by T. B. Harms, and later by Chappell and Co., all three directed by Max Dreyfus. During this period, Rodgers' music for the screen was published by other companies, those affiliated with the studios for which he was working.

Even before *Oklahoma!* was produced, Rodgers—who was the only one to insist that the play would be a sensation—became convinced that its music had incalculable commercial value. "We'd be suckers if we didn't publish it ourselves," he told Hammerstein one day. They decided to visit Dreyfus at his home in Bronxville to discuss this matter, preparing beforehand arguments proving the justification and feasibility of their plan. To their surprise they needed none of these arguments. Dreyfus agreed wholeheartedly that they should now be their own publishers and even offered to cooperate fully.

In 1944, Rodgers and Hammerstein formed the music publishing house of Williamson Music, Inc., so named because they were both the sons of fathers named William. It became an adjunct of Chappell and Company, and its first publication was the music of *Oklahoma!*. A subsidiary Dreyfus enterprise—Crawford Music Company—was used for promotion purposes exclusively. Dreyfus charged Rodgers and Hammerstein a percentage for the use of his office, staff, and distribution and promotion facilities. Williamson Music, Inc., which has since published all the Broadway music of Rodgers and Hammerstein, has remained a Chappell subsidiary, though it is owned by the writers. (The use of the Crawford Music Company for promotion was dispensed with after *Oklahoma!*.) A London branch was also founded at the same time, affiliated with Chappell's English branch, Chappell, Ltd.

Another enterprise of the new Rodgers and Hammerstein empire was the establishment of a firm in 1944 to produce plays by other writers. A small office was set up in Room 511 of the RKO Building in Radio City, a few doors down the corridor from Chappell. Maurice Jacobs was its business manager; the only other employee was Lillian Leff, as secretary.

On October 19, 1944, this new organization presented its first play, *I Remember Mama*, by John van Druten. Since this play won several prizes and had a New York run of 714 performances, the producing firm of Rodgers and Hammerstein was launched with flying colors. But the organization did even better with its very next production, a year and a half later, growing out of a plan to put on a new musical comedy with Jerome Kern's score. When Kern died suddenly in 1945, before completing any of this music, Irving Berlin was brought in as Kern's replacement. The musical, *Annie Get Your Gun*, which starred Ethel Merman, remained in New York for 1147 performances, and in London for 1304 performances; a second American company toured the country from October 3, 1947, to May 28, 1949; a Paris company presented it in a French translation in 1950. (Of parenthetical interest is the fact that this was probably the first time that one leading Broadway composer produced a musical show by one of his leading competitors. The relationship between Rodgers and Irving Berlin was untouched by discord of any kind. Rodgers—even though his approach to the problems of writing music for the stage was different from Berlin's— never attempted to give Berlin suggestions, just as Berlin gave Rodgers a completely free hand in the production.)

Of the five succeeding Rodgers and Hammerstein productions by writers other than themselves, three were also successes: *Happy Birthday*, a comedy by Anita Loos starring Helen Hayes (564 performances); *John Loves Mary*, by Norman Krasna (421 performances); and Samuel Taylor's *The Happy Time* (614 performances).* The income from Broadway and out-of-town presentations from the five successes was handsomely supplemented by revenue from Hollywood

---

* The two failures were Graham Greene's *The Heart of the Matter*, which played for two and a half weeks in Boston in 1950 and never came to New York; and John Steinbeck's *Burning Bright* (13 performances), also in 1950.

for the motion-picture rights, piling profits upon profits with prodigal abundance. "In the matter of contemporary success," *Business Week* was able to report on August 11, 1951, "Richard Rodgers and Oscar Hammerstein II are at the peak of their profession. Their income as a team is believed to be somewhere over $1,500,000 a year, or roughly $31,000 a week before taxes. . . . Since forming their production partnership in 1944, the two have become the most successful firm on Broadway."

In addition to plays by others, the Rodgers and Hammerstein office has produced all their own musicals after *Allegro*. When in 1953 and 1955 it bought from the Theatre Guild its interest in *Oklahoma!* and *Carousel* respectively, the producers became the exclusive owners of every musical they had written together. They were now in the favorable position of being able to form the Rodgers and Hammerstein Picture Corporation for the sale of the motion-picture rights to their plays for the unprecedented figure of 40 per cent of the profits.

The Rodgers and Hammerstein firm now occupies a suite of ten rooms at 488 Madison Avenue. A staff of between ten and twelve carry on the varied activities of the organization that annually grosses about $15,000,000. The staff includes the two who first opened the office—Maurice Jacobs and Lillian Leff—and with them a librarian, casting director, receptionist, and assistant.

Rodgers' office, at the end of the corridor, is spacious and handsomely outfitted with a concert grand Steinway piano, desk, books and music, and attractive drawings on the walls. The Venetian blinds are always drawn to insure his privacy against the buildings nearby. Rodgers' table (he never uses a desk anywhere) is always meticulous in its neatness—each pencil, eraser, memorandum, letter in its proper place even after he has been working for hours.

The organization has a London branch called Williamson Music Ltd., with a staff of about twenty headed by Jerome Whyte as production supervisor. This firm first came into existence in 1950 when Rodgers and Hammerstein, in conjunction with Emile Littler, presented *Annie Get Your Gun* in London. Its first production without outside collaboration was *South Pacific* one year later. Since that time it not only is the agency for producing any Rodgers and Hammerstein play given in London—such as *The King and I* in 1953 —but it is also the English producing firm for several successful American plays for which it has acquired European rights: *Teahouse of the August Moon* and *Can Can* in 1954; *Damn Yankees* in 1957. It also had financial interests in several London productions, including *Plain and Fancy* and *The Desperate Hours.*

The year in which they organized their firm—1944— Rodgers and Hammerstein also worked for 20th Century-Fox. Their assignment was to write the screen play, lyrics and music for *State Fair.* This was the best-selling novel by Phil Stong which in 1933 had been filmed with Will Rogers, Janet Gaynor, and Lew Ayres. It was now being remade into a musical, in a production by William Perlberg, and starred Dick Haymes with Vivian Blaine and Jeanne Crain. Since its locale was a small-town fair out West, the Hollywood executive considered the authors of *Oklahoma!* best suited to make the adaptation.

State Fair is one of the best original scores Rodgers wrote for motion pictures, and he is as proud of it as he is of many of his musical plays. He wrote six numbers. One was a large opening routine, "Our State Fair." Three others were hits in varying degrees: "That's for Me," "It's a Grand Night for Singing," and "It Might as Well Be Spring." When, in November, 1945, "It Might as Well Be Spring" and "That's for Me" were joined on the Hit Parade by "If I Loved You" from *Carousel,* it was the first time that this radio program had three songs by the same composer and lyricist on the same evening.

When *State Fair* was released in 1945, Kate Cameron said: "The audience literally floats out of the theatre on the strains of the Rodgers music." And Rose Pelswick wrote: "The Rodgers and Hammerstein score is in great measure responsible for the picture's charm; unlike most film songs . . . these stem directly from and became a part of the story itself."

"It Might as Well Be Spring" won the Academy Award on March 7, 1946, as the best song written that year for the movies. Since it is the only Rodgers song thus far to achieve this distinction—and since both in lyrics and music it is one of the best by Rodgers and Hammerstein—its history deserves telling. In trying to write his lyrics, Hammerstein was temporarily stymied. Margy is a young girl afflicted with the blues—and for no good reason since she is about to go to the state fair. Hammerstein felt that her mood required a song; and in thinking the matter over it seemed to him that Margy's temper resembled spring fever. But state fairs are held in the fall and not in the spring. He consulted Rodgers and asked if it is possible to have a lyric in which Margy opines that it might be autumn but that the way she feels it might as well be spring. "That's it," Rodgers said. "That's just it." Hammerstein recalls: "All my doubts were gone. I had a partner behind me."

Hammerstein completed his lyric in about one week— the complete master now not only of his technique but also of poetic expression:

I'm as restless as a willow in a windstorm,
I'm as jumpy as a puppet on a string!
(I'd say that I had spring fever,
But I know it isn't spring.)
I am starry-eyed and vaguely discontented,
Like a nightingale without a song to sing.
(Oh, why should I have spring fever
When it isn't even spring?)

I keep wishing I were somewhere else,
Walking down a strange new street,
Hearing words that I have never heard
From a man I've yet to meet.

I'm as busy as a spider, spinning daydreams,
I'm as giddy as a baby on a swing.
I haven't seen a crocus or a rosebud
Or a robin on the wing,
But I feel so gay—in a melancholy way—
That it might as well be spring . . .
It might as well be spring.

One day, in their office at the RKO Building, Hammerstein handed this lyric over to Rodgers. He then stepped down the corridor to talk to Max Dreyfus. When he returned, about an hour later, Rodgers had completed his melody in its final form. "This is the annoying part of our collaboration," Hammerstein confesses. "It takes me a week, and sometimes three weeks, to write the words of a song. After I give them to him, it takes him an hour or two and his work is over."

4

"WE ARE STUBBORNLY ROMANTIC"

During the run of *Oklahoma!* Rodgers, Hammerstein, and Theresa Helburn would hold weekly luncheon meetings at Sardi's restaurant, which they called "the gloat club," to gloat over the fabulous success of the play. During one of these lunches, Helburn asked them about making Ferenc Molnar's *Liliom* into a musical. The Theatre Guild had produced it successfully in 1921; and as recently as 1940 it had been revived on Broadway with Ingrid Bergman and Burgess Meredith. It was Helburn's thought that the Hungarian background and characters, and the play's flight into fantasy, were ideal for musical treatment. Hammerstein knew and liked the play; but he also believed the international situation during those war years made the use of a Budapest setting highly impractical.

Three lunches later at Sardi's, Helburn returned to *Liliom*.

Why not, she asked, change the setting from Budapest to New Orleans? Hammerstein wanted to consider this suggestion further. But after reading up on that city he rejected the plan. He did not feel he could learn to use the New Orleans vernacular with facility.

The *Liliom* matter seemed to have been dropped for good when, at another of these lunches, Rodgers suddenly inquired why they could not use New England as a setting. He does not now remember what made him bring up this suggestion when he did, since he had not given it any previous thought. Hammerstein and Helburn both seized upon the idea. Hammerstein recognized that such a setting could provide ensembles basic to the the play—sailors, fishermen, mill girls—and that New England speech would come easily to him.

They talked a great deal about this project during the next few weeks. "When we wrote our first number—it was the 'Soliloquy'—we knew we had the play licked," recalls Rodgers. "We signed a contract with the Theatre Guild and went to work."

With Ferenc Molnar out of New York, negotiations had to be undertaken with him by long-distance communication. Giacomo Puccini had once approached Molnar about turning *Liliom* into an opera and had been politely turned down. "I want *Liliom* to be remembered as a Molnar play, not as a Puccini opera," the dramatist explained. But he was now much more amenable to the Theatre Guild, recognizing the commercial value of having *Liliom* become a Rodgers and Hammerstein musical.

Hammerstein started writing his book and lyrics. The title *Liliom* became *Carousel*; Liliom himself, Billy Bigelow. The setting was shifted from Budapest to a coastal New England town in 1873. In Hammerstein's first version, a scene in heaven consisted of a New England cottage inhabited by Mr. and Mrs. God. "The whole concept was pretty terrible," Hammerstein concedes. When the play tried out in Boston, Rouben Mamoulian, the stage director, suggested that both the cottage and Mr. and Mrs. God be completely eliminated, to be replaced by the Starkeeper in a nebulous heaven setting. Mamoulian also introduced the highly effective prop of a clothesline, from which the stars hang out to dry.

As we have already remarked, Hammerstein's first lyric was the "Soliloquy," in which Billy speaks of his joy at being a father and anticipates what his son will be like. After Hammerstein read his lyric to Rodgers, the latter (doting father of two daughters) asked if it might not be more effective to add a second part in which Billy suddenly realizes he might get a daughter, and soon finds things in that prospect to warm his heart. Theresa Helburn was with Rodgers when Hammerstein read him his revised lyric. "I saw his face light up at the new part," she says. "I feel that it is from this moment on that Rodgers fell hopelessly in love with his play." It had taken Hammerstein three weeks to write his lyric; Rodgers' music came in about three hours.

Once the first song was completed, the rest came easily. "It's like opening a bottle of olives," explains Rodgers. "Remove the first, and the others follow without trouble." One of the big numbers, "June Is Bustin' Out All Over," took Rodgers only about twenty minutes. Dorothy Rodgers left the house to drive her children to a nearby movie. When she returned, less than half an hour later, she found Rodgers had completed his song, which had not even been begun when she had left.

Two weeks after *Carousel* went into rehearsal, and at its first run-through, Ferenc Molnar, now in New York, had his first glimpse of how his play had been revised. Naturally both Rodgers and Hammerstein were apprehensive; the changes, particularly in the ending of the play, had been drastic. "Molnar was sitting in the back row," recalls Rodgers, "his overcoat draped over his shoulders, his monocle jutting from his right eye—the apotheosis of the implacable Hungarian playwright. I shivered. Oscar shivered. The run-through started. We still hadn't met the man. When the second act was over, Langner took us up the aisle to meet Molnar. He was beaming. He thought it was wonderful, he said. 'And best of all,' he added, 'I like the new ending.' "

The first reports about *Carousel* from out of town were not good. In fact the initial response in Boston had been so hostile that, says Rodgers, "you'd have thought we brought the thing in to insult the Pilgrim Fathers."

Rodgers witnessed the New York opening, on April 19, 1945, from the vantage point of a stretcher in back of some draperies that hung down from an upper box in the Majestic Theatre. A few days earlier, coming back from Boston, he had ripped a lumbar muscle carrying his heavy suitcase from train to taxi. (The war had virtually eliminated the porter.) He had had to conduct the performance at the final New York rehearsal from a stretcher. On opening night he watched from a horizontal position, his brain befuddled by a heavy dosage of morphine. "I remember two reactions from the drug: (a) I couldn't hear any laughter or applause and was convinced that the show was laying an egg, and (b) I couldn't have cared less. The soft, gray cloud I was on was floating high above either exultation or despair."

Carousel did not "lay an egg." Handsomely produced by the Theatre Guild, brilliantly staged by Mamoulian, and profiting from the attractive choreography of Agnes de Mille and the warm and poignant performances of John Raitt and Jan Clayton in the two leading roles, *Carousel* won the hearts of the critics completely. John Chapman saw it as "one of

the finest musical plays I have ever seen, and I shall remember it always." To Robert Garland it was "an evening
of sheer theatrical entertainment . . . romantic, melodra-
matic, fantastical, colorful, comic, tragic, melodic. When
somebody writes a better play than *Carousel*, Richard Rodgers
and Oscar Hammerstein will have to write it."

Carousel received the New York Drama Critics Award
as the best musical of the season and the Donaldson Awards
in eight categories. It stayed on Broadway a little over two
years (890 performances); went on tour from May 29, 1947,
to February 28, 1949; had a run of 566 performances at the
Drury Lane in London, with a special company touring the
rest of England; was successfully revived in New York City in
1954, staged by Oscar Hammerstein's son William; and in
1955 was given a lavish screen production by 20th Century-
Fox in Cinemascope '55, Gordon MacRae and Shirley Jones
taking the leads.

Carousel was a forward step in the history of the American musical play. From many points of view it is better than
Oklahoma! even if its performance history is less spectacular.
The text has greater depths of feeling, a more encompassing
humanity, and greater universality— with tragic overtones not
often encountered on the musical stage. Hammerstein uses
the vernacular in dialogue and lyrics gracefully and naturally.
The fusion between music and the text is even more sensitive
here than in *Oklahoma!*. Song flows into speech and speech
into song; melody and text become one. Extended sequences
combine prose, verse, and speech, or recitative with melody.
The orchestra often becomes an eloquent commentator on
what has just happened or is about to happen.

In *Carousel* Rodgers' artistic horizon is extended. Here
he is much more than the shaper of fresh, original, and beautiful melody; he is a musical dramatist. It is this fact that led
Otis Guernsey, Jr., to suggest that *Carousel* "proved that

music and real drama can be combined outside opera with very good entertainment results," and Ward Morehouse to say of Rodgers' score that it is "some of the most beguiling music of his career." Aware of the growing dimensions of his musical thinking, Rodgers demanded an orchestra twice the size usually encountered in the Broadway theater. Then he began his score with a series of vertiginous waltzes, symphonic in breadth, which was played under the opening scene, in which a carousel is spinning in an amusement park. This music had not actually been written for the play. It was a *Waltz Suite* composed by Rodgers for Paul Whiteman, who never performed it. Its mood and movement so happily caught the gay and colorful feeling of the opening carousel scene that Hammerstein persuaded Rodgers to use it for the play.

There were also new horizons in Rodgers' melodic writing. The form and style of his windswept melodies and his expansive musical scenes, now unhampered by structural limitations, were dictated by the requirements of the text without concern for convention or tradition. The deservedly famous "Soliloquy" is a seven-minute narrative of operatic dimensions, made up of eight different melodic fragments. And what a wealth of tenderness, sweetness of sentiment, and feeling was brought into the concluding part, in which Billy reconciles himself to a daughter (beginning with the lines "My little girl, pink and white, as peaches and cream is she")! The "Mr. Snow" sequence is made up of accompanied speech, scenes, and melody, and so is the "Carrie and Mr. Snow" sequence, which like the "Soliloquy" also has a section of irresistible charm and touching beauty, "When the Children Are Asleep." The lyrical richness Rodgers had poured into *Oklahoma!* and into so many earlier musicals is also present in *Carousel.* Some of the songs are among the best Rodgers has written: "If I Loved You," still one of his most moving love songs; "June Is Bustin' Out All Over," which brims over with the effervescence of the vernal season; "You'll Never Walk Alone," which has a spirituality that once led Cole Porter to say of Rodgers' best songs that they have "a kind of holiness about them."

But Rodgers goes beyond distinguished lyricism and toward a dramatic expressiveness which at times penetrated to the very core of a character or situation. We get a new insight into some of the finer qualities of Billy Bigelow—his pride and fiery independence—in "The Highest Judge of All." We understand the extent of Julie's devotion to Billy through her moving exposition, "What's the Use of Wond'rin'." This last song, incidentally, deserved a far greater popularity than it has achieved, for it is in one of Rodgers' most affecting, most winning veins of tenderness. It is Oscar Hammerstein's belief that its failure away from the play is due entirely to the single word "talk," with which the lyric ends abruptly. "The trouble with this word is the hard 'k' sound at the end of it," Hammerstein explains in *Lyrics*. "The last two lines of the refrain are 'You're his girl and he's your feller, and all the rest is talk.' This is exactly what I wanted the character to say. . . . I realized that I was defying convention in ending with the word "talk" but I had a perverse desire to try it anyway."

Both Hammerstein and Rodgers have always been particularly partial to *Carousel*. Of all their brainchildren, this is still their favorite. When Hammerstein saw the 1954 revival, he confesses he went home and cried through half the night. "They were tears of gratitude. I was *so* glad to have written it." Rodgers revealed an equally sentimental attachment to the play, but in another way. Early in 1953 he brought Jan Clayton to the Majestic Theatre to hear some auditions. They came early and the theater was still deserted. Though neither said a word they both suddenly remembered that this was the theater in which *Carousel* had played, and that it was Jan Clayton who had played Julie. "The idea occurred to us simultaneously," recalls Rodgers. "Jan stood on the same spot on the stage where she'd stood nine years before, and I went to the piano. She sang 'What's the Use of Wond'rin' ' to the empty seats. I don't mind saying we were both a little teary."

Two plays like *Oklahoma!* and *Carousel* coming in succession brought their authors to an unrivaled position among those writing for the American musical theater. It was, then, to be expected that they now were frequently approached with possible plays, books or ideas to which they might be sympathetic. "We have never profited a great deal from the advice well-meaning friends have given us," Rodgers explains, "even when these people are knowledgeable and discriminating. It just doesn't seem to work out. The trouble seems to be that these people want us to repeat our last success and they offer us ideas like the one in which we were last successful. But we cannot repeat something we have already done. We have to seek out something new, fresh, and unexpected before we can become sufficiently excited to go to work."

And in seeking out a fresh subject for their next musical, Rodgers and Hammerstein departed just as sharply from *Carousel* as *Carousel* had differed from *Oklahoma!*. For a long time Hammerstein had nursed an ambition to write a play tracing the career of one man from birth to death. He asked Rodgers if such a venture might appeal to him. When Rodgers said it did, Hammerstein started writing *Allegro*. This was his first attempt at writing an original play for Rodgers' music, and "I put a great deal of myself in it." He traces the life and career of Joseph Taylor, Jr., son of a small-town physician, born in 1905, raised in his home town, and become wealthy in Chicago through a large practice of wealthy neurotics and hypochondriacs. The realization how empty his life and career have become sends him back to his small town and to a comparatively humble practice.

Everything about the play delighted Rodgers. Once when Hammerstein, on vacation in Australia, sent him a batch of lyrics and some pages of dialogue, Rodgers wired him back, YES, YES, A THOUSAND TIMES YES.

In their discussions of the play, Rodgers and Hammerstein agreed that what they were writing was in essence a modern morality play and that consequently it called for unorthodox methods and techniques. Joe's biography, they decided, would be told principally through music and the dance, and the music would consist not only of songs and orchestral interludes but also of large choral numbers. The opening of the play, Joe's birth, thus became an elaborate cantata for solo voices, chorus and orchestra, and so later in the play was Joe's marriage. And Joe's playtime at school is told in terms of the ballet, the music consisting of a series of variations on the nursery tune "Here We Go Round the Mulberry Bush."

They introduced a kind of Greek chorus to comment (sometimes in song, sometimes in speech) upon what was going on and to act as an audible conscience of one of the characters. During Joe's boyhood, the chorus serves as Joe's nursemaid; when Joe is a success in Chicago, the chorus points out to the audience the plight of the doctor who has lost his sense of true values.

They reduced sets, costumes, and properties to a minimum, with lighting doing most of the work. Frequently the action took place on a bare stage. Colors were thrown on a large screen backstage to intensify moods while loudspeakers served to amplify Joe's more inspiring thoughts. "We just took a story and worked it out to what we thought was its logical conclusion," Rodgers explains, "and the hell with the old type of show with its sequence of scene, song, and dance."

They worked out their ideas with freedom and became increasingly bold and iconoclastic as they went along. They had defied musical-comedy convention in *Oklahoma!* by including a murder and in *Carousel* by killing off their hero midway in the play. In *Allegro* they went one step further by bringing back on the stage both Grandma and Mama Taylor after their deaths—not as ghosts but as "presences," almost conventional characters. They become Joe's alter ego, to tell him what is right and to advise and encourage him in his wiser decisions.

The Rodgers score was unconventional also in that most of the important songs were assigned to comparatively minor characters. If there is any single hit song in *Allegro* it is "A Fellow Needs a Girl"—once again, as with "You'll Never Walk Alone" from *Carousel,* a melody rich with spiritual overtones; it is sung by Joe's parents. The other important numbers were "So Far," "I Know It Can Happen Again," and "The Gentleman Is a Dope" (the last deriving unusual musical interest from the even four-quarter-note phrases in the accompaniment of the verse followed by the richer harmonic background of the chorus). Among the principal numbers, Joe, Jr. participates in only one—the title song, a vivacious cakewalk, which does not appear until almost the end of the play and then leads directly into a psychiatric ballet. The score is also unusual in that the Freshman Dance Music quotes an old Rodgers and Hart song, "Mountain Greenery" —at one point translated into Dixieland tempo—to evoke the climate of the 1920's.

While Rodgers and Hammerstein planned *Allegro* as a serious play with deeply tragic incidents and highly charged dramatic climaxes, they were too astute to sidestep comedy completely. An extended scene, "Yatata Yatata," is a delightful satire on cocktail parties, while in another part of the play there is a hilarious takeoff on a Hollywood producer.

Every detail of the production was carefully planned by Rodgers and Hammerstein before they tied *Allegro* up neatly into a single package and turned it over to the Theatre Guild. A huge cast was assembled, none of them stars. Half had never appeared on the Broadway stage before, and some of the others were unknowns. "One or two big names," says Rodgers, "would have thrown us completely off balance." William Ching was the father; Annamary Dickey, who had appeared at the Metropolitan Opera between 1939 and 1944, the mother; John Battles and Roberta Jonay, Joe and Jennie. In the minor roles were two to whom success in the theater world would come at a later day: Lisa Kirk and John Conte. In addition to the regular cast there was a large chorus and an equally large dance corps. Agnes de Mille was in charge not only of the choreography but also (for the first time in her career) of the stage direction.

The misfortunes that beset *Allegro* on its out-of-town try-outs were perhaps an unhappy portent. When it opened at the Shubert Theatre in New Haven on September 3, 1947, accident followed accident. The first-act scenery collapsed; then Lisa Kirk lost her footing and fell into the orchestra pit; finally, smoke from the burning of some trash outside the theater led some in the audience to suspect fire and rush to the exits. At the Boston première, at the Colonial Theatre on September 10, the audience included some labor-union leaders come to the city for a convention. Being in a holiday mood some of them were obstreperous, disturbing the play with loud laughter, whistles, and comments. Not until Hammerstein yelled out "Shut up!" from his seat did the disturbance subside.

Allegro turned out to be the first failure by Rodgers and Hammerstein. The forty-week Broadway run which began at the Majestic on October 10, and the thirty-one-week tour that followed, would have insured a financial success for most musicals. But despite an advance sale of $700,000, it represented a financial loss due to the immense running expenses incurred by the huge cast and the musical forces.

It was also for the most part an artistic failure—even though it received Donaldson Awards in three categories (book, lyrics, and musical score). It had flashes of beauty and brilliance which made Brooks Atkinson say that the first half had "the lyric rapture of a musical masterpiece," and Robert Coleman describe much of it as "a stunning blending of beauty, integrity, imagination, taste, and skill." Perhaps the most serious indictment against it was that it was too pretentious in treatment of what was essentially a simple story. Too much of the warmth and humanity of the dialogue was smothered under the weight of the elaborate format. The experimental stage tricks and techniques, however interesting in themselves, usurped attention that should have gone to the homespun wholesomeness of the subject.

Beyond this, the thinking of Agnes de Mille as stage director was too strongly influenced by Agnes de Mille the choreographer; the ballet carried too much of the weight of the dramatic action. And the emphasis on lighting worked against the play; the colors were too often drab and somber, intensifying the depressing moods.

Finally, as Hammerstein now remarks sadly: "Many of the critics completely misunderstood what I was saying. They seemed to find in my play an indictment of the city doctor as opposed to the country doctor. This was not my intent at all. The fault was not theirs, but mine. If a writer's aim is misread, it can only be because he has not written clearly enough. Also, I think the play suffered because I did not carry my hero to the end of his life as I first intended, but stopped short when he had reached his decisive crossroad."

But if *Allegro* was a failure, it was an interesting and provocative failure, and one to which both Rodgers and Hammerstein look back with affection and pride. Some day they would like to return to it and repair some of its shortcomings, for they still feel that Joe Taylor's story has the makings of a deeply moving musical play.

It is not hard to see why the subject of *Allegro* had such a strong appeal to Rodgers. As the son and brother of doctors, he had personally known the inner struggle of physicians in choosing between serving humanity and their own personal ambitions. Consciously or otherwise he identified Joe Taylor, Jr., with his own father. In Joe's personal triumph over the materialistic forces that surrounded him, Rodgers probably saw his own father's humanitarian conduct during and immediately after World War II.

By a strange and tragic coincidence, this play in which the central character had so much of Dr. William Rodgers was also the last Rodgers and Hammerstein play Dr. Rodgers lived to see. A victim of cancer, Dr. Rodgers died in his apartment at the Hotel Croydon in New York on November 17, 1948. He had had the rich satisfaction of having lived to see that his high principles in allowing his son to follow a musical career without interference had yielded rich fruit; and he had known the pure joy of having associated himself intimately and identifying himself closely with that career.

His cousin, Hannah Harris, recalls that on the day of his funeral, a few yards from the funeral parlor, an organ grinder (one of the last survivors of this calling) was churning the strains of "Oh, What a Beautiful Mornin'."

Dr. Rodgers' last request was that he be cremated and that his ashes be scattered on the high seas. The summer after his death, Mortimer Rodgers fulfilled his father's last wish. At that time, Mortimer and his family were spending the summer in East Hampton, Long Island. Early one morning, while his family was still asleep, he went out on an inlet and scattered his father's ashes over the water.

The administration of the producing organization of Rodgers and Hammerstein, writing the music for his plays, helping produce the plays by other writers—all this did not keep Richard Rodgers from assuming other obligations. From 1941 to 1947 he was a member of the board of directors of the American Society of Composers, Authors, and Publishers (ASCAP); he had previously held the same post for a single year in 1929-1930. From 1945 to 1949 he was president of the Dramatists Guild.

In 1948 he became involved in a project that absorbed his interest and enthusiasm for several years. The drama department of Columbia University invited several Broadway personalities, Rodgers among them, to discuss the possibility of expanding the department to include more courses in the dramatic arts. Rodgers left the meeting feeling that the measures brought up by the conference only scratched the surface of what had to be done. What his alma mater needed, he felt, was not an enlarged drama department but an entire school of the theatre, both for undergraduate and postgraduate work, which would embrace not only drama but also music, art, sculpture, and the dance; which would draw its faculty and program from the professional Broadway theater, concert hall, opera house, ballet company, and leading museums.

With this idea in mind, he consulted the Board of Trustees of Columbia University as well as Dwight D. Eisenhower, then president of the university. The reaction was enthusiastic; Rodgers was encouraged to develop his plans further. These assumed such ambitious proportions—including a fifteen-story building to be erected on Amsterdam Avenue between 116th and 117th streets—that ten million dollars were required for its realization.

On February 8, 1950, Dean Leopold Arnaud of the School of Architecture selected a nine-man committee, headed by Rodgers, to plan the new art center in detail; among the members were Lawrence Tibbett, Alfred de Liagre, Jr., Douglas Moore, and Eli Jacques Kahn. But an insurmountable obstacle was posed by the financing. When the allocation of endowments and funds took place, there were always departments at Columbia where the need seemed more pressing at the moment.

When on November 23, 1953, Rodgers saw President Eisenhower in Washington, at the dinner at which Rodgers and Hammerstein produced a show in Eisenhower's honor, the President inquired how the art center was progressing. When Rodgers revealed that it was going slowly, the President expressed his disappointment and confided that it had been close to his heart from the moment Rodgers had proposed it to him.

5

1925 ENCHANTED EVENINGS

In 1948, Joshua Logan suggested to Richard Rodgers the advisability of making a musical play out of one of the stories from James Michener's *Tales of the South Pacific*. Michener, formerly an editor of the publishing house of Macmillan, had served in the Navy in the South Pacific during the war. He used his own experiences and incidents for a series of sketches which he assembled into a book, published by Macmillan early in 1947.

An advance copy of the book reached Carol Brandt, the New York story editor of M.G.M. She found it so interesting that she turned it over to the studio story head, Kenneth MacKenna, who finally rejected it as unsuitable for the screen. One evening, however, while dining with Jo Mielziner and Joshua Logan, MacKenna mentioned the Michener book to Logan as a possibility for dramatization. Logan was convinced, and soon afterwards he won the interest of Leland Hayward, a producer with whom at the time he was bringing *Mister Roberts* to Broadway, and together they entered into an agreement with Michener for the stage rights.

Logan now wanted Rodgers to become interested in it, since both he and Hayward believed that the stage adaptation should include music. Logan told Rodgers that he was particularly interested in the sketch "Fo' Dolla'." In his little black book Rodgers carefully noted down the titles of the sketch and the book and the name of the author. One day, thumbing through his notebook, he came upon this notation and decided to follow it up at once. "I fell in love with the darned thing," he says. He now acquainted Hammerstein with the project, who readily agreed that Michener's book was the kind of material he liked to work with. Since they had already decided after *Allegro* to produce their own shows, they entered into a deal with Logan and Hayward whereby Rodgers and Hammerstein acquired the dramatic rights; in return, Logan would be stage director, and Logan and Hayward would join as co-producers. Soon after these negotiations were consummated, Michener's *Tales of the South Pacific* received the Pulitzer Prize for fiction.

When Michener saw Rodgers and Hammerstein for the first time, he found them "inwardly burning because of the reception accorded to *Allegro*." He remarked at the time that "those fellows are so mad they could make a great musical out of three pages from the Bronx telephone directory." Michener left this initial meeting confident that they would make a great musical out of his story.

Hammerstein began planning an outline, a task that consumed four months. At first he thought of dramatizing the entire book but rejected this because "we would have had an impossible crazy-quilt kind of story." Then, as Logan had suggested, he decided to concentrate on "Fo' Dolla'," the tale that emphasized the love of Lieutenant Joseph Cable of the Marines for the native girl Liat. This also worried him. "People would call it *Madame Butterfly* all over again," he complained, "just because the girl had slanting eyes, and the boy was a naval officer."

Work on the outline was interrupted when Rodgers and Hammerstein left for Los Angeles for the opening of *Annie Get Your Gun*. On their first day in Beverly Hills, while sunning themselves at the pool of the Bel-Air Hotel and discussing ways of adapting the Michener book, Rodgers and Hammerstein suddenly seized upon the idea of using a second sketch, "Our Heroine," which related the love of Nellie Forbush, an American nurse, and Emile de Becque, a local planter of French extraction. "We now began to flirt with the idea of making the Frenchman the leading character."

A few days later, they were approached by an agent, Edwin Lester, who explained he had Ezio Pinza, the distinguished basso of the Metropolitan Opera, under contract for a Broadway play. The play was not ready, however, and Lester wondered if Rodgers and Hammerstein could possibly use the singer for one of their own musicals. "We had heard Pinza at the Metropolitan," says Rodgers, "so we knew he was one opera singer who didn't act like one. And of course his voice—there was no doubt about that. But we still hadn't heard him sing in English. So we bought a copy of the only record he made in English. It turned out to be a Negro Spiritual. If you can imagine Pinza with an Italian accent trying to sound like a Down South Negro, you'll get some notion of what the record was like. But we decided nevertheless to start negotiations." These continued a month later when Pinza came to New York for a radio broadcast. That evening, at the studio for Pinza's broadcast, Rodgers saw "the way the audience

reacted not only to his singing but also to his personality."
He consulted Hammerstein, and they decided then and
there to close the deal with Pinza.

Getting Pinza as their star clarified the creative problems
in the adaptation. Hammerstein decided to use some of the
characters from several of the sketches, but the basic plot
would be taken from "Our Heroine" and the subsidiary plot
from "Fo' Dolla'." A logical means of consolidating the two
stories into one was achieved through the interpolation of
an episode of his own invention—sending Cable and De
Becque together on a dangerous war mission.

His outline now ready, Hammerstein retired to his Doylestown farm to collaborate with Logan on the actual adaptation. Their sleeping and working habits conflicted: Logan
was the night owl who did his best work in the late hours;
Hammerstein preferred going to bed early and beginning
work the first thing in the morning. They compromised. The
two men worked until about two in the morning, after which
Hammerstein retired. Logan would continue working but
would not have to get up until the following afternoon. At
that time they revised the typed transcript of everything they
had dictated into a dictaphone the preceding evening. They
called their completed adaptation *South Pacific*.

In progressing to any logical point demanded by a text,
Rodgers and Hammerstein never lacked the courage of their
convictions. As Rodgers puts it: "You can do anything in the
theater—just so long as you do it right." They did not lack
such courage in *South Pacific*. Placing the central love interest in a middle-aged man with graying hair was a bold
undertaking for the musical stage, which had always glorified
youth. But bolder still was their effort to make the secondary
love plot—that of Cable and Liat—a plea for racial tolerance.
To preach this moral, they wrote for Cable a song, "You've
Got to Be Taught":

You've got to be taught to be afraid
Of people whose eyes are oddly made,
And people whose skin is a diff'rent shade,
You've got to be carefully taught.

Pressure was put on Rodgers and Hammerstein to eliminate this number, since the feeling was prevalent that social problems had no place in the musical theater. Michener has written: "The authors replied stubbornly that this number represented why they had wanted to do the play and that even if it meant failure of the production it was going to stay in. And as the well-wishers foresaw, many of the major reviews panned the song as an intrusion. [Two legislators in Georgia also issued a vehement protest against it.] But as the play matured, it was found that this song was more often praised than any other. . . . Courage and determination such as this counts for something in art."

The music Rodgers finally wrote might not be indigenous to the South Pacific—it resembled nothing but Richard Rodgers—but it was an effort to make the music reflect the deeper currents in the personalities of the characters who sang them. Rodgers said:

I tried to weave De Becque's character into his songs—romantic, rather powerful, but not too involved—and so I wrote for him "Some Enchanted Evening" and "This Nearly Was Mine." Nellie Forbush is a Navy nurse out of Arkansas, a kid whose musical background probably had been limited to the movies, radio, and maybe a touring musical comedy. She talks in the vernacular, so her songs had to be in the vernacular. It gave me a chance for a change of pace, and the music I wrote for her is light, contemporary, rhythmic: "A Cockeyed Optimist," "I'm Gonna Wash That Man Right Outa My Hair," "I'm in Love with a Wonderful Guy." Cable's songs—"Younger than

Springtime" and "You've Got to Be Taught"—are like the man, deeply sincere, while Bloody Mary's songs, "Bali Ha'i" and "Happy Talk," try to convey some of the languor and mystery of her race.

This score, like any other by Rodgers, came easily. Some of the songs were written at a white heat. "Bali Ha'i" was completed in five minutes. Rodgers was dining with some friends at Logan's apartment. When coffee was served, Hammerstein arrived with the lyrics of "Bali Ha'i." Rodgers looked at the typewritten sheet, pushed aside his coffee, and started writing. He was through in a matter of minutes, and he never changed a single note of what he put down on paper.

"Happy Talk," which Bloody Mary chants to Cable and Liat, was done in about twenty minutes. A messenger brought the lyric to Rodgers while the latter was sick in bed with a cold. Less than a half hour later Hammerstein telephoned to inquire if Rodgers had received the verse. "I not only received it," Rodgers answered, "but I also have the music."

With two of the songs—"This Nearly Was Mine" and Cable's love song "Younger than Springtime"—the melody came before the lyric. That of "Younger than Springtime" had originated in *Allegro* but had been discarded. Hammerstein had always been fond of it. The love music Rodgers had written for Cable did not seem to convey the feelings of tenderness and ecstasy that were needed. Hammerstein encouraged Rodgers to replace it with the song he had previously intended for *Allegro*.

Some of Rodgers' most effective writing came in orchestral passages and interludes, which he used to carry the drama along. He interpolated episodes to introduce a character, set the mood for an approaching scene, or to comment on a preceding event. In each instance he succeeded in bringing to the play a new dimension.

Just as Rodgers had each character vividly in mind when he wrote his music, so he and Hammerstein knew—as the play was being written—who would play the leading parts. Ezio Pinza had already been contracted before the final adaptation was made. In the same way, the names of Juanita Hall and Betta St. John came up for the parts of Bloody Mary and Liat long before *South Pacific* had been completely written. Juanita Hall was no novice, but Betta St. John was. She had come to Rodgers as a slight, undernourished fifteen-year-old ballet dancer while he was casting *Carousel.* He had to turn her down. A year later she returned for a second audition. This time Rodgers hired her to work in the chorus of *Carousel* and to be Bambi Linn's understudy; when *Carousel* went on tour, she took over the part of Louise for a year and a half. She did not have to ask for a part in *South Pacific;* Rodgers had had her in mind for Liat from the very beginning.

The selection of Mary Martin as costar with Pinza was also made long before *South Pacific* was on paper. Oscar Hammerstein had seen her in *One Touch of Venus,* where in the final scene she appeared dressed in a simple gingham dress. He turned to his wife and said, "This is the real Mary Martin, a corn-fed girl from Texas—and that's the kind of part she should play." When the role of Nellie Forbush (a corn-fed girl from Arkansas) was discussed, both Hammerstein and Rodgers knew that this was for Mary Martin. Actually, she was at that time working for them, playing the lead in the national company of *Annie Get Your Gun.* When that company was in San Francisco, Rodgers telephoned her to tell her that Pinza had been engaged for *South Pacific* and that he and Hammerstein wanted her to play opposite him. "Why do you need *two* basses in the show?" Mary asked. She did not conceal the fact that she was scared to her very skin at the thought of playing opposite a Metropolitan Opera star. She promised to visit Rodgers as soon as she came East to discuss this matter further.

When she arrived in New York she went with her husband, Richard Halliday, to Rodgers' country place in Connecticut. Logan read her the first scene, and Rodgers played four songs —all that thus far had been completed. She was enchanted, but still greatly disturbed about how her voice would sound in conjunction with Pinza's. "I've thought it out carefully, Mary," Rodgers told her soberly. "You will never have to sing with Pinza in *opposition* to him. You'll sing in *contrast* to him." Mary Martin understood, and finally said she would like seventy-two hours to think the matter over. "We went home," her husband says, "and sat up all night talking about it, very excited and very happy with the whole idea of the show. The next day was Saturday. I phoned Rodgers at nine-thirty in the morning and said to him, 'Look, do we have to wait until Monday to tell you that Mary will take the part?' "

The business of finally getting Mary's signature on a contract was a delicate one which Howard Reinheimer, the Rodgers and Hammerstein lawyer, performed with extreme tact. Since in her own field she was as important as Pinza was in opera, the greatest discretion had to be used that neither got any precedence over the other in any way—in billing, length of role, importance of songs, or even the size of their biographies in the program. While it was agreed that Mary's name appear first in the billing alongside that of Pinza, in deference to her sex, it was also decided that the conjunction "and" between the two names be carefully omitted, so as to leave no false impression that Pinza's position was secondary to Mary Martin's. Another problem had to be solved. Now that a star like Mary Martin had been chosen to appear opposite Pinza, the percentage previously allotted to him had to be trimmed (and Mary Martin had to take an equal fee, smaller than was customary with her), otherwise their combined weekly income would have upset the budget. So eager were Pinza and Mary Martin to work with each other, and in *South Pacific*, that from neither one came the slightest murmur of discontent about their revised, and lowered, income.

The first time Mary Martin sang the song from *South Pacific* with which she has since become so completely identified—"I'm in Love with a Wonderful Guy"—was at Logan's apartment at two o'clock in the morning. "I almost passed out," she confesses. "I was so excited. After the repeats I fell off the piano bench and I remember that the management had to call up to complain of the noise."

The first rehearsal began on February 2, 1949. To insure the unity of the production—recognized as its strong point—the decision had been reached to rehearse the entire show from the beginning in a single place rather than allow different sections to work out their parts in different places before being assembled for later rehearsals.

Public curiosity in the production was aroused from the very first rehearsals. The play was based on a Pulitzer Prize book; it was a Rodgers and Hammerstein production; and, for their first time, it had stars of the first importance. Rumor and inside information about the play kept sharpening this curiosity. Those who were fortunate enough to catch glimpses of some of the rehearsals started using extravagant terms to describe it, adding to the rapidly mounting hullabaloo surrounding the play. By the time *South Pacific* opened out of town—and as glowing reports from New Haven and Boston flooded New York—*South Pacific* had become the talk of theatrical circles. There was an advance sale of almost a million dollars before the curtain first rose at the Majestic Theatre in New York on April 7, 1949.

So confident were Rodgers and Hammerstein of the merits

of their play, and of the public and critical reaction to it, that, in conjunction with Logan and Hayward, for the first time they arranged in advance a gala party for the cast, collaborators and friends at the St. Regis Hotel following the première. They were convinced that they would have good cause for celebration.

After all the preliminary talk, rumor, and anticipation, *South Pacific* easily might have proved a disappointment, but—as *Variety* noted—it lived up to all the advance build-up, "and then some." Arthur Hammerstein, who had been in the professional theater for over half a century, left the Majestic muttering that he had finally seen the perfect musical. (Surely it must have been no small personal satisfaction to him to recall that it was he who had given his nephew his first opportunity to work in the theater!) Michael Todd unequivocally called it the greatest show he had ever seen. These were only two of many similar reactions from the theater folk that crowded the Majestic that evening. They had good reason for enthusiasm. This was as ideal a production as money, creative talent, stage technique, imagination, and artistic courage could make it. For the first time in a Rodgers and Hammerstein play, there was no ballet. Ballet, felt the authors, belonged more in a fantasy than in a production about the war. The dancing was confined to little tap dances and other simple routines consistent with the characters. In line with the unity of purpose of the entire production, no single number was allowed to milk an audience for applause and disturb the continuity of the stage action. Veteran showmen that they were, Rodgers and Hammerstein knew well that a song like "Some Enchanted Evening" —especially when sung by Pinza—could arouse in the audience a demand for encores. But they also felt that the artistic whole was more important than any of its parts. Consequently, before the demand for encores could be expressed,

Rodgers used a transitional passage in the orchestra to lead the play firmly from the ending of that song to the change of scene.

The critical response to *South Pacific* was even better than even the most sanguine had expected. "A magnificent musical drama," Brooks Atkinson called it, "as lively, warm, fresh and beautiful as we all hoped it would be." "A show of rare enchantment," exclaimed Howard Barnes, "novel in texture and treatment, rich in dramatic substance, and eloquent in song." "The finest kind of balance between story and song, and hilarity and heartbreak," wrote William Hawkins. "A thrilling and exultant musical play," according to Ward Morehouse, and to Richard Watts, Jr., "an utterly captivating work of theatrical art . . . a work of great style and loveliness that is yet gay, vigorous, and vital."

The excitement over *South Pacific* mounted as the weeks and the months passed. Tickets became so rare that having seen the show became a mark of social achievement. Fact and fiction were joined in the stories now circulated to prove what precious commodities these tickets had become. (Leonard Lyons published an entire column of these tales.) The Marquis of Milford-Haven said the wedding gift to which he was most partial was a pair of seats; Justice Hugo Black preferred a pair of tickets to a fee for a speaking engagement; General Carlos P. Romulo, speaking at a luncheon attended by Rodgers and Hammerstein, said, "Let's hope the Lord will make it easier for these two gifted men to get into Heaven than it is for us to get into *South Pacific*"; the concert singer Igor Gorin refused to substitute for the indisposed Lawrence Tibbett in Carnegie Hall unless the tickets he had for *South Pacific* that evening were exchangeable for others in the near future.

Oklahoma! had had a legendary history. *South Pacific* almost equaled it. *South Pacific* had the second longest run of any Broadway musical (its 1925 performances being only 323 fewer than the record formerly piled up by *Oklahoma!*); it was seen in New York by 3,500,000 theatergoers who paid $9,000,000. A national company began a several year tour in Cleveland on April 24, 1950. An all-time box-office record was set, and $500,000 in mail orders had to be returned for lack of seats. "Not in twenty-five years has a theatrical production caused such a furor," reported the New York *Times*. What happened in Cleveland was repeated in most of the other cities this company visited later on. In its first twenty-six weeks on the road the company netted a profit of $647,000 (only $24,000 less than the New York company in a similar period of time); after a year, the gross was $3,300,000 and the profit close to $1,500,000. The backers who had contributed the $225,000 for production costs received their money back in four months. After a year their return was ten to one, while before the final count is in the odds will probably leap to fifty to one. By January, 1957, the profit was just under five billion dollars—not counting the revenue from the motion picture adaptation.

In London, *South Pacific* opened at the Drury Lane on November 1, 1951. Though the critics were annihilating— one of them referred to it as "South Soporific"—the play found enough public backing to stay on two and a half years and then go on tour for an additional year and a half. Australian and Danish companies each opened on the same day —September 8, 1952—and stayed on for several years. In 1955, a Spanish troupe gave it at the old Teatro de la Zarzuela in Madrid to score what the local newspapers said was the greatest success in Spanish theatrical history. In 1955 and again in 1957 it returned to New York in highly acclaimed revivals, and in 1956 it was sold to 20th Century-Fox for screen adaptation in the Todd-AO process.

The sheet-music sale in America passed the two million mark. The long-playing recording of the score with the original cast sold over a million copies; the income from this single venture ($4,500,000) was probably more than the total earnings of many successful musicals. The name "South Pacific" was licensed for use by cosmetics, compacts, dresses, coats, lingerie, hairbrushes, and other commodities.

Every theatrical award in sight had been absorbed. In 1950 it won the Pulitzer Prize in drama (only the second time a musical production had thus been honored, the first time being in 1932 with Gershwin's *Of Thee I Sing*), and the New York Drama Critics Circle Award as the season's best musical. It received Antoinette Perry Awards in seven departments, and Donaldson Awards in nine.

The 1925th—and last—New York performance of *South Pacific,* on January 16, 1954, was justly an event to evoke deep sentiment. Only fourteen of the original cast were still playing their parts, but these did not include the two leads. Mary Martin had given her farewell performance in New York on June 2, 1951, six months before opening in London; Ezio Pinza had left the cast a year earlier. On this final night, their parts were being played by Martha Wright and George Britton.

Later that evening, until the early hours of dawn, Rodgers and Hammerstein gave a champagne party for the cast. Mary Martin distributed plaques to the fourteen who had been with *South Pacific* from the beginning. Then various performers from other Rodgers and Hammerstein shows, joined by Joshua Logan and Rodgers and Hammerstein themselves, performed skits burlesquing some of the scenes from the play.

But before this party took place, and right after the final curtain, Myron McCormick, who had appeared as Luther Billis since the first performance, stepped to the front of the stage and asked the audience to join the cast in singing "Auld

Lang Syne." The curtain had not been lowered, and it stayed up as the audience sang. Even after the theater had been finally emptied of both audience and performers, the curtain stayed up. It was almost as if to say that a final curtain can never be lowered on *South Pacific*.

6

"A FLOWERING OF ALL THE ARTS"

Before advancing from *South Pacific* to the next musical play, Richard Rodgers had several opportunities to throw a nostalgic glance backwards in his career toward some of his past achievements.

The year of 1950 marked the twenty-fifth anniversary of his first successful appearance on Broadway with the *Garrick Gaieties*. This birthday was not ignored. On May 17, the Theatre Guild held a reception in Rodgers' honor at its offices on 53rd Street. The hosts were Theresa Helburn, and Lawrence Langner and his wife. Among the guests were Mary Martin, Helen Hayes, Charles MacArthur, Lisa Kirk, Deems Taylor, Rouben Mamoulian, Libby Holman, Hildegarde Halliday, Betty Starbuck, Edith Meiser and Sterling Holloway, the last five of whom had appeared in the revue. Three Rodgers songs from the *Gaieties* were heard, one of them

—"Manhattan"—sung by Holloway, who had introduced it. The festivities were topped off by a parody of "Ol' Man River" by Benjamin Kaye, called "Ol' Man Rodgers." ("He don' write novels, He don' write drama, He ain't no wizard, On words or grammar, but Ol' Man Rodgers, His songs go rollin' along.") As a memento of this sentimental occasion Rodgers was presented with a sterling silver platter on which were inscribed the titles of songs he had written for Theatre Guild productions.

Still another moving tribute came to him on October 22, 1950, when Dwight D. Eisenhower, then President of Columbia University, presented him with the award of the Hundred Years Association, a group of century-old business enterprises and institutions in New York. This honor was conferred on Rodgers for his distinguished contributions to the American theater. In making the presentation, Eisenhower said, "Except for the award of a decoration to a worn and weary soldier on the battlefield—one who has laid everything on the line for his country—I don't think the award of medals ever gave me more pleasure and pride than this."

During this period Rodgers' achievements with Hammerstein were given a panoramic review by symphony orchestras throughout the country with programs devoted entirely to music from their plays. *Variety* was able to report on July 26, 1950, that "so far this year about fifteen . . . concerts have been done. . . . The demand for tickets is so great that the program was repeated two or three times. Seating capacity in most situations played is around 10,000. In most cases, the program played to SRO."

One of these concerts took place at the Lewisohn Stadium in New York on August 6, inaugurating a tradition that would continue there from that time on, namely, including a Rodgers and Hammerstein evening in its season of summer concerts. Despite the threatening weather, nineteen thousand music lovers jammed the stadium for this first Rodgers and Hammerstein program. Six minutes before the concert began, a heavy downpour drenched the stadium. But the huge crowd refused to be discouraged. They waited patiently for the rain to subside. As it happened, the rain did stop in about six minutes, and the concert was then able to begin and to proceed through the entire program. During the intermission, Oscar Hammerstein II made a brief speech calling the audience "the best twenty thousand sports I know." From this evening on, the annual Rodgers and Hammerstein evening at the Lewisohn Stadium was an invitation to tremendous turnouts which, in one or two instances, smashed all existing box-office records in the auditorium.

The receptivity of audiences everywhere to these Rodgers and Hammerstein nights led, in 1951, to the organization of a complete unit, managed by James A. Davidson, which toured the country for an entire season in a program made up of twenty-two numbers from six Rodgers and Hammerstein plays. The first performance took place in Pittsburgh on October 8, 1951. The performers included Leigh Allen, Andrew Gainey, Carol Jones, Earl William, and an orchestra and chorus conducted by Crane Calder.

Even more comprehensive than any of these programs in its sweeping survey of Rodgers' career was "An Evening of Richard Rodgers," presented in honor of his twenty-five years in the professional theater over the NBC television network, on Sunday evening, March 4, at 9:00 P.M. The program began with "It's a Grand Night for Singing" and ended with "Oh, What a Beautiful Mornin'." In between there were fifteen other Rodgers favorites, from both the Hart and Hammerstein eras, presented by a galaxy of stars that included Mary Martin, Bing Crosby, Alfred Drake, Vivienne Segal, and Celeste Holm. "In bringing a full hour of your lovely music to millions of American men and women this evening," said

Mary Martin, presenting Rodgers with a silver bowl on which were engraved the names of all participants in the telecast, "we—your colleagues in the professional theater—hope to emphasize once more the tremendous contribution that you have made to the lyric stage of our country during the past twenty-five years. You have wrought melodies of the purest beauty and the quality of your music has had a constancy that has won the respect of the entire world. We salute your great accomplishment and ask you to accept, in terms of our warmest admiration, this bowl . . . a memento from all of us to you."

After *South Pacific*, Rodgers and Hammerstein were in a situation not unlike that of the performer who offered a vaudeville booking agent an act in which he commits suicide on the stage. "What will you do for an encore?" the agent asked. Or that of the circus performer who was asked, after he had succeeded standing on one finger, what he could do to top that performance.

What could Rodgers and Hammerstein possibly do for an "encore" after an achievement like *South Pacific?* The answer was—to be sure—they would once again do something completely different; something in which they would once again attempt the unorthodox, perform the unexpected, achieve the seemingly impossible.

But even those now familiar with the Rodgers and Hammerstein pattern of refusing to conform to patterns could not be prepared for anything so far off the beaten track as *The King and I*. Here was a play with a setting in (of all places!) Bangkok, Siam, in the early 1860's; with characters made up mostly of Orientals, and including four Anglo-Saxons none of whom was American; a play that had already been a successful motion picture (motion pictures came from successful plays—who ever heard of reversing this procedure?); a play in which no traditional love interest involved the two leading characters (they do not even kiss); a play which ends with the death of the hero.

The entire subject was so unusual, and seemingly alien to their talent, that Rodgers and Hammerstein for a while resisted it. Their respective wives read Margaret Landon's novel, *Anna and the King of Siam*—which, in turn, was based upon a true episode in Siamese history—soon after its publication in 1944. They suggested it to their husbands for a musical play. But Rodgers and Hammerstein rejected it individually and collectively; they said that it was not their meat. In 1946 the novel was made into an attractive motion picture starring Rex Harrison and Irene Dunne and became a huge box-office success. Gertrude Lawrence saw the picture, then read the book. Seeing herself as Anna, she asked her lawyer, Fannie Holtzman, to try to convince Rodgers and Hammerstein to convert it for her into a Broadway musical. The deal was finally consummated through the William Morris Agency before either Rodgers or Hammerstein put down a single note or word on paper. "Why did we undertake to make a musical play out of Margaret Landon's book when we realized that the story presented unusually difficult problems?" Rodgers, who asks this question, also provides the answer. "Because we are allergic to formulae and because of the attractions of its Oriental setting and unusual characters." He might have added that he and Hammerstein had seen the motion picture and had succumbed to its exotic charm and subtle spell; and that, showmen that they were, they knew what a strong asset Gertrude Lawrence would be for one of their plays.

It was, as Rodgers stated, not an easy play to write. "I did not want to tread on any Oriental toes," explains Hammerstein. "I had to be careful about gags about the huge number of wives in the royal family. What was required was the

Eastern sense of dignity and pageantry—and none of this business of girls dressed in Oriental costumes and dancing out
onto the stage and singing 'ching-aling-aling' with their
fingers in the air."

Rodgers had problems of his own in trying to write music
for a Far Eastern play. "I never heard music of the Far East.
Probably I never shall. I couldn't write an authentic Far
Eastern melody if my life depended upon it. If I could, I
wouldn't. A too-accurate re-creation of Siamese music would
have jarred the ears of an American audience and sent it
out of the theater into the streets shrieking with pain." He
resolved this difficulty in the only way it could be done, by
not trying to write Oriental music. He did sprinkle through
his music intervals of seconds, open fourths and fifths in the
harmony, unexpected intervallic leaps in the melody, the
tones of the flute and the harp in the instrumentation. These
were the spice to give his music a Far Eastern tang and flavor,
but the dish itself remained Western. "What I tried to do was
to say what the Far East suggests to me musically, to write a
score that would be analogous in sound to the look of a series
of Siamese paintings by Grant Wood. I myself remained a
Broadway character, not somebody disguised in Oriental
getup."

The casting presented another obstacle. For the part of
the King a singing actor was needed who looked Oriental and
had the swagger, pompousness, and the callous brutality of the
traditional Eastern potentate. Rodgers and Hammerstein felt
that Alfred Drake would do well. But during lunch at the
Hotel Plaza, Drake told them that he wanted a straight
dramatic part for his next play. Somewhat downhearted,
Rodgers and Hammerstein went on to the nearby theater
where auditions for their play were taking place. One of
those trying out for a part was a huge man with an Oriental-
shaped head, slanted eyes, thick lips, and a regal bearing. He

was sitting crosslegged on the floor, singing gypsy songs to his own guitar accompaniment. "There's *our* king," Rodgers whispered to Hammerstein. They learned his name was Yul Brynner, that he had played with Mary Martin in *The Lute Song,* which had had a brief career on Broadway, and that more recently he had been successful directing plays over television.

Hammerstein's script did not basically change the original story in Margaret Landon's novel and as it was later translated to the motion-picture screen. "I've tried to tell this story through music," says Rodgers. *"The King and I* is truly a musical drama with every song advancing the plot. We ask the audience to believe that these people on the stage, who face many serious problems of life, will suddenly stop talking and burst into song. We tried to avoid destroying the reality by the singing, and the singing by the reality."

The aim to combine action with musical continuity is realized more successfully in *The King and I* than in any other preceding Rodgers and Hammerstein play. In the fifteen numbers, two finales, and forty-six musical cues, Rodgers now achieves complete assurance in his technique of getting a song to spring effortlessly from a situation or a sequence of dialogue; in interrupting a song with dialogue and then re-turning to song; in providing an instrumental background to dialogue when a scene requires the atmospheric or emotional support of music. Instruments are used tellingly at the be-ginning of the play, when Anna first comes to Siam and must speak through an interpreter; the interpreter and the king's minister remain silent, but a clarinet or bassoon speaks for them. (Once the audience becomes used to the incongruity of Siamese people being able to speak in perfect English, this device can be abandoned.) Bits and brief snatches of orches-tral music continue to point up a piece of stage action: the fragments of melody in flute, viola and cello when Anna proves to Thiang that her own shape does not conform to the ample circumference of her hoop skirt; the saucy, Prokofiev-like little Oriental march that accompanies the appearance of the royal princes and princesses, its dynamics proportionate to the increasing size of the children, and the delightful Oriental vignette and dance at the beginning of the play; the fleet, highly descriptive background music for the feverish party plans discussed by Anna and the king; musical bits that continually tie scenes together and with which at times a character makes an appearance or exit.

Rodgers' songs include numbers like "I Whistle a Happy Tune" and "Shall We Dance?" which are unmistakably Rodgers in their felicitous and light-hearted lyricism. But his songs also show an increasing sympathy for and appreciation of the poetic text. Rodgers has now become the compelling musical dramatist. His narrative writing is more articulate and intense, as in "A Puzzlement" and "My Lord and Master," and demonstrate new dramatic powers. And his lyricism has gained in expressive beauty. "Hello, Young Lovers" has caught the soaring poetic lift of the verses so wonderfully that it is more of an aria than a popular song (the delicate staccato notes that introduce the song like aural stardust!). The freshness and individuality of lyricism and harmonic background that touch this number with such magic are also to be found in three other songs: "We Kiss in a Shadow," "I Have Dreamed," and "Something Wonderful."

The large cast of children presented an unforeseen difficulty. Just before *The King and I* opened in New Haven, an epidemic of colds broke out among the youngsters which soon spread even to some of the adults. At the New Haven opening performance, on February 26, 1951, Gertrude Lawrence went through her part with a fever of 103 degrees.

But, Miss Lawrence's indisposition notwithstanding, this opening was one of the happiest of any Rodgers and Hammerstein out-of-town tryouts. So carefully had the play been planned, written, staged, and directed that no drastic revision was required. The only job facing Rodgers and Hammerstein was that of cutting about forty-five minutes from the play— a not completely unwelcome task. "The flops always end on time," says Rodgers, "but when you start cutting off the things you love you're down to pretty high standards."

The cuts, made in Boston, were ample enough to permit the inclusion of three new songs. One was "Getting to Know You," inserted at the request of Gertrude Lawrence, who felt that the first act needed a number between herself and the royal children. This melody was an older one which Rodgers had written as the love song for Cable in *South Pacific* and which had been discarded for "Younger than Springtime."

When *The King and I* arrived in New York on March 29, it came to the same theater—the St. James—in which *Oklahoma!* had opened eight years earlier almost to the day. Nobody in the audience had reason to look back nostalgically to *Oklahoma!*. The new play was, as Danton Walker reported with excitement, "a flowering of all the arts of the theater, with moments . . . that are pure genius." Other critics might like to single out some one earlier Rodgers and Hammerstein play they liked better, but nobody could deny that *The King and I* was a triumph, sensitively beautiful to the eye and ear, a consummate achievement in the synchronization of play and music.

Six carloads of Oriental sets, designed by Jo Mielziner, and brilliantly decorated costumes made from rare silks imported from Thailand and designed by Irene Sharaff helped make it a lavish and exciting spectacle. Five years later, when *The King and I* was revived in New York City, William Hawkins still remembered "the stunning decors and costuming," saying, "There has never been a show more beautiful to look at than the first *The King and I.*"

But the visual splendor did not by any means submerge the simple charm and poetry of Hammerstein's writing, the human equations in the story, the eloquence of Rodgers' music, or, finally, the integrity with which the East was portrayed. In the words of Richard Watts, Jr., it was "an East of frank and unashamed romance, seen through the eyes of . . . theatrical artists of rare taste and creative power, and it [was] made something far more than a lovely exotic panorama by the ability of the authors to create characters possessing human dignity."

Nor did the pomp and pageantry in any way diminish from the significance of John Van Druten's imaginative stage direction—this was the first time he had directed a play other than his own, and this was his first experience with a musical—nor from the inspiration of Jerome Robbins' choreography. The principal ballet, "The Small House of Uncle Thomas," was a choreographic recreation of *Uncle Tom's Cabin* in terms of the Siamese dance and proved to be the tour de force of the entire production. The charm and humor of the literalness of the conception, and the ingenuousness of the overall approach, helped to create pictures unforgettable for their beauty and touching in their bare simplicity. "One is tempted to describe each delicious detail of this enchanting ballet," the New York *Herald Tribune* said, "but its subtleties are so many, its humor so fleet that one is hard put to select the key moments of a dance pattern so wholly absorbing." With a remarkable sense of dramatic appropriateness, Rodgers used percussive effects of woodblocks and ancient cymbals to punctuate the commentary of the spoken chorus;

the musical settings of the various choreographic episodes consciously aspired for the amusing, childlike realism which was in keeping with the style of the ballet as a whole.

In *The King and I* a new star was born in Yul Brynner, while another star, Gertrude Lawrence, shone with altogether new splendor. "He plays the snarling, swaggering, likable king," reported *Life,* "as if he had a string of firecrackers under his royal panung"; *Look* remarked tersely, "He *is* the king." For Gertrude Lawrence, the role of Anna was destined to be her last. Just as the sunset is sometimes more brilliant than the full day, so her last stage portrait was in many ways the most radiant of all her interpretations. "She came to the stage with a new and dazzling quality," says John Van Druten, "as though an extra something had been added to the brilliance of her own stage light. . . . Her comedy was in part gentler, Victorian, almost evasive, and her touch on the sweeter and more personal notes were stronger and surer than New York had ever seen."

The King and I stayed on Broadway three years (1246 performances). A half year before the end of this run, on September 6, 1952, Gertrude Lawrence died of cancer. Just before her death she asked that Yul Brynner be given star billing and that Constance Carpenter be selected to replace her.

The stunning visual beauty of the original stage production of *The King and I* was magically recaptured and even enhanced in the motion-picture adaptation produced by 20th Century-Fox with Deborah Kerr playing Anna, while Yul Brynner reassumed his stage role of the King. Receiving its world première at the Roxy Theatre in New York on June 28, 1956, the picture remained, as William K. Zinsser pointed out, "a fascinating performance." Bosley Crowther went on to say: "Whatever pictorial magnificence *The King and I* may have had upon the stage—and goodness knows, it had plenty, in addition to other things—it has twice as much in

the film version. . . . It also has other things. . . . Done
with taste in decoration and costuming that is forceful and
rare, the whole thing has a harmony of the visual that is
splendid in excellent color and Cinemascope." Less than a
year after its release, *The King and I* was selected as the best
motion picture of the year in a poll conducted by the *Film
Daily* among 357 critics; and it received Academy Awards
in half a dozen categories, including one to Yul Brynner.

7

SILVER JUBILEE

The year 1952 was Rodgers' fiftieth. In many ways it was one of the happiest of his life.

The year began significantly for him with the triumphant revival of *Pal Joey* on January 3. This was a boundless source of satisfaction to him. To discover that after twelve years its dialogue was still fresh, its plot still refreshing, and its characterizations still impertinent—and that everybody was now ready to acclaim them—was justification of his own faith in a play both he and Hart had loved from its inception.

While *Pal Joey* flourished at the Broadhurst, Rodgers had three formidable attractions running simultaneously on 44th Street (*South Pacific* was approaching the end of its third year at the Majestic and *The King and I* was rounding out its first year at the St. James). "The western end of 44th Street between 7th and 8th Avenues," reported the New

York *Times* on January 13, "has become a Rodgers music festival." Nobody enjoyed this festival more than Rodgers himself. After finishing his evening meal he would often slip off to 44th Street and walk into each of the three theaters to sample now a piece of one play, now a piece of another.

He had other reasons for deep personal gratification during the celebration of his fiftieth birthday. Not even an annoying back ailment which frequently kept him in bed could mar his delight at the magnificent tribute paid him over television on the Ed Sullivan "Toast of the Town" program over CBS. For two consecutive Sunday evenings— on June 15 and 22—the entire program was given over to "The Richard Rodgers Story," one evening to Rodgers and Hart, the second to Rodgers and Hammerstein. Among the participants were Jane Froman, Lisa Kirk, William Gaxton, Vivienne Segal, Martha Wright, Ray Middleton, Yul Brynner, John Raitt, and Rodgers himself.

At the end of the same month, the birthday festivities reached a climax with a surprise party given him by the Oscar Hammersteins. An excursion boat, with Emil Coleman's orchestra on board, was chartered to sail up the Hudson, carrying a caravan of the great of the theatrical world and many other friends. About midnight, the boat docked for a while at the 134th Street pier and members of the cast of *The King and I* serenaded the composer with his music.

The year of 1952 brought still other rewards. On August 3, the fifth annual Rodgers and Hammerstein program at the Lewisohn Stadium attracted one of the largest audiences in its history; and for this occasion Rodgers conducted the world première of his "Guadalcanal March" from *Victory at Sea*. And on November 18 Rodgers received an award from the class of 1923 at Columbia College for "outstanding achievement." The silver plaque was presented to him by

Oscar Hammerstein II at a reunion dinner at the Columbia Club.

On December 29, *Life* magazine did the unusual by publishing an original song for the first time. It was "Happy Christmas, Little Friend," by Rodgers and Hammerstein, which had been commissioned late that spring. Both Rodgers and Hammerstein agreed, while working at this song, that it should involve children, be about them and for them, and be written so simply that it could be sung and played by them. Hammerstein wrote the lyrics in about three weeks in August; Rodgers completed the music early one morning at a single sitting. The payment received from this assignment was used by the writers to inaugurate a venture they had been discussing for months: the Rodgers and Hammerstein Foundation to provide help for talented youngsters aspiring for the musical stage.

Before Rodgers' silver-jubilee year had ended, he experienced what he himself has often said was one of the thrills of his life: he conducted the St. Louis Symphony Orchestra in a program of his own music for the benefit of the orchestra. This event took place at Convention Hall in St. Louis on February 22, 1953.

Whenever Rodgers took up a baton to lead an orchestra he became a different man. Joshua Logan has described the expression of his face while conducting as "incandescent." Mary Martin has said, "You're looking at another man. The walls are down and you see something of what lies beneath the surface. The expression of his face—it isn't happiness or sadness, but rather an expression of utter tranquillity, of completeness." He had conducted his music frequently before 1953; but never before had he conducted one of America's great symphony orchestras in an entire program of his works.

The program in St. Louis was made up of ten sections comprehensively spanning Rodgers' creative history. The artists were Marguerite Piazza, Thomas Hayward, Claramae Turner and Robert Weede, and the orchestra was supplemented by a mixed chorus of thirty directed by Crane Calder.

From this concert Rodgers the conductor emerged with almost as much glory as Rodgers the composer. (Whether with baton or at the piano, he has always been an ideal interpreter of his own music.) Francis A. Klein said in the *Globe-Democrat:* "Ordinarily a composer is not the best conductor of his own works, but Mr. Rodgers happily proved the exception. He's a past master at it." Charles Menees said in the *Post-Dispatch:* "Mr. Rodgers moved the program right along. Always he was in close rapport with the orchestra, soloists, and chorus."

Three days before the concert, the St. Louis Symphony honored Rodgers at a dinner in which he voiced one of his favorite musical credos. "Music lovers," he said, "should not cling to the belief that music is either too good to be popular or too popular to be good. What we need is more people who appreciate equally an Irving Berlin song and a Vivaldi concerto."

He was even more exhilarated a year and a half later when he was invited to conduct a Pension Fund Concert of the Philharmonic-Symphony Society of New York with a program of his works at Carnegie Hall on November 15, 1954. His friends insist that of all the experiences in Rodgers' career none made him happier than this—so much so that he now spoke at length of fulfilling other engagements as conductor with American symphony orchestras in similar programs. His soloists in New York were Annamary Dickey, Claramae Turner, Davis Cunningham, and John Raitt; once again the chorus was directed by Calder. "The program was like a sentimental stroll down memory lane," wrote Howard Taubman in the New York *Times.* "A Carnegie Hall *aficionado* imagining that a succession of Broadway tunes could become tiresome, had to be surprised by the freshness and variety of these songs. Such a concertgoer . . . had to respect the precision and aplomb with which Mr. Rodgers conducted."

After the concert, at a supper party, Floyd Blair, president of the Symphony Society, presented Rodgers with an illuminated scroll in gratitude for his contribution to the orchestra Pension Fund. For Rodgers would take no fee for his performance (the concert yielded the highest possible gross of which Carnegie Hall was capable); and when a long-playing recording was made by Columbia of some of the highlights of the concert with Rodgers conducting, Rodgers once again arranged for all proceeds to go to the Pension Fund.

But let us return to the silver-jubilee year of 1952.

It brought to completion Rodgers' most ambitious and artistically most significant score—the background music to the documentary motion picture *Victory at Sea.* Nothing he has written away from the stage, and few scores for the stage, mean as much to him personally as this music does.

In the preceding decade—since the ballet *Ghost Town*—Rodgers had written nothing not intended for either the stage or screen. In 1949, he received a tempting commission from the Metropolitan Opera Association to write an opera with Oscar Hammerstein II based on *Moby Dick.* He turned it down, however, because he felt that the subject of Melville's classic was "too austere"; because he did not care to write the kind of formalized opera the Metropolitan would want to produce; and finally, if he did write an opera, he would prefer to see it on a regular Broadway run than have it receive a few sporadic performances as part of a season's repertory.

He was almost as ready at first to dismiss the proposition that he write the music for *Victory at Sea.* For some time

Henry Salomon—a historian who during the war had served in the Navy—had been gathering and editing some sixty million feet of motion picture films about naval operations conducted during World War II. These films consisted of numerous reels from the archives of the military and naval branches of ten Allied and enemy countries. Salomon's plan was to prepare for television a documentary giving a detailed, first-hand photographic account of the operations of the American and Allied naval forces from 1939 until the end of the war. In this project he had the cooperation of Robert Sarnoff (son of the RCA head), a young television executive with NBC. The work consumed about four years and cost $500,000. Finally, when 60,000 feet of film were combined with a narrative by Salomon and Richard Hanser, a program was evolved that was to be presented over the NBC television network in weekly half-hour installments over a twenty-six-week period.

"There was something the pictures by themselves could not convey," said Salomon, "a subtle, spiritual dimension needed to give them—and the entire drama—its ultimate meaning." In short, Salomon knew his picture needed an appropriate musical setting, not the mechanical musical material any skillful artisan could provide on order, but something that could recreate and underline the profound emotional and dramatic surges of the mighty episodes on the screen. Salomon adds: "Since Rodgers is America's foremost musical spokesman, it was of him I thought when I first grasped the full implication of *Victory at Sea*."

Rodgers was no more willing to go to work on this background music than he had been to write an opera for the Metropolitan, especially since the film called for thirteen hours of music. But he did consent to see a run-through of the picture, and it won him over completely. Rodgers now said he would be willing to take on the job if he was given full freedom to write a spacious score instead of being confined to a routine scoring assignment, and if Salomon stood ready and willing, if necessary, to make adjustments in the film for the sake of the music. (Actually such adjustments had to be made in the episode utilizing the music of the "Guadalcanal March.")

Eight months were required to bring this musical assignment from first sketches to final orchestration. Perhaps too much awe has been aroused by the monumental length of the completed score. In his book on Rodgers and Hammerstein, *Some Enchanted Evenings,* Deems Taylor is so impressed by the sheer bulk of the music that he italicized the "thirteen hours" it requires for performance. He then adds: "While Dick has never claimed to be the peer of Richard Wagner he can, if he chooses, point out that the score of *Victory at Sea* equals in running time the combined scores of *Tristan und Isolde, Die Meistersinger,* and *Parsifal*—and it took Wagner a total of twelve years to write them!"

Fortunately the writing of music is not an endurance contest; and the value of Rodgers' music certainly does not lie in its quantity. Besides, simple honesty dictates the admission that much of the thirteen hours of music was created not by Rodgers but by his orchestrator, Robert Russell Bennett, who not only provided the orchestral dress but also many of the transitional passages. What Rodgers wrote were the chief melodic episodes for the major incidents in the film, together with some of the subsidiary material; he also suggested the harmonization, orchestration, and the way some of his thematic material should be developed. It is the uniformly high inspiration of these episodes, and the way they capture the essence of the pictorial sequences, that gives the entire score its intrinsic value.

The first installment of *Victory at Sea* received its first telecast on October 26, 1952, over NBC, Leonard Graves serving as narrator. The musical background had been recorded by the NBC Symphony Orchestra under Bennett. Acceptance of *Victory at Sea,* both as history and as cinematic art, was immediate and unqualified. Jack Gould wrote in the New York *Times: "Victory at Sea . . .* is a documentary film of rare power and poetry . . . told with moving simplicity and restrained majesty." Bernard De Voto wrote in *Harper's Magazine:* "It is a drama, a work of imagination, art of a high order. And it is new under the sun." *Victory at Sea* subsequently received the two highest awards that could be conferred on a television program: the George Foster Peabody citation and the Sylvania Award. It was televised in England by the British Broadcasting Company. On July 13, 1954, it was released as a motion picture at the Trans-Lux Theatre in New York.

Much of the acclaim that went to *Victory at Sea* was apportioned to Rodgers for his music—a remarkable fact when one bears in mind that the background music for motion pictures is rarely noticed or commented on. Mr. Gould said of it: "Hardly enough can be said for the score of Mr. Rodgers. . . . Especially the portions accompanying the scenes of the sea and the tension of the battle, his work has a compelling beauty and vigor that adds incalculably to the emotional intensity of the series." Archer Winsten found that Rodgers' score "contributes to the drama and the grandeur of the photography without being too persistent." Otis L. Guernsey remarked that "the celebrated score . . . suggests courage, self-sacrifice, and the indomitable spirit of the free man." A critic on the *New Yorker* described the music as "a seemingly endless creation, now martial, now tender, now tuneful, now dissonant . . . memorable and tremendously moving." *Time* said that the "music is often the only description that action needs"; *Variety* called the score "the finest original work of its kind produced by an American composer." The

George Foster Peabody citation went out of its way to refer to the score as "magnificent."

For his part in this project, the composer was awarded in 1953 the Distinguished Public Service Award by the United States Navy, which (as Rodgers told Edward R. Murrow on the "Person to Person" program over television) has since become one of his proudest possessions.

The basic material of this thirteen-hour score can be found in a nine-movement suite arranged by Robert Russell Bennett and recorded by him with the NBC Symphony for Victor. This material is all Rodgers—and it is all gold. It opens with "The Song of the High Seas," a description of the ships sailing on the dangerous waters, menaced by U-boats, in the early period of the war when Great Britain stood alone against the enemy. A convoy of British ships is attacked by enemy submarines, which leave behind them death and desolation. This section opens with a theme suggesting the swelling sea—a chromatic surge and sweep of sound—which leads to a Wagner-like passage for brasses that speaks with pride of the British fleet. An ominous section tells of the presence of U-boats and is followed by a stormy page depicting the battle. A poignant theme for solo trumpet, against a rumbling bass, brings up a picture of the havoc that follows.

"The Pacific Boils Over" opens with a tourist-poster description of the delights of Hawaii in a melody for the woodwinds with overtones of Hawaiian song and dance. A dissonant section breaks up this idyllic mood: Pearl Harbor is attacked. This part ends on a note of sadness but also hope— with a rich melody in the strings culminating in resounding chords—as the air base prepares to repair the damage.

The third part is one of the two most celebrated portions of the entire score, the stirring "Guadalcanal March." This march, which has greater symphonic dimensions than most marches, has since become a staple of brass-band repertories. It received its world première before the television broadcasts, at the Lewisohn Stadium on August 3, 1952, when Rodgers conducted it.

The fourth section, "D Day," has as its principal subject a muscular theme for the brass which, in a more subdued but no less determined mood, returns in the woodwind. Here we are given a picture of the build-up of men and materials for the great assault on Europe. The attack on France erupts with full fury. Then the opening melody returns majestically in the strings, against figurations in the woodwind, to point up the triumph of the invading forces.

The next part, "Hard Work and Horseplay," offers a contrast to the horrors of war. This is a description of the life, routine, work, and play of American soldiers scattered throughout the Pacific both on their ships and on numerous islands and atolls in rear-area bases. This section begins with a stern, martial melody in the strings; life may not be dangerous but it is hard. But there are lighter moments, too, as a sprightly dance tune in the violins informs us.

"Theme of the Fast Carriers" now evokes a tonal picture of a task force on its way to attack enemy-held islands. The battle rages furiously. A solemn, deeply moving funeral march speaks of the terrible price of victory.

The second of the two familiar parts of the score is contained in "Beneath the Southern Cross." This is a scene in the South Atlantic, far removed from the grim realities of war. Its principal theme is a seductive tango melody which Rodgers later adapted into the song "No Other Love," a hit in a later musical play.

With "Mare Nostrum" we are back in the thick of the fighting. First the music evokes a tranquil scene—the Mediterranean in its peacetime beauty. Suddenly the serenity is destroyed. A storm gathers, collects its forces, then erupts with violence as the fleet attacks North Africa, Sicily, Salerno, Anzio. Then, almost like a tropical hurricane that has spent its wrath, serenity returns to the sea.

The concluding movement, "Victory at Sea," is a paean to victory. A brief quotation of the tango melody from "Beneath the Southern Cross" leads to a solemn hymn of thanksgiving, and a repetition of the "Guadalcanal March" is a reminder of past deeds. The tango returns to bring the score to its close, now become a culminating song of joy and triumph. The men —so long separated from loved ones, so long surrounded by fear and death and devastation—can now go home and enjoy a peace they have won and richly deserve.

"SAY THAT I'M A GUY WHO'S IN LOVE WITH THE THEATER"

Rodgers is sometimes asked why, in view of the huge income he receives from various enterprises, he continues working. The tax structure being what it is, there is not much he can gain financially from another box-office triumph. His answer is quick and decisive: "Say that I'm a guy who's in love with the theater. If you're really in love you don't start adding up the profits or losses to be derived from going out with your girl. What would I do with myself if I didn't keep on writing for the stage? I just can't sit in my Connecticut place, much as I love it, and watch the grass grow. Besides, when an idea for a new show seizes me it will just leave me no peace or rest until I have fulfilled it." Oscar Hammerstein has sometimes confided to friends that now that he is past sixty and no longer dependent on his writing for a livelihood he would be glad to retire—if Rodgers did not continually stir him into action.

Rodgers has many interests. The theater is his single passion. He attends all the principal New York shows each season. "I can't imagine a life without the stage," he told an interviewer. Once, pointing to an empty stage just before a rehearsal, he commented, "See that back there? Doesn't it look drab? Props scattered all about. Scenery backed up against the brick wall. Yet I love it. I know that 8:30 in the evening the same spot will be transported into a magical loveliness."

Writing for the theater is what he wants to do for the rest of his life. As he puts it, "If there ever comes a time when there are only five legitimate playhouses in New York, I'd love to have one of them. And if we ever get down to only one, I'd want that to be mine." He has no inner compulsion to write symphonies, concertos or operas. "This doesn't mean I wouldn't get the kick of my life hearing the New York Philharmonic-Symphony under Mitropoulos playing one of my symphonies, or hearing an opera of mine at the Metropolitan. But when I say this I'm talking simply about personal vanity, not about artistic necessity. I have never had the artistic motivation to write serious abstract music in large designs, or a formal grand opera, having always found complete satisfaction in getting my musical stimulation from a play or a motion picture. The only inspiration I need comes from a plot and the lyrics—and occasionally from a member of the cast whose personality may suggest an added development of character."

About his career, he once confided to a friend, "I'm just about the luckiest man in the world. I'm working for the theater, the only place I really want to be, and I guess the only place I belong. I'm writing the kind of music I want and I have made a big success at it. Sometimes I want to pinch myself to be sure I'm not dreaming."

His great love for the stage is the reason why he never allows his pride in a particular piece of music to interfere with good theater. When a number (even one to which he is particularly partial) slows down the action of a play he is the first to insist on its deletion. "I may be in love with my music, but I'm not married to any of it." The requirements of the stage are always uppermost in his mind. He knows those requirements thoroughly. His coworkers in the theater—people like Hammerstein, George Abbott, Joshua Logan—have frequently remarked on Rodger's knowledge of every phase of stagecraft.

His love for the stage is also a reason why he never writes a song solely with the idea of making it popular and then trying to find a spot in the show where it can have the proper showcase. Almost every song he writes is designed, he explains, "to fill an essential role in a play whose story line and character delineations depended at least as much on its musical-lyrical structure as on the spoken word. The fact that such songs afterward become individually accepted as simply a pleasantly rewarding happenstance." Unlike so many other composers for the popular musical stage, he avoids inciting an audience to applause with a sure-fire tune, since this will only arrest the play's action; when he knows he has written a big number that can create instantaneous enthusiasm he will employ subtle musical and stage techniques to allow the play to continue without encores.

Perhaps one of the reasons why he has been able to accomplish as much as he has is that he has an unwavering conviction that the American musical comedy, or play, could be an art. He has said: "A show, if it is any good at all, must have a theater line, and everything had better hew to it. Only then does one get a thoroughly integrated evening in the theater, where the scenery looks the way the music sounds and the clothes look as if they belonged to the characters rather than the management." He has also said: "There is a great need

for a form of musical theater more serious in intent and more
lasting in its nature than that to which we have become accustomed. . . . It could be an extension of musical comedy into
a field where music has emotion as well as rhythm, where
lyrics become poetry, where design has artistry, and where
dancing has meaning and is not a succession of hammer blows
on a wooden stage."

He believes strongly that stage music, to be artistically
valid, must be written for the play for which it is intended—
not fitted conveniently because it happens to be available.
How else, he argues, can the music hope to reflect sensitively
every mood and feeling of the words? (There have been times,
as we have seen, when Rodgers did use in one production a
song originally written and meant for another—but these
have been so few and far between that they do not negate the
sincerity of his credo.)

He has a profound respect for the intelligence and discrim-
ination of theater audiences, and for this reason has been able
to write for them to the fullest capacity of his talent and
imagination. "I suspect that the limitations of any art form
are set by its creators and not by the public, and I can think
of no field in which the viewpoint can be better substantiated
than in the musical theater. Too often I have heard the producer say in all his expansive smugness, 'If I don't understand
it neither will the public.' What he doesn't understand is that
the public is a lot smarter than he is, or I am, for that matter.
Its taste is enormously catholic, and in its choice of entertainment it is precise and knowing. To the public *Parsifal* is good
and so is *My Fair Lady*. The range is large, and the entertainment need only be good of its kind to attract hordes of people. The public is not only willing but anxious to go along
with us in the theater in search for better things, if we continue that search with honesty."

The excitement the theater always arouses in Rodgers became the inspiration for a new musical comedy. *Me and Juliet*, which opened at the Majestic on May 28, 1953, was described by one critic as "a love letter to the theater." It was a story of theater life—onstage and backstage; in the orchestra pit and on the electrician's bridge; in dressing rooms, the smoking room, and the company manager's office; at an audition, an actual performance, and during intermission at a candy counter; in the back alley outside the theater and inside a nearby bar. It tells of the reactions of performers not only to their own craft and to themselves but also to their audiences; and of the reactions of audiences to a play and its songs. It carries passing reminders of Hammerstein's early career as stage manager. Through it all it sounds a message that the theater is a place of magic and wonder where "year after year, there is something to cheer."

For Rodgers and Hammerstein, *Me and Juliet* represented a return to old patterns and stage aesthetics discarded a decade earlier. As they took pains to point out in the program, *Me and Juliet* was not a "musical play" but a "musical comedy." For some time now Rodgers had been absorbed in reviving *Pal Joey*. It reawakened a nostalgia for the kind of musical theater he had once collaborated on with Hart. He suggested to Hammerstein that they temporarily abandon the "musical play" and instead do a "musical comedy" together. Rodgers had another idea, nursed for quite some time, of doing a show about the theater itself and going from one place to another in the theater while telling a story.

Hammerstein agreed, for he felt that this would be a way to retain their freshness. They hit upon the plan of showing what goes on in a theater during a prosperous run of a musical comedy, showing the little people, their problems and personal involvements. New production ideas leaped to their minds—a scene on an electrician's bridge; a spotlight gone awry.

In doing such a musical play, Rodgers and Hammerstein scrupulously avoided the customary clichés about show business and show people. As Hammerstein said: "We steered clear of the kindly old stage-door man called Pop, the pretty little understudy who replaces the star on opening night, the backstage story of a company putting on a new show with all the anxieties of actors and producers—will the show make a hit? Will the little understudy make good? Will she marry the songwriter?" They also had no intention of succumbing to some of the old-fashioned malpractices of stilted characterizations, lack of realism and authenticity in the story; and they did not completely abandon techniques they had been using in their recent plays for making their songs and dance routines arise logically out of the story pattern.

Yet they *were* creating a musical comedy. They decided to engage collaborators whose specialty was the musical-comedy field rather than that of the musical play: George Abbott to direct; Robert Alton to stage the dances and musical numbers; Don Walker to prepare the orchestrations. As for the music, Rodgers remained mindful of the needs of the musical-comedy theater. He used a smaller orchestral ensemble than the one he had been utilizing in the past ten years, with fewer strings, more brass, and some saxophones. His songs were fashioned more in the smart, slick vein he had once tapped while working with Hart than in the subtle, evocative style he had brought to Hammerstein's words. He did not hesitate to employ the standard musical-comedy procedure of fitting a ready-made song into the context instead of writing one especially to fit the text. "No Other Love," a rich-blooded tango and the big hit of the show, came from *Victory at Sea*. A song like "Keep It Gay" had the kind of sophistication for which

Rodgers and Hart had once been so famous—not only in the sprightly melody but even in Hammerstein's lyric, where "gambit" is made to rhyme with "damn bit" and "mongoose" with "a gone goose." "It's Me" and "We Deserve Each Other" were two other breezy numbers bringing nostalgic reminiscences of another era. But there were also other songs in which later musical innovations were retained: a recitative-like melody, "The Big, Black Giant," describing how the audience appears to people on the stage; and a large sequence, "Intermission Talk," combining dialogue with song.

Me and Juliet did not quite accomplish what it set out to do, even though the play moved swiftly, maintained its interest throughout, and had numerous episodes and incidents that were by turns amusing and spellbinding. There were so many things happening all the time, during the many changes of scene, that the overall effect was one of confusion. The many varied elements never quite jelled into a consistent whole. And the middle section—the play within a play—lacked conviction. Walter F. Kerr put it well when he said: "Like a lot of lovers bent on declaring their passion, the authors strike a point at which they become tongue-tied. They want to say so much, they want to say it burstingly, they want to be sure that no heartfelt endearment is omitted anywhere, that they wind up gasping for breath, and making slightly disconnected sounds."

For anyone else but Rodgers and Hammerstein, *Me and Juliet* would have represented a success. It ran over a year and returned a profit of over $100,000 for an investment of $360,-000. "No Other Love," was, for a while, a song strong enough in popularity to achieve a prominent position on the Hit Parade for several weeks running. Finally there was much in the production to win the praise of the critics, even though they were all quick to add that this was sub-standard Rodgers and Hammerstein. But after *Oklahoma!, Carousel, South*

Pacific, and *The King and I,* anything less than a monumental triumph was thought of as a failure. One unidentified columnist summed up the situation neatly: "They never used to cheer when Babe Ruth hit a double."

Despite the apparent failure of *Me and Juliet,* Rodgers stood at the height of his career—the foremost musical figure in the American theater. This fact received official recognition toward the end of 1953. The week beginning August 31 was proclaimed by Mayor Vincent R. Impellitteri of New York "Rodgers and Hammerstein Week," the reason being that four Rodgers and Hammerstein plays (*South Pacific, The King and I, Me and Juliet,* and, beginning a five-week revival at the New York City Center on August 31, *Oklahoma!*) were now running concurrently on Broadway. The Mayor presented a scroll to Rodgers and Hammerstein at City Hall while their wives, and stars from the various productions, looked on. "We might as well have called the whole 1943–1953 period the Rodgers and Hammerstein decade," Walter F. Kerr commented expansively. "No one working in the field of musical entertainment has been uninfluenced by the Rodgers and Hammerstein vision. The fact of musical comedy itself has changed beyond recognition." In acknowledging the honor of having a week dedicated to them—the first of its kind to honor any writer—Rodgers and Hammerstein gave voice to their gratitude in an advertisement which appeared in the Sunday newspapers in New York on August 30.

Other events followed in rapid succession to accentuate further Richard Rodgers' unique position in the theater. On October 12, 1953, there was released at the Astor Theatre a motion-picture documentary called *Main Street to Broadway,* produced by M.G.M. for the Council of Living Theatre to pay homage to the Broadway stage. Both Rodgers and Hammerstein appeared in it, and Mary Martin sang their new song, "There's Music in You." In another sequence, a portion of *The King and I* was presented. Appearing with Rodgers and Hammerstein were such luminaries of the stage as Ethel Barrymore, Helen Hayes, Gertrude Lawrence, Mary Martin, Tallulah Bankhead, and Joshua Logan.

Six weeks later, Rodgers and Hammerstein went to Washington, D.C., to help honor President Eisenhower, recipient of America's Democratic Legacy Award for 1953 of the Anti-Defamation League in commemoration of its fortieth anniversary. This event was celebrated at the Mayflower Hotel on November 23, and Rodgers and Hammerstein presented a program, "Dinner with the President," starring Eddie Fisher, Jane Froman, Helen Hayes, Ethel Merman, Lucille Ball, Desi Arnaz, and Jackie Robinson. The production, together with other proceedings at the dinner, was televised at various times during the evening by the three major networks.

The honors to Rodgers continued to mount. An honorary doctorate in Music was given him and a Doctor of Letters degree to Hammerstein, by Columbia University on January 11, 1954. The presentation was made by Dr. Grayson Kirk, who described Rodgers as "a maker of songs which have touched the hearts of countless Americans." Another honorary degree, a doctorate of Humane Letters, was conferred on him and Hammerstein at the University of Massachusetts at Amherst on March 31. "For more than a decade your collaboration has been a continuing source of artistry which has enriched the musical life both here and abroad," read a part of the citation.*

On December 7, 1954, Rodgers was elected to the board of directors of the Philharmonic-Symphony Society of New

---

* These were not the first honorary degrees bestowed on Rodgers. On November 4, 1949, he had been awarded a degree of Doctor of Law at Drury College in Springfield, Missouri. On that occasion, an all-Rodgers and Hammerstein concert was given in the city and was broadcast over the ABC radio network, and subsequently throughout the world by the Voice of America.

York. The year before, he had been elected a member of the board of trustees of Barnard College for a seven-year term. On May 25, 1955, he was elected to the National Institute of Arts and Letters on a life tenure. On April 4, 1956, he received, along with Hammerstein, the Alexander Hamilton Award, the highest honor Columbia University bestows on an alumnus for "distinguished service and accomplishment in any field of human endeavor." The dinner on this occasion, held at the Waldorf-Astoria, consisted of dishes named after Rodgers and Hammerstein productions; the entertainment was made up of their compositions, including "Room for One More," a song they had written together for Rodgers' first Columbia Varsity Show.

Television did not fail to join in these varied tributes. On November 6, 1954, Rodgers and his wife were interviewed in their country home in Connecticut by Edward R. Murrow on his "Person to Person" program. During a twelve-minute conversation Rodgers explained how he worked with Hammerstein while Dorothy revealed something about Rodgers' life in the country.

One of the most distinguished tributes ever paid by television to a composer came on March 28, 1954, in a program sponsored by General Foods on the occasion of its twenty-fifth anniversary. The hour-and-a-half presentation of excerpts from their plays and motion pictures was carried simultaneously by the four principal television networks comprising 245 stations. No entertainment had ever before or since received such coverage, and it was estimated that almost half of the entire country saw the production. "It would be hard," said Harriet van Horne, radio and television critic, "to recall a more enchanted evening by the home screen." Among those who either performed or made an appearance were Gordon MacRae, Florence Henderson, John Raitt, Jan Clayton, Mary Martin, Ezio Pinza, Bill Hayes, Janice Rule, Yul Brynner,

Patricia Morison, Tony Martin, Rosemary Clooney, Jack Benny, Groucho Marx, Edgar Bergen, and Ed Sullivan.

Another "first" came one year later on July 18, 1955. At the concluding half of its thirty-seventh season, the St. Louis Municipal Opera, under the management of Paul Beiman, created an unprecedented Rodgers and Hammerstein festival, lasting six weeks, beginning on July 18. The festival opened with a week's performance by a symphony orchestra of a Rodgers and Hammerstein program. Then followed performances of *Carousel, Allegro, The King and I,* and *South Pacific*—the first three given for one week each, and the last for two.

To return to the theater and to music some of the munificent rewards he has received from them, Rodgers has established various endowments and awards. The Rodgers and Hammerstein Foundation, launched with the money received from *Life* for their Christmas song, was only one of these, and not the first. In 1948, Rodgers, with Hammerstein, had established at the Juilliard School of Music an annual scholarship to deserving New York public high school graduates, in the name of Irving Berlin on the occasion of the latter's sixtieth birthday. This was the first of three Juilliard scholarships. In 1953, Rodgers alone set up a second endowment of a permanent scholarship to be given annually to a talented musician; in 1954 he and Hammerstein financed a scholarship in perpetuity endowed in the name of Max Dreyfus, on his eightieth birthday, to be given each year to a talented singer.

In addition to these benefactions, Rodgers and Hammerstein established two scholarships to provide a year's tuition in the Professional Wing Training Program of the American Theatre Wing to gifted young performers. And, through the agency of the League of Composers, Rodgers and Hammerstein commissioned one of America's foremost composers,

Aaron Copland, to write an opera, *The Tender Land,* introduced by the New York City Opera Company on April 1, 1954.

A gift of another kind was made by Rodgers in 1954 to the Congressional Library in Washington, D.C.: he presented all his manuscripts, everything of importance he has written from the *Garrick Gaieties* to *Victory at Sea.* He had long been thinking of donating these manuscripts to the Juilliard School of Music. But when Harold Spivacke, the head of the music division of the Congressional Library, told him of his efforts to procure complete manuscript libraries of America's foremost composers and asked Rodgers to cooperate with him, Rodgers decided to turn over his manuscripts to the Library. It became the core of a "retrospective exhibition" of the career of Richard Rodgers, arranged by L. Quincy Mumford and Deems Taylor at the Library of Congress from April 4 to July 30, 1955—the second time that a composer of nonclassical music was chosen there for such a display (the first was Stephen Foster). "The exhibit," a Library press release explained, "testified to the part he has played in the history of the American musical theatre and shows how fittingly his scores have interpreted the American scene. Rodgers' career is represented in its varying aspects in the exhibit; a major part of the display consists of the original manuscripts written by the composer. In addition . . . the exhibition includes numerous original drawings and designs for the Rodgers productions by such artists as Jo Mielziner, George Jenkins, Lemuel Ayers, and Oliver Smith. A number of the awards and citations bestowed on the composer . . . have also been lent by Mr. and Mrs. Rodgers."

9

EBB TIDE AND HIGH TIDE

In the spring of 1955, Rodgers began to suffer pain in his left jaw. The pain continued throughout the summer and was finally diagnosed by Rodgers' physician, Dr. Milton Rosenbluth, as a cancer of the gum posterior of the last tooth. A serious operation of the neck and jaw was successfully performed by Dr. Hayes Martin at Memorial Hospital on September 25, in which the left jaw bone and glands in the neck were removed. The prognosis was favorable. The cancer had not spread, and its removal gave every assurance that Rodgers' recovery would be complete.

The months of pain and the suffering that followed the operation were borne by Rodgers with fortitude. He was an uncomplaining patient who accepted stoically every demand made upon him by his physicians, and every postoperative discomfort. "On the eighth day following the operation I went for a ride in the park with my wife. I hated it. On the ninth she took me to a movie. I bore it. On the tenth, still living at the hospital, I went to rehearsal. I loved it." Before that rehearsal, he gathered around him his cast and coworkers and said simply: "Look, I know that *you* know what has happened to me, and what I suffered from. I don't want any of you going around sympathizing with me, or pulling long faces, or whispering. If there's anything you want to know about my condition, don't ask each other but come to me and I'll tell you. Period. Now let's get down to work." He had to supervise rehearsals while suffering postoperative pains, and had to keep a handkerchief continually to his lips to arrest an uncontrollable flow of saliva. He could not even speak properly, "because my tongue hadn't learned to behave." His physical discomfort was still intense when he attended the tryouts of *Pipe Dream* in New Haven and Boston.

Pipe Dream was based on John Steinbeck's novel *Sweet Thursday*. The plan to use the Steinbeck story for a musical originated not with Rodgers and Hammerstein but in the producing offices of Feuer and Martin, who asked Steinbeck to prepare his own adaptation and who sought out Frank Loesser, the composer of *Guys and Dolls,* for the music. When this project collapsed, Feuer and Martin communicated with Rodgers and Hammerstein to inquire if they might be interested in his book. The setting of Cannery Row, a somewhat disreputable section of Monterey, California—and the odd assortment of social misfits who populated it—appealed strongly to both Rodgers and Hammerstein, who expressed their interest. While they were in London in 1953 to prepare the production of *The King and I,* they received parts of Steinbeck's script piecemeal. Immediately, Hammerstein began to prepare the text.

The kindly tolerance and gentleness Hammerstein brought to the delineation of his lowly characters are also found in Rodgers' music. Suzy's lament, "Everybody's Got a Home but Me," has that touch which so often gives to a Rodgers song an incomparable incandescence; and the principal love song, "All at Once You Love Her"—lightly marked by a Mexican flavor—is in Rodgers' most appealing and tender vein. Both these songs have become popular. But several others were no less distinguished: "Suzy is a Good Thing," with its surprising chromaticisms; the lovable ballad "The Next Time It Happens"; the sprightly "Sweet Thursday," with its infectious cakewalk rhythm; the poignantly nostalgic "The Man I Used to Be." A score like this, in the variety of expression and inventiveness of thought, need not assume the unhappy status of a stepchild among Rodgers' creations; it finds him in the fullness of his creative powers.

The casting was marked by an act of discovery, on the one hand, and an act of courage, on the other. The discovery was Judy Tyler, in the principal role of Suzy, whom Rodgers had seen on television as a princess in the Howdy-Doody program and who had had only four weeks of stage experience in a summer operetta circuit. The courageous move was to select a great lady of Wagnerian music drama, Helen Traubel, for the part of a bordello madame. While Judy Tyler was a winner in every way, Helen Traubel's performance never quite came off. She had the lusty vigor and expansive manner for her part, but somehow she continued to remain too much of Brünnhilde or Isolde to feel completely at ease as Fauna. "The joke of casting a musical heroine as the keeper of a squalid bordello is cute rather than hearty," remarked Brooks Atkinson.

Pipe Dream opened at the Shubert Theatre in New York on November 30, 1955, with the largest advance sale of any Rodgers and Hammerstein play ($1,200,000). There were some things in the production that pleased the critics—Rodgers' music received virtually a unanimous verdict in its favor. But the consensus as a whole was that the play represented Rodgers and Hammerstein "in a minor key," as Atkinson said, and that, in the words of Richard Watts, Jr., it "hardly reveals the Masters at the peak of their distinguished form." *Pipe Dream* had the shortest run of any Rodgers and Hammerstein play (246 performances) and incurred the greatest financial loss.

Both Rodgers and Hammerstein—who are ready to concede the many shortcomings of *Me and Juliet* and recognize their own responsibilities for them—are convinced that *Pipe Dream* is better than it has been judged to be. Hammerstein feels the play suffered most from serious production errors. "I'll put it this way," he says. "If anybody else had produced the play we'd say these are producers we wouldn't like to work with again." Rodgers remarks sadly that too much is expected of them, and quotes a line from his song "The Next Time It Happens": "Who expects a miracle to happen every day?"

Several important things helped to dissipate Rodgers' disappointment over *Pipe Dream*. On December 10, 1956, he received from Dr. Hayes Martin assurance of good health. This was the first time he became completely convinced that he was well again and need be apprehensive no longer about the return of his cancerous condition. Six weeks later, on January 22, 1957, he appeared as guest conductor of the Philadelphia Orchestra in an all-Rodgers concert for the benefit of the orchestra Pension Fund. This was his first appearance on a conductor's podium since his illness, and it put to final rest the fears he had long entertained that his operation had brought his baton career to an end.

Most important of all, as a composer he was now asked

to meet a new challenge—and an artistic challenge was something that always aroused and stimulated him. He was deep at work again, this time on the score for an original musical play for television, the first time that he and Hammerstein were writing directly for that medium.

One day in June, 1956, Jerome Whyte met Lou Wilson, the American representative of Julie Andrews, the brilliant English star of *My Fair Lady*. Wilson was interested in a television spectacular for his client and he inquired from Whyte whether he knew of a composer and lyricist interested in writing the songs and book. "Why don't you ask Rodgers and Hammerstein?" inquired Whyte. Wilson was taken aback; he considered Rodgers and Hammerstein unapproachable for such an assignment. "There's only one way to find out," Whyte suggested, "and that is by asking them."

When Rodgers and Hammerstein expressed their enthusiasm a deal was worked out with the Columbia Broadcasting System for a ninety-minute production. The vehicle planned for Julie Andrews was the Cinderella fairy tale.

There was a kind of logic in having Julie Andrews star in the first original television play by Rodgers and Hammerstein. The first important musical she ever saw was *South Pacific*, in London. She recalls that after the performance her manager, Charles Tucker, remarked: "Rodgers and Hammerstein will some day write a show for you." Curiously, this prophetic remark was almost realized in *My Fair Lady*. This project—before Frederick Loewe and Alan Jay Lerner accepted it—had been considered by Rodgers and Hammerstein, but was finally turned down by them as unsuitable to their kind of creative talent.

It took Rodgers and Hammerstein six months to write the book and songs of *Cinderella*. Four weeks were consumed by the tryouts and casting, and another six weeks in rehearsals. The telecast finally took place on Sunday evening, March 31,

1957, from 8:00 to 9:30 P.M. over the CBS network and carried to practically the entire North American continent by a chain of 245 stations, the largest number ever assembled by a network for a single program. It was estimated that between 75,000,000 and 100,000,000 watched the broadcast, probably the largest audience ever to witness an entertainment program. Julie Andrews, as Cinderella, was supported by a glittering array of stars. Howard Lindsay and Dorothy Stickney were the king and queen; Ilka Chase was Cinderella's stepmother; Kaye Ballard and Alice Ghostley were the stepsisters; Edith Adams was the Fairy Godmother. The only newcomer was Jon Cypher in the role of the Prince.

Hammerstein made no basic departure from the Cinderella story as it was originally told by Charles Perrault in the seventeenth century. "The traditional Cinderella has done very well," he explained. "Why should we trick her up? We decided at once Cinderella would not become a shop girl from Macy's who is spotted by the proprietor's son and wafted to El Morocco. There will be absolutely no updating, no naturalistic or Freudian explanations. We wanted to do a musical version of the story that everyone remembers from childhood." The only major alteration was in the transformation of the stepsisters from cruel characters into comic caricatures, a change which to Jack Gould and several other television critics "threw the story's focus a little askew."

Music had to carry the main burden of providing the fairy tale with a fresh and vibrant new interest for a modern-day audience. And there can be little question but that it is through the music that this Rodgers and Hammerstein television play acquires its magic. Every number, without exception, is in his most attractive creative vein. Rodgers has always been particularly tender and ingratiating when he wrote about little girls. He is so once again in the two love songs of Cinderella and the Prince, "Ten Minutes Ago" and "Do

I Love You?", the latter the big song of the entire production; in Cinderella's two poignant songs, "In My Own Little Corner" and "A Lovely Night"; and in the three main orchestral sections, the pert opening march that follows Cinderella and her mother, the gavotte, and the whirling waltz at the ball.

10

COLLABORATORS

If Rodgers had deliberately set out to find himself a working partner as different in personality, temperament, and daily habits from Lorenz Hart—and at the same time as much like himself—as was humanly possible, he could not have been more successful than with Oscar Hammerstein II. Where Hart had been a five-foot organism of exposed nerves and explosive moods, Hammerstein is a huge, gangling, six-foot-one, two-hundred-pound hulk of calmness. Hart had made Rodgers appear like the epitome of normalcy and repose, but compared to Hammerstein, Rodgers is like a seething volcano. Even the quiet and systematic dispatch with which Rodgers attends to the business of living and working seems frenetic when compared with Hammerstein's outer placidity, inner tranquillity, and extreme composure and grace under pressure.

In working habits, Hammerstein is also Hart's opposite. Hammerstein is not a man whose production depends upon whim or mood. Like Rodgers, he always performs his tasks punctiliously; he always completes the job expected of him on time; he is always there when he is needed. Hammerstein's orderly approach to the problems of collaboration represented for Rodgers a welcome revolution from the anarchy of Hart's methods and behavior. Perhaps one of the reasons why Rodgers has done his best work with Hammerstein is that Hammerstein's is the kind of law and discipline under which Rodgers functions to maximum capacity. "I needed a little calm in my life after twenty-five years," said Rodgers, "and I got it with Hammerstein. When Oscar says I'll meet you at two-thirty, he is there at two-thirty. That had never happened to me before."

Hammerstein is always so methodical and punctual that Rodgers has said of him he is probably the only man alive who knows where he will be on November 16, 1960, at 3:30 P.M. It has been said that Hammerstein looks like a construction engineer. Maybe so—but he surely lives like one. His daily life is untouched by the much publicized diversions and temptations of stage life. He rises each day early at 7:30, finishes his breakfast an hour later, and by 9:00 is at his desk in his study for a full day of work. After he has finished the day's stint and has partaken of a leisurely dinner, he likes to spend the evening quietly, watching television, reading, or puttering around in his study—that is, if there is no theater performance to attend. Like Rodgers, Hammerstein is no enthusiast for night life or night clubs; unlike Rodgers, he does not even like to give or attend large dinners and mingle with important people. While his friends are legion—including for the most part theatrical people—he prefers to spend his free hours with his rather ample family: his three children by both marriages, his two stepchildren and their nine children. It is an unusual occasion for him if he is not in bed by midnight. If he is visiting friends or entertaining them, he begins by 11 o'clock at night to perform what Jerome Kern once described as "the Hammerstein glide"—edging slowly and surely toward the door until he can make a swift and discreet exit.

"Ock," as his friends like to call him, is a large and bulky man with broad shoulders and gangling movements that are usually slow and sedate. His sensitive blue eyes register kindliness and tolerance, and his forehead always seems to be contracted into a frown. A shy smile creeps across his lips frequently as he talks, touching his round, rugged, and pockmarked face with a gentleness that are duplicated in his speech and manner. He always speaks in a softly modulated voice, rarely loses his temper, and is never temperamental. There is about him the air of a poet and a dreamer—but, as Rodgers hastens to add, "a very careful dreamer"—whose head might sometimes be up in the clouds but whose feet are always firmly on the ground.

Hammerstein met his present wife, Dorothy, in 1928 aboard the *Olympic* on its westbound voyage from Europe. They fell in love during that trip but, since both were married at the time, had to wait for their respective divorces. They were married in New York City on May 14, 1929. Dorothy, née Blanchard, was Australian by birth, but many years of her life were spent in London. Her Old World dignity and Australian accent, and the engravings and portraits of Queen Victoria, Prince Albert, and Lord Nelson hanging on the walls of her home, are present-day reminders of her background. She has had some experience in the theater, having been both a bit player and Gertrude Lawrence's understudy in *Charlot's Revue*, with which she came to the United States in 1924.

Several years after marrying Hammerstein, she became interested in interior decoration and built up a highly profitable enterprise. Among her accounts were the Australian Embassy in Washington, D.C., the Milton Blow advertising agency in New York, Eleanor Holm's apartment, and the homes of many friends of the stage. Dorothy's brother-in-law handled all the business details for her. When he died in 1942, she decided to close her firm. Since then her major interests, outside her husband and his career, have been Welcome House, an agency organized by Pearl Buck to find homes for unwanted children of mixed marriages of Americans and Orientals; continually refurnishing her homes; gardening; keeping up a copious correspondence with friends and relatives all over the world; and reading.

The Hammersteins, like the Rodgerses, maintain two homes. A five-floor brick house on East 63rd Street off Fifth Avenue is their town house, on the ground floor of which is a room serving as the office for Hammerstein's business affairs. Inside the residence itself an impressive circular stairway winds through the five floors. The rooms are beautifully outfitted with old English furniture and American antiques in a setting enlivened by brightly colored accessories. The pictorial decorations on the walls do not consist of famous paintings but of family photographs. "Oscar," Dorothy explains, "simply has no feeling for the graphic arts."

The country place, called "Highland Farm," stands atop a hill on seventy-three acres of land in Doylestown, Buck County, Pennsylvania. It is a functioning farm. Black Angus cattle, turkeys and chickens are raised and sold; and alfalfa, wheat, and corn and other crops are grown. But the place also includes a swimming pool with an adjoining bathhouse, a tennis court with special cork composition surface (both Hammersteins like playing the game), and a small summer house presented to them one Christmas by the Rodgerses.

When Hammerstein has a commitment to meet he likes best to work in Doylestown. There, on the second floor, is a huge workroom the length of the house; it has an adjoining balcony, presented him by his wife on their twenty-fifth wedding anniversary. The walls are decorated with some of the citations and awards his plays have received. With them is a small framed card from the New York Board of Education attesting to the fact that Oscar Hammerstein, while attending P.S. 9, was "a good boy." The room is lined with bookcases and has an open fireplace along one of the walls.

Hammerstein works best in a standing position. When he is trying to solve an immediate problem he likes to pace restlessly, either on the balcony outside his room, up and down the room, or outdoors on a lonely road. When he is writing he stands in front of an erect old-fashioned bookkeeper's desk presented him by Jerome Kern. He prefers working on dialogue by using a dictating machine, a practice he learned from Joshua Logan and began with *South Pacific*. His dictation is then transcribed by his secretary on paper to await his revisions. For his lyrics, he always does his writing in longhand. He stops from time to time to act out a scene aloud in order to hear how the dialogue sounds to the ear. When he is engaged on a comedy scene, he enacts it, laughing uproariously when he finds a situation funny; for romantic incidents he makes an effort to put himself into a sentimental frame of mind. For his lyrics he makes up dummy tunes. "Those dummy tunes," reveals Dorothy, "are so terrible they make you want to cry."

For Hammerstein the process of creation is long and laborious. In contrast to Rodgers, who often produces a gem in minutes, it takes Hammerstein a few weeks to write a single lyric. He weighs each word and phrase carefully. The deceptive simplicity of his writing comes only after the most painstaking selection and revision.

While writing verses Hammerstein sometimes reaches for Loring's *Rhymer's Lexicon*. However, "a rhyming dictionary should be used as a supplement to one's own ingenuity and not as a substitute for it," he informs us. "I do not open mine until I have exhausted my own memory and invention of rhymes for a word." In his lyrics, he is never particularly interested in unusual rhymes or rhythms, unexpected phrasing, scintillating alliterations, or other virtuoso effects. He wants the lines of his verse to flow as naturally and as easily as his dialogue, to be simple and precise in its expression, to employ the vernacular. In his opinion, one of the best lyric lines ever written is also one of the simplest: it is "All alone by the telephone," by Irving Berlin. Hammerstein has definite ideas on how a good lyric should be written. "A rhyme should be unassertive, never stand out too noticeably. It should, on the other hand, not be a rhyme heard in a hundred other popular songs of the time, so familiar that the listener can anticipate it before it is sung. There should not be too many rhymes. In fact, a rhyme should appear only where it is absolutely demanded to keep the pattern of the music. If a listener is made rhyme conscious, his interest may be diverted from the story of the song. If, on the other hand, you keep him waiting for a rhyme, he is more likely to listen to the meaning of the words. . . . The job of the poet is to find the right word in the right place, the word with the exact meaning and the highest quality of beauty or power. The lyric writer must find this word, too, but it must also be a word that is clear when sung and not too difficult for the singer to sing on that note which he hits when he sings it."

If he knows what makes a good lyric, he also knows how to turn a good lyric into poetry. For these reasons, many of his rival lyricists often refer to him as the "Master." With a true poet's capacity to seize beauty and truth, Hammerstein is able to bring to his lyrics lines which, for all their disarming economy and lack of pretention, soar. It is a poet, not a functional lyricist, who has written lines like these:

When I think of Tom, I think about a night
When the earth smelled of summer and the sky was streaked
with white.
And the soft mist of England was sleeping on a hill.
I remember this—and I always will.

Or these:

And somewhere a bird who is bound to be heard,
Is throwing his heart at the sky.

Or these:

I walk in the loneliness of the evening,
Looking out on a silver-flaked sea,
And ask the moon:
Oh, how soon, how soon,
Will my love come home to me?

The working arrangements of Rodgers and Hammerstein differ radically from those previously employed by Rodgers and Hart. Carrying a show from the initial planning to the first-night curtain is, with Rodgers and Hammerstein, a carefully calculated process. Months are spent in conferences before a single word or melodic phrase is set down on paper. Not only every detail of the writing of the play but every aspect of the production itself is meticulously planned and agreed upon. In these discussions they do not remain exclusively in their own fields. Rodgers may make important suggestions for lyrics and give advice upon the development of a character or a situation. Hammerstein may sometimes provide significant ideas for the kind of song that is needed or the style called for in a certain orchestral transition.

Once the detailed plans are crystallized, actual writing

begins. Hammerstein is the first to go to work, retiring to the privacy of his study in Doylestown. Once again a method formerly adopted by Rodgers and Hart has been altered. With Hart, as we have seen, the lyrics usually came after the music; with Hammerstein it is the lyrics that usually come first.

Like Hammerstein, Rodgers prefers to have no one around him when he is working, not even within hearing distance of his piano. His family learned long ago to stay clear of him until he is through. He is also reticent about playing his latest songs for the first time—even for his wife. But once that first hearing is over, he finds considerable exhilaration and pleasure in exhibiting his new music at special auditions and parties, either solo, or with Margot Hopkins at a second piano.

The hardest part of the work comes at rehearsal time. Rehearsals usually consume about five weeks. In that time, Rodgers and Hammerstein work twelve hours a day, seven days a week, supervising every detail and making the many adjustments in text and music that are always required before a production is ready. Here as in the earlier writing they work in complete harmony. Their press representative, Michael Mok, has said: "I can't show one of them a window card for a Chinese laundry without his calling the other for an opinion."

At rehearsals, Hammerstein is a pillar of repose. He stays quietly in one seat, absorbing everything that is happening and making mental notes of criticisms he will ultimately make. These are given softly and politely, not as a command but as discreet suggestions.

Rodgers, however, is in a perpetual state of motion and agitation, using his fullest mental and physical resources. His coat is off; his tie is loosened; his collar is open; his shirt sleeves are rolled up. He wanders restlessly from one part of the theater to another to test acoustics, to get a fresh angle on a piece of stage business, to inspect the lighting. No element of sight or sound seems to escape his ever-vigilant eye and ear. When he gives instructions to an actor or actress, his remarks are, as Hammerstein points out, "the models of clarity." He knows what he wants, and he knows how to express himself succinctly and forcefully. A perfectionist, he demands the best of everybody working with him. He is a stickler for having his music sung and played the way he wrote it. "If you change one note," recalls Diana Costello, who played in the road company of *South Pacific,* "he gets irritated. When you're singing along and thinking what a nice voice you have, he is apt to say, 'Don't fall in love with your voice.'" As the rehearsal proceeds, the expression on his face becomes so serious and intense that he often frightens those with whom he is working. "That is because he goes into a little chamber," explains Joshua Logan. "He's putting himself into the audience so he can better judge the effect of a scene or a song objectively."

On opening nights, Rodgers and Hammerstein exchange temperaments. Rodgers is now the imperturbable one, sitting quietly with his wife in the last row of the theater, giving everybody around him the impression that he is extremely confident. Hammerstein also gives the outward impression of being free of jitters—but this is entirely deceptive. The truth is that this is the one time Hammerstein is a victim of nerves. He sweats so profusely that by the time the performance is over he must change his clothing completely. "He is all on edge inside," says his wife. "If there seems to be a delay in the changing of the scene, he begins to curse under his breath. He says some really terrible things." Hammerstein himself has said of opening nights that they are like "jumping off a precipice," or like "a nightmare about being caught naked in public."

11

SONGS BY RODGERS—A FINAL WORD

The speed with which Richard Rodgers produces a song masterpiece is deservedly the source of awe and envy among his fellow composers—and the despair of Hammerstein. Some of Rodgers' best songs have been completed in ten minutes, twenty minutes, half an hour, as we have already pointed out in earlier chapters. Lillian Leff, who has sometimes been a witness to his production, says, "Creatively, he's kind of frightening."

His own modest explanation of his creative facility is that Hammerstein writes the kind of lyrics that simply lend themselves to music. "There is an almost inevitable musical pathway leading from his words," he tells us. "All you have to do with a Hammerstein lyric is to put it on the piano—and the song writes itself." But Rodgers wrote with equal rapidity when he was Hart's partner, when he did not have a lyric to help him along. Another Rodgers explanation is perhaps closer to the truth. "When I sit down to the actual business of writing notes, I already know all the governing circumstances—the scene, the mood, the singer, the subject, and even what kind of a song it will be." And again: "I have a story. I see a stage. I know what my settings are going to be. I know in most cases who will be the performers. I am standing in the orchestra pit. The lights are beginning to dim, the curtain is going up. I must have a song with the proper mood. I sit down and write that song. It's as simple as all that." Finally, Rodgers has said: "The time it takes to write a song should not be computed by the amount of minutes spent at the piano putting the notes together, but from the minute the song is first discussed."

In writing his songs, Rodgers works best at the piano, playing the harmonic accompaniment with both hands while whistling or singing the melody. When he has his melody clearly and completely formulated he prepares a "lead sheet," in which the lyrical line is written out and the harmony and orchestration are suggested. Later on, he does a complete piano arrangement, a chore he detests. The song is then turned over to the orchestrator, who fills in the details. Rodgers has worked with several orchestrators through the years: Roy Webb, Hans Spialek, Don Walker, and, most frequently, Robert Russell Bennett.

As Lorenz Hart's collaborator, Rodgers was essentially a child of Tin Pan Alley, working within the formal structure of the popular song, even while bringing to it a dignity of melodic writing, a freshness of viewpoint, and most of all a personal identity. Little stylistic idiosyncrasies personalize the songs Rodgers wrote to Hart's lyrics, and set them sharply apart from the stereotype utilized by so many other popular composers. Many of Rodgers' choruses are partial to melodies built from an ascending or descending scale, sometimes to both as in "Mountain Greenery," where a descent is made in the first three bars, and an ascent in the next two. Surprise often comes in the melody or harmony through the unexpected introduction of notes foreign to the scale, or through sudden modulations without the expected preliminaries. The canvas of the song form is enlarged beyond the traditional thirty-two-bar chorus through unusual releases as in "There's a Small Hotel" and "Where or When?" or through protracted endings or self-sufficient trios tacked on to the chorus, as in "On a Desert Island with Thee," "Mountain Greenery," "Johnny One Note," and "Little Girl Blue."

Deems Taylor once said that Rodgers' songs are so simple that we forget they are also great. This is particularly true of the songs he wrote with Hart. His vocal range is limited, his melody has a minimum of ornamentation, his tonality is restricted. These songs are not encumbered by any elaborate harmonic backgrounds—often Rodgers uses only two harmonic patterns for a song—or complicated rhythmic schemes. He never strives for interest by superimposing an unusual chord on a melody or altering it through changes of meter and rhythm. The interest lies exclusively in the lyricism. A song like "The Girl Friend," which derives its effect from syncopation, or "Johnny One Note" and "That Terrific Rainbow," which have a dynamic rhythmic drive, are exceptions to the rule. Rodgers more often alternates between a brisk and invigorating air of sophistication and wit and soft-spoken tender feelings in a lyricism which, while remaining simple and direct, never lack variety of mood or feeling.

In collaborating with Hart, he achieved his best vein— purity and sweetness—through tight-lipped restraint and understatement. With rare exceptions, his love songs written to Hart's lyrics attempt to caress and beguile, not to excite or overwhelm. Hart often avoided an open avowal of love, preferring to speak of it through circumlocution, innuendo, suggestion. ("This can't be love because I feel so well"; or "You took advantage of me"; or "Caring too much is just a juvenile fancy"; or "I'm a sentimental sap that's all, what's the use of trying not to fall.") In the same way, Rodgers usually touches ever so lightly on emotion, only infrequently becoming passionate or deeply personal—though there are songs like "My Heart Stood Still," "Where or When?," and "My Romance," which are exceptions. Yet the emotional gamut of his love songs remain wide: naïve and uncomplicated in "There's a Small Hotel"; sophisticated in "I Could Write a Book"; earthy in "Bewitched, Bothered and Bewildered"; as delicate as a Japanese print in "My Funny Valentine."

But with Hammerstein he became a completely different composer. The piano study he had undertaken just as his career with Hart was drawing to a close brought him new values and concepts in writing melody and harmony. His contact with the simple eloquence of Hammerstein's poetry and the humanity of Hammerstein's philosophy brought new sensitivity and refinement and radiance to his musical writing. And he was, of course, strengthened in his creative powers through the maturity that comes to a composer who all the while has been continuously developing and growing.

As Hammerstein's collaborator, Rodgers no longer is willing to adapt his music to the limitations of the popular song form. He is now a composer who makes his structure adapt itself resiliently to the flow of his musical ideas and to the requirements of his text. Gone forever are the formal verse and chorus relationships; the thirty-two-bar melody evenly partitioned into symmetrical phrases. Instead we have a song which becomes an art song in the freedom of its construction, in the deepened expressiveness of the lyricism, the independence of the harmony, and most of all in the capacity of the melody to catch the most elusive mood and emotional vibration of the lyric. Like the celebrated *Lied* composers of Germanic tradition from Schubert through Richard Strauss, Rodgers often becomes a story teller in music, a dramatist in miniature. He makes his music serve the poetry so completely that it becomes its inextricable partner. Like Hugo Wolf, he becomes a musician so concerned with the poetic and dramatic expression that he is ready to sacrifice lyricism for declamation, and declamation for accompanied speech.

If his career had terminated after his quarter-of-a-century collaboration with Hart, Rodgers would still have found a secure place with George Gershwin, Jerome Kern, Cole Porter and Irving Berlin among the most significant popular composers of our generation. But that he has been able to go on from this point to a still richer, more productive and artistically more important career with Oscar Hammerstein— that he was able to develop from a great composer of popular songs into a great writer of the American *Lied*—gives him a unique place in American music.

Appendixes

i

STAGE PRODUCTIONS
WITH MUSIC BY RODGERS

1   with Lorenz Hart

1920

POOR LITTLE RITZ GIRL. A "musical novelty" with book by George
Campbell and Lew Fields. Presented by Lew Fields at the Cen-
tral Theatre on July 28 (119 performances). Production staged
by Ned Wayburn. Cast included Charles Purcell, Eleanor
Griffith, Lulu McConnell, and Andrew Tombes. Additional
eight songs by Sigmund Romberg.
Musical Numbers: Mary, Queen of Scots; Love Will Call; You
Can't Fool Your Dreams; What Happened Nobody Knows; All
You Need to Be a Star; Love's Intense in Tents; The Daisy and
the Lark.

The following songs were also included during the Boston
tryout at the Wilbur Theatre on May 28, 1920, but were re-

moved to make room for Romberg's songs: The Midnight Supper; Lady Raffles—Behave; The Gown Is Mightier than the Sword; Drink Into Your Eyes; Will You Forgive Me; Souvenirs; The Lord Only Knows; The Boomerang; I Surrender.

1924

THE MELODY MAN. A comedy by "Herbert Richard Lorenz" (Herbert Fields, Richard Rodgers, and Lorenz Hart). Presented by Lew Fields at the Ritz Theatre on May 13 (56 performances). Staged by Lawrence Marston and Alexander Leftwich. Cast included Lew Fields, Sam White, and Eva Puck.
Musical Numbers: Moonlight Mama; I'd Like to Poison Ivy.

1925

THE GARRICK GAIETIES. A musical revue. Presented by the Theatre Guild sponsoring the Theatre Guild Junior Players at the Garrick Theatre on May 17 (161 performances). Produced by Philip Loeb. Sketches and additional lyrics by Benjamin Kaye, Louis Sorin, Sam Jaffe, Newman Levy, and Morrie Ryskind, among others. Dances arranged by Herbert Fields. Cast included Sterling Holloway, Romney Brent, June Cochrane, Betty Starbuck, Philip Loeb, Edith Meiser, and Hildegarde Halliday.
Musical Numbers: Gilding the Guild; Sentimental Me; Manhattan; Do You Love Me?; April Fool; An Old-fashioned Girl; On with the Dance. *The Joy Spreader,* described as an "American jazz opera," libretto by Hart, appeared in the first two performances.

DEAREST ENEMY. "An American musical comedy," with book by Herbert Fields. Presented by George Ford at the Knickerbocker Theatre on September 18 (286 performances). Staged by John Murray Anderson. Dances and ensembles directed by Carl Hemmer. Cast included Helen Ford, Charles Purcell, and Flavia Arcaro.

Musical Numbers: Heigh-Ho, Lackaday!; War Is War; I Beg Your Pardon; Cheerio; Full Blown Roses; The Hermits; Here in My Arms; Gavotte; I'd Like to Hide It; Where the Hudson River Flows; Bye and Bye; Old Enough to Love; Sweet Peter; Here's a Kiss.

1926

THE GIRL FRIEND. A musical comedy with book by Herbert Fields. Produced by Lew Fields at the Vanderbilt Theatre on March 17 (409 performances). Production supervised by Lew Fields. Musical numbers arranged and staged by Jack Haskell. Cast included Sam White, Eva Puck, June Cochrane.
Musical Numbers: Hey! Hey!; The Simple Life; The Girl Friend; Good-bye, Lenny!; The Blue Room; Cabarets; Why Do I?; The Damsel Who Done All the Dirt; He's a Winner; Town Hall Tonight; Good Fellow, Mine; Creole Crooning Song; I'd Like to Take You Home; What Is It?.
"Pipes of Pansy" was deleted during the out-of-town tryouts.

THE GARRICK GAIETIES, Second Edition. A revue. Presented by the Theatre Guild at the Garrick Theatre on May 10 (174 performances). Staged by Philip Loeb. Dances and musical numbers staged by Herbert Fields. Sketches by Benjamin Kaye, Newman Levy, Herbert Fields, and Philip Loeb among others. Cast included Romney Brent, Hildegarde Halliday, Sterling Holloway, Philip Loeb, Edith Meiser, Betty Starbuck, and Lee Strasberg.
Musical Numbers: Allez Up; Gigolo; Mountain Greenery; Rose of Arizona; Four Little Song Pluggers; What's the Use of Talking; Keys to Heaven.

LIDO LADY (London). A musical comedy with book by Guy Bolton, Bert Kalmar and Harry Ruby. Produced by Jack Hulbert at The Gaiety, London, on December 1 (259 performances). Cast included Jack Hulbert and Phyllis Dare.

Musical Numbers: A Little Flat in Soho; Atlantic Blues; Here in My Arms; What's the Use?; I Want a Man; Lido Lady; Try Again Tomorrow; My Heart is Sheba Bound; I Must Be Going.

PEGGY-ANN. A musical comedy with book by Herbert Fields based on *Tillie's Nightmare* by Edgar Smith. Presented by Lew Fields and Lyle D. Andrews at the Vanderbilt Theatre on December 27 (333 performances). Production supervised by Lew Fields. Musical numbers and dances arranged by Seymour Felix. Cast included Helen Ford, Lester Cole, Lulu McConnell, and Betty Starbuck.

Musical Numbers: Hello; A Tree in the Park; Howdy Broadway; A Little Birdie Told Me So; Charming, Charming; Where's That Rainbow?; In His Arms; Chuck It!; I'm So Humble; Havana; Maybe It's Me; Give This Little Girl a Hand.

"Maybe It's Me" appeared originally in the *Fifth Avenue Follies,* a night-club revue produced by Billy Rose at the Fifth Avenue Club in 1926. With lyrics by Donovan Parsons, and called "I'm Crazy 'Bout the Charleston," it appeared in Cochran's 1926 Revue in London.

BETSY. A musical comedy with book by Irving Caesar and David Freedman, revised by Anthony Maguire. Presented by Florenz Ziegfeld at the New Amsterdam Theatre on December 28 (39 performances). Production supervised by Florenz Ziegfeld. Staged by Sammy Lee. Cast included Belle Baker, Allen Kearns, Bobbie Perkins and Al Shean.

Musical Numbers: The Kitzel Engagement; My Missus; Stonewall Moskowitz March; One of Us Should Be Two; Sing; In Our Parlor on the Third Floor Back; This Funny World; Follow On; Push Around; Bugle Blow; Cradle of the Deep; If I Were You; Leave it to Levy (lyrics by Irving Caesar); Birds on High; Shuffle; The Tales of Hoffmann (lyrics by Irving Caesar and A. Segal).

Irving Berlin's "Blue Skies," written expressly for Belle Baker, was interpolated into the production.

1927

ONE DAM THING AFTER ANOTHER (London). A musical revue by Ronald Jeans. Presented by Charles B. Cochran at the London Pavilion on May 20 (237 performances). Dances and ensembles by Max Rivers. Cast included Jessie Matthews and Sonny Hale.

Musical Numbers: I Need Some Cooling Off; My Lucky Star; My Heart Stood Still; Paris Is Really Divine; Gigolo; Sandwich Girls; One Dam Thing After Another; Danse Grotesque à la Nègre; Idles of the King; Make Hey! Make Hey!; Shuffle.

A CONNECTICUT YANKEE. A musical adaptation of Mark Twain's *A Connecticut Yankee in King Arthur's Court,* with book by Herbert Fields. Presented by Lew Fields and Lyle D. Andrews at the Vanderbilt Theatre on November 3 (418 performances). Production supervised by Lew Fields. Staged by Alexander Leftwich. Dances by Busby Berkeley. Cast included William Gaxton, Constance Carpenter, and June Cochrane.

Musical Numbers: A Ladies' Home Companion; My Heart Stood Still; Thou Swell; At the Round Table; On a Desert Island with Thee; Nothing's Wrong; I Feel at Home with You; The Sandwich Men; Evelyn, What Do You Say?.

"I Blush" and "Someone Should Tell Them" were deleted during the out-of-town tryouts.

Revival: Presented by Richard Rodgers at the Martin Beck Theatre on November 17, 1943 (135 performances). Directed by John C. Wilson. Dances by William Holbrook and Al White, Jr. Cast included Dick Foran, Vivienne Segal, and Robert Chisholm. *New musical numbers:* This Is My Night to Howl; To Keep My Love Alive; Ye Lunchtime Follies; Can't You Do a Friend a Favor?; You Always Love the Same Girl; The Camelot Samba.

1928

SHE'S MY BABY. A musical farce comedy with book by Guy Bolton, Bert Kalmar and Harry Ruby. Presented by Charles Dillingham at the Globe Theatre on January 3 (71 performances). Production staged by Edward Royce. Tiller dances arranged by Mary Read. Cast included Jack Whiting, Beatrice Lillie, Clifton Webb, Irene Dunne.

Musical Numbers: This Goes Up; My Lucky Star; You're What I Need; Here She Comes; The Swallows; When I Go on the Stage; Try Again Tomorrow; John Tiller's Lillie Cocktails; Camera Shoot; Where Can the Baby Be?; I Need Some Cooling Off; A Little House in Soho; A Baby's Best Friend; Whoopsie; Wasn't It Great.

"Morning Is Midnight," "Pipes of Pansy," "If I Were You," and "How Was I to Know?" were deleted during out-of-town tryouts.

PRESENT ARMS. A musical comedy with book by Herbert Fields. Presented by Lew Fields at the Lew Fields' Mansfield Theatre on April 26 (155 performances). Production supervised by Lew Fields. Staged by Alexander Leftwich. Musical numbers staged by Busby Berkeley. Cast included Charles King, Flora Le Breton and Busby Berkeley.

Musical Numbers: Tell It to the Marines; You Took Advantage of Me; Do I Hear You?; A Kiss for Cinderella; Is It the Uniform?; Crazy Elbows; Down by the Sea; I'm a Fool For You; Blue Ocean Blues; Hawaii; Kohala.

CHEE-CHEE. A "musical narrative" adapted from Charles Petit's novel, *The Son of the Grand Eunuch,* with book by Herbert Fields. Presented by Lew Fields at the Lew Fields' Mansfield Theatre on September 25 (31 performances). Production supervised by Lew Fields. Staged by Alexander Leftwich. Dances and ensembles by Jack Haskell. Cast included Helen Ford, William Williams, George Hassell and Betty Starbuck.

Musical Numbers: "The musical numbers, some of them very short, are so interwoven with the story that it would be confusing for the audience to peruse a complete list. Among the principal numbers are: I Must Love You; Dear, Oh Dear!; Moon of My Delight; Better Be Good to Me; The Tartar Song; Singing a Love Song." (Note in program.)

1929

SPRING IS HERE. A musical comedy with book by Owen Davis. Presented by Alex A. Aarons and Vinton Freedley at the Alvin Theatre on March 11 (104 performances). Staged by Alexander Leftwich. Dances and ensembles by Bobby Connolly. With Glenn Hunter, Lillian Taiz, Inez Courtney, and Charles Ruggles.

Musical Numbers: Spring Is Here; Yours Sincerely; You Never Say Yes; With a Song in My Heart; Baby's Awake Now; Red Hot Trumpet; What a Girl; Rich Man! Poor Man!; Why Can't I?.

HEADS UP. A musical comedy with book by John McGowan and Paul Gerard Smith. Presented by Alex A. Aarons and Vinton Freedley at the Alvin Theatre on November 11 (144 performances). Dances and ensembles by George Hale. Cast included Jack Whiting, Barbara Newberry, Victor Moore, Betty Starbuck, Ray Bolger, and Janet Velie.

Musical Numbers: You've Got to Surrender; Play Boy; Mother Grows Younger; Why Do You Suppose?; Me for You; Ongsay and Anceday; It Must Be Heaven; My Man Is On the Make; The Lass Who Loved a Sailor; A Ship Without a Sail; Knees.

"Sky City" and "I Can Do Wonders with You" were deleted during out-of-town tryouts.

1930

SIMPLE SIMON. A musical comedy with book by Ed Wynn and Guy Bolton. Presented by Florenz Ziegfeld at the Ziegfeld Theatre on February 18 (151 performances). Ensembles and dances staged by Seymour Felix. Cast included Ed Wynn, Ruth Etting, and Harriet Hoctor.

Musical Numbers: Coney Island; Don't Tell Your Folks; Magic Music; Ten Cents a Dance; Send for Me; Dull and Gay; Sweetenheart; Hunting the Fox; Hunting Ballet; Mocking Bird; I

Love the Woods; On with the Dance; I Want That Man;
Lonely Days and Lonely Nights; Roping; Kissing Forest
Ballet; Rags and Tatters; Cottage in the Country.

"Dancing on the Ceiling" was deleted during out-of-town
tryouts and used in *Evergreen,* produced in London; "I Can
Do Wonders with You" was also deleted out of town.

EVERGREEN (London). A musical comedy with book by Benn W.
Levy. Presented by Charles B. Cochran at the Adelphi Theatre,
London, December 3 (254 performances). Production supervised by Charles B. Cochran. Staged by Frank Collins. Dances
and ensembles by Buddy Bradley and Billy Pierce. Cast included Jessie Matthews and Sonny Hale.

Musical Numbers: Harlemania; Doing a Little Clog Dance;
Dear, Dear; Nobody Looks at the Man; Waiting for the
Leaves to Fall; No Place But Home; The Lion King; Quand
Notre Vieux Monde Etait Tout Neuf; La Femme A Toujours
Vingt Ans (Lovely Woman's Ever Young); The Color of Her
Eyes; In the Cool of the Evening; Dancing on the Ceiling; Je
M'en Fiche du Sex Appeal; If I Give In to You.

1931

AMERICA'S SWEETHEART. A musical comedy with book by Herbert
Fields. Presented by Laurence Schwab and Frank Mandel at
the Broadhurst Theatre on February 10 (135 performances).
Produced under the supervision of Bobby Connolly. Book
directed by Monty Woolley. Cast included Jack Whiting,
Harriet Lake (Ann Southern), Inez Courtney and Virginia
Bruce.

Musical Numbers: Mr. Dolan Is Passing Through; In Califor-
n-i-a; My Sweet; I've Got Five Dollars; Sweet Geraldine;
There's So Much More; We'll Be the Same; How About It?;
Innocent Chorus Girls of Yesterday; A Lady Must Live; You
Ain't Got No Savoir Faire; Two Unfortunate Orphans; I
Want a Man; Tennessee Dan.

1935

JUMBO. A spectacular musical comedy with book by Ben Hecht and Charles MacArthur. Presented by Billy Rose at the Hippodrome on November 16 (233 performances). Production staged by John Murray Anderson. Book directed by George Abbott. Equestrian, acrobatic and aerial ballets by Allan K. Foster. Rhythmic movement and dance impressions by Marjery Fielding. Cast included Jimmy Durante, Gloria Grafton, Donald Novis, and Paul Whiteman and His Orchestra.

Musical Numbers: Over and Over Again; The Circus Is on Parade; The Most Beautiful Girl in the World; Laugh; My Romance; Little Girl Blue; The Song of the Roustabouts; Women; Memories of Madison Square Garden; Diavolo; The Circus Wedding.

1936

ON YOUR TOES. A musical comedy with book by Rodgers and Hart and George Abbott. Presented by Dwight Deere Wiman at the Imperial Theatre on April 11 (315 performances). Staged by Worthington Miner. Choreography by George Balanchine. Cast included Ray Bolger, Tamara Geva, Doris Carson, Luella Gear, and Monty Woolley.

Musical Numbers: Two-a-day for Keith; The Three B's; It's Got to Be Love; Too Good for the Average Man; There's a Small Hotel; The Heart Is Quicker Than the Eye; Quiet Night; Glad to Be Unhappy; On Your Toes; Slaughter on Tenth Avenue.

Revival: Staged and revised by George Abbott at the Forty-sixth Street Theatre on October 11, 1954 (64 performances). Dances by George Balanchine. Cast included Bobby Van, Vera Zorina, Kay Coulter, and Elaine Stritch. "You Took Advantage of Me" was lifted from *Present Arms* and interpolated for Elaine Stritch in the final scene.

1937

BABES IN ARMS. A musical comedy with book by Rodgers and Hart. Presented by Dwight Deere Wiman at the Shubert Theatre on April 14 (289 performances). Staged by Robert Sinclair. Choreography by George Balanchine. Cast included Mitzi Green, Alfred Drake, Wynn Murray, and Ray Heatherton.

Musical Numbers: Where or When?; Babes in Arms; I Wish I Were in Love Again; All Dark People; Way Out West; My Funny Valentine; Johnny One Note; Imagine; All at Once; Peter's Journey Ballet; The Lady Is a Tramp; You Are So Fair.

I'D RATHER BE RIGHT. A musical comedy by George S. Kaufman and Moss Hart. Presented by Sam H. Harris at the Alvin Theatre on November 2 (290 performances). Book staged by George S. Kaufman. Choreography by Charles Weidman. Cast included George M. Cohan, Austin Marshall, Joy Hodges, and Florenz Ames.

Musical Numbers: A Homogenous Cabinet; Have You Met Miss Jones?; Take and Take and Take; Spring in Vienna; A Little Bit of Constitutional Fun; Sweet Sixty-Five; We're Going to Balance the Budget; American Couple; Labor Is the Thing; I'd Rather Be Right; Off the Record; A Baby Bond.

1938

I MARRIED AN ANGEL. A musical comedy from the play by John Vaszary, with book by Rodgers and Hart. Presented by Dwight Deere Wiman at the Shubert Theatre on May 11 (338 performances). Staged by Joshua Logan. Choreography by George Balanchine. Cast included Dennis King, Vera Zorina, Vivienne Segal, Audrey Christie, and Walter Slezak.

Musical Numbers: Did You Ever Get Stung?; I Married an Angel; The Modiste; Honeymoon Ballet; I'll Tell the Man in the Street; How to Win Friends and Influence People; Spring Is

Here; Angel Without Wings; A Twinkle in Your Eye; At the Roxy Music Hall.

THE BOYS FROM SYRACUSE. A musical comedy based on Shakespeare's *A Comedy of Errors,* with book by George Abbott. Presented by George Abbott at the Alvin Theatre on November 23 (235 performances). Directed by George Abbott. Choreography by George Balanchine. Cast included Jimmy Savo, Teddy Hart, Eddie Albert, Ronald Graham, Muriel Angelus and Marcy Wescott.

Musical Numbers: I Had Twins; Dear Old Syracuse; What Can You Do with a Man?; Falling in Love with Love; The Shortest Day of the Year; This Can't Be Love; Let Antipholus In; Ladies of the Evening; He and She; You Have Cast Your Shadow; Come with Me; Big Brother; Sing for Your Supper; Oh, Diogenes.

1939

TOO MANY GIRLS. A musical comedy with book by George Marion, Jr. Presented by George Abbott at the Imperial Theatre on October 18 (249 performances). Directed by George Abbott. Dances by Robert Alton. Cast included Richard Kollmar, Desi Arnaz, Eddie Bracken, Diosa Costello, and Mary Jane Walsh.

Musical Numbers: Heroes in the Fall; Tempt Me Not; My Prince; Pottawatomie; 'Cause We Got Cake; Love Never Went to College; Spic and Spanish; I Like to Recognize the Tune; Look Out; The Sweethearts of the Team; She Could Shake the Maracas; I Didn't Know What Time It Was; Too Many Girls; Give It Back to the Indians.

1940

HIGHER AND HIGHER. A musical comedy with book by Gladys Hurlbut and Joshua Logan, based on an idea by Irvin Pincus. Presented by Dwight Deere Wiman at the Shubert Theatre on April 4 (108 performances). Staged by Joshua Logan. Dances by Robert Alton. Cast included Jack Haley, Marta Eggert, Shirley Ross, and Leif Erickson.

Musical Numbers: A Barking Baby Never Bites; From Another World; Mornings at Seven; Nothing But You; So Disgustingly Rich; Blue Monday; Ev'ry Sunday Afternoon; Lovely Day for a Murder; How's Your Health?; It Never Entered My Mind; I'm Afraid.

PAL JOEY. A musical comedy based on a series of stories by John O'Hara with book by O'Hara. Presented by George Abbott at the Ethel Barrymore Theatre on December 25 (270 performances). Production staged by George Abbott. Dances by Robert Alton. Cast included Gene Kelly, June Havoc, Vivienne Segal and Leila Ernst.

Musical Numbers: You Mustn't Kick It Around; I Could Write a Book; Chicago; That Terrific Rainbow; What Is a Man?; Happy Hunting Horn; Bewitched, Bothered and Bewildered; The Flower Garden of My Heart; Zip; Plant You Now, Dig You Later; In Our Little Den of Iniquity; Do It the Hard Way; Take Him.

Revival: Presented by Jule Styne and Leonard Key in association with Anthony B. Farrell at the Broadhurst Theatre on January 3, 1952 (542 performances). Production supervised by Robert Alton. Book directed by David Alexander. Dance and musical numbers staged by Robert Alton. Cast included Harold Lang, Helen Gallagher, Vivienne Segal, and Pat Northrop.

1942

BY JUPITER. A musical comedy based on Julian F. Thompson's *The Warrior's Husband,* with book by Rodgers and Hart. Presented by Dwight Deere Wiman and Richard Rodgers in association with Richard Kollmar at the Shubert Theatre on June 2 (427 performances). Staged by Joshua Logan. Dances by Robert Alton. Cast included Ray Bolger, Benay Venuta, Vera-Ellen, Ronald Graham, and Constance Moore.

Musical Numbers: For Jupiter and Greece; Jupiter Forbid; Life with Father; Nobody's Heart Belongs to Me; The Gateway of the Temple of Minerva; Here's a Hand; No, Mother, No; The Boy I Left Behind Me; Ev'rything I've Got; Bottoms Up; Careless Rhapsody; Wait Till You See Her; Now That I've Got My Strength.

2 with Oscar Hammerstein II

1943

OKLAHOMA!. A musical play based on Lynn Riggs' *Green Grow the Lilacs,* with book and lyrics by Oscar Hammerstein II. Presented by the Theatre Guild at the St. James Theatre on March 31 (2248 performances). Production directed by Rouben Mamoulian. Dances by Agnes de Mille. Cast included Alfred Drake, Joan Roberts, Celeste Holm, Betty Garde, Joan Mc-Cracken, Bambi Linn, Howard da Silva, and Joseph Buloff.

Musical Numbers: Oh, What a Beautiful Mornin'; The Surrey with the Fringe on Top; Kansas City; I Cain't Say No; Many a New Day; It's a Scandal!; People Will Say We're in Love; Pore Jud; Lonely Room; Out of My Dream; Laurey Makes Up Her Mind; The Farmer and the Cowman; All 'er Nothin'; Oklahoma!.

"Boys and Girls Like You and Me" was deleted during out-of-town tryouts.

Revivals: Reproduced by Jerome Whyte at the Broadway Theatre on May 28, 1951, for eight weeks. A New York engagement of the National Company. Cast included Ridge Bond, Patricia Northrop, Jacqueline Sundt and Jerry Mann. Presented by Rodgers and Hammerstein at the New York City Center on August 31, 1953, for five weeks. Cast included Ridge Bond, Florence Henderson, Barbara Cook, and David Le Grant.

1945

CAROUSEL. A musical play based on Ferenc Molnar's *Liliom,* with book and lyrics by Oscar Hammerstein II. Produced by the

Theatre Guild at the Majestic Theatre on April 19 (890 performances). Staged by Rouben Mamoulian. Dances by Agnes de Mille. Cast included John Raitt, Jan Clayton, and Jean Darling.

Musical Numbers: Waltz Suite; You're a Queer One, Julie Jordan; When I Marry Mr. Snow; If I Loved You; June Is Bustin' Out All Over; When the Children Are Asleep; Blow High, Blow Low; Soliloquy; This Was a Real Nice Clam Bake; Geraniums in the Winder; There's Nothin' So Bad for a Woman; What's the Use of Wond'rin'; You'll Never Walk Alone; The Highest Judge of All.

Revivals: Produced by the Theatre Guild at the New York City Center on January 25, 1949 (49 performances). Cast included Stephen Douglass and Iva Withers. Produced by the New York City Light Opera Company. Staged by William Hammerstein. Restaged by Robert Pagent. Cast included Chris Robinson and Jo Sullivan.

1947

ALLEGRO. A musical play with book and lyrics by Oscar Hammerstein II. Produced by the Theatre Guild at the Majestic Theatre on October 10 (315 performances). Stage production supervised by Lawrence Langer and Theresa Helburn. Choreography by Agnes de Mille. Cast included John Battles, Roberta Jonay, William Ching and Annamary Dickey.

Musical Numbers: Joseph Taylor, Jr.; I Know It Can Happen Again; One Foot, Other Foot; A Fellow Needs a Girl; Freshman Dance; As They Imagine They Are; A Darn Nice Campus; The Purple and Brown; So Far; You Are Never Away; What a Lovely Day for a Wedding; It May Be a Good Idea for Joe; Wedding; To Have and to Hold; Wish Them Well; Money Isn't Everything; Hazel Dances; Yatata, Yatata; The Gentleman Is a Dope; Allegro; Come Home.

1949

SOUTH PACIFIC. A musical play adapted from James A. Michener's *Tales of the South Pacific,* with book by Oscar Hammerstein II and Joshua Logan. Presented by Rodgers and Hammerstein in association with Leland Hayward and Joshua Logan at the Majestic Theatre on April 7 (1,925 performances). Book and musical numbers staged by Joshua Logan. Cast included Mary Martin, Ezio Pinza, William Tabbert, Juanita Hall, and Betta St. John.

Musical Numbers: Dites-Moi Pourquoi; A Cockeyed Optimist; Some Enchanted Evening; Bloody Mary Is the Girl I Love; There Is Nothing Like a Dame; Bali Ha'i; I'm Gonna Wash That Man Right Outa My Hair; I'm in Love with a Wonderful Guy; Younger than Springtime; Soft Shoe Dance; Happy Talk; Honey Bun; You've Got to Be Taught; This Nearly Was Mine.

"Loneliness of Evening" and "My Girl Back Home" were deleted during out-of-town tryouts.

Revivals: Produced by the New York City Light Opera Company at the New York City Center on May 4, 1955, for two weeks. Staged by Charles Atkin. Cast included Sandra Deel, Richard Collett, Sylvia Sims and Herb Banke. Produced by the New York City Light Opera Company at the New York City Center on April 24, 1957, for three weeks. Directed by John Fearnley. Cast included Mindy Carson and Robert Wright.

1951

THE KING AND I. A play with music based on the novel *Anna and the King of Siam* by Margaret Landon, with book and lyrics by Oscar Hammerstein II. Presented by Rodgers and Hammerstein at the St. James Theatre on March 29 (1246 performances). Directed by John Van Druten. Choreography by Jerome Robbins. Cast included Gertrude Lawrence, Yul Brynner, Dorothy Sarnoff, and Doretta Morrow.

Revival: Produced by the New York City Light Opera Company at the New York City Center on April 18, 1956, for two weeks. Directed by John Fearnley. Cast included Jan Clayton and Zachary Scott.

Musical Numbers: I Whistle a Happy Tune; My Lord and Master; Hello, Young Lovers; The Royal Siamese Children; A Puzzlement; The Royal Bangkok Academy; Getting to Know You; We Kiss in a Shadow; Shall I Tell You What I Think Of You?; Something Wonderful; Western People; I Have Dreamed; The Small House of Uncle Thomas; Shall We Dance?.

1953

ME AND JULIET. A musical comedy with book and lyrics by Oscar Hammerstein II. Presented by Rodgers and Hammerstein at the Majestic Theatre on May 28 (358 performances). Directed by George Abbott. Dances and vocal numbers staged by Robert Alton. Cast included Isabel Bigley, Bill Hayes and Joan McCracken.

Musical Numbers: A Very Special Day; That's the Way It Happens; Dance Impromptu; Overture to Me and Juliet; Opening of Me and Juliet; Marriage Type Love; Keep It Gay; The Big, Black Giant; No Other Love; It's Me; First Act Finale of Me and Juliet; Intermission Talk; It Feels Good; Sequence in Second Act of Me and Juliet; The Baby You Love; We Deserve Each Other; I'm Your Girl; Second Act Finale of Me and Juliet; Finale of Our Play.

1955

PIPE DREAM. A musical play based on *Sweet Thursday,* by John Steinbeck, with book and lyrics by Oscar Hammerstein II. Presented by Rodgers and Hammerstein at the Shubert Theatre on November 30 (246 performances). Staged by Harold Clurman. Choreography by Boris Runanin. Cast included Helen Traubel, Bill Johnson, and Judy Tyler.

Musical Numbers: All Kinds of People; The Tide Pool; Everybody's Got a Home but Me; A Lopsided Bus; Bum's Opera; The Man I Used to Be; Sweet Thursday; Suzy is a Good Thing; All at Once; The Happiest House on the Block; The Party That We're Gonna Have Tomorrow Night; Will You Marry Me?; Thinkin'; How Long?; The Next Time It Happens.

1957

CINDERELLA (A production for television). Based on the fairy tale by Charles Perrault. Produced by Richard Lewine over the CBS-TV network on March 31. Directed by Ralph Nelson. Cast included Julie Andrews, Howard Lindsay, Dorothy Stickney, Ilka Chase, Kaye Ballard, Alice Ghostley, Edith Adams, and Jon Cypher.

Musical Numbers: Mother and Daughter March; In My Own Little Corner; The Prince Is Giving a Ball; Impossible; Gavotte; Ten Minutes Ago; Stepsisters' Lament; Do I Love You?; Waltz for a Ball; A Lovely Night; Finale.

ii

OTHER MUSIC BY RODGERS

1936

ALL POINTS WEST, a symphonic narrative with text by Lorenz Hart. Orchestrated by Adolph Deutsch. Première: Philadelphia Orchestra under Paul Whiteman, with Ray Middleton, Philadelphia, November 27.

1938

NURSERY BALLET, a suite for piano orchestrated by Roy Bargy. I. March of the Clowns; II. A Doll Gets Broken; III. Little Girls Don't Fight. Première: Paul Whiteman and Orchestra, Carnegie Hall, New York, December 25.

1939

GHOST TOWN. An American Folk Ballet in one scene, prologue and epilogue. Libretto by Rodgers and Marc Platoff. Presented by S. Hurok, and produced by the Ballet Russe de Monte Carlo at the Metropolitan Opera House on November 12. Choreography by Marc Platoff. Cast included Mia Slavenska and Frederic Franklin.

1952

VICTORY AT SEA. Orchestral suite arranged by Robert Russell Bennett from the musical background to the documentary film *Victory at Sea*. I. The Song of the High Seas; II. The Pacific Boils Over; III. Guadalcanal March; IV. D Day; V. Hard Work and Horseplay; VI. Theme of the Fast Carriers; VII. Beneath the Southern Cross; VIII. Mare Nostrum; IX. Victory at Sea. Première: "Guadalcanal March," Lewisohn Stadium Orchestra under Rodgers, Lewisohn Stadium, New York, August 3. (See also Original Scores for Motion Pictures.)

iii

STAGE PRODUCTIONS
WITH INTERPOLATED SONGS

1 with Lorenz Hart

1919

A LONELY ROMEO. A musical comedy with book by Harry B. Smith and Lew Fields, music by Malvin F. Franklin, and lyrics by Robert B. Smith. Produced by Lew Fields at the Casino Theatre in August (87 performances). Cast included Lew Fields, Herbert Fields, Alan Hale and Frances Cameron.
Musical Number: Any Old Place with You.

1935

SOMETHING GAY. A play by Adelaide Heilbron. Presented by the Shuberts at the Morosco Theatre on April 29 (72 perform-

ances). Staged by Thomas Mitchell. Cast included Tallulah Bankhead, Walter Pidgeon and Nancy Ryan.
Musical Number: You Are So Lovely and I'm So Lonely.

1936

THE SHOW IS ON. A revue. Presented by the Shuberts at the Winter Garden on December 25 (237 performances). Entire production conceived, staged, and designed by Vincente Minnelli. Dances and principals' numbers staged by Robert Alton. Sketches by David Freedman and Moss Hart. Music and lyrics by Vernon Duke and Ted Fetter, Hoagy Carmichael and Stanley Adams, Arthur Schwartz and Howard Dietz, George and Ira Gershwin, Harold Arlen and E. Y. Harburg, Herman Hupfeld, Will Irwin, and Norman Zeno.
Musical Number: Rhythm.

2 with Oscar Hammerstein

1948

HAPPY BIRTHDAY. A play by Anita Loos. Presented by Rodgers and Hammerstein at the Broadhurst Theatre on October 31 (564 performances). Directed by Joshua Logan. Cast included Helen Hayes and Louis Jean Heydt.
Musical Number: I Haven't Got a Worry in the World.

iv

MOTION-PICTURE ADAPTATIONS
OF STAGE PRODUCTIONS

1930

SPRING IS HERE. A Warner Brothers-First National Picture. Directed by John Francis Dillon. Screenplay by James A. Starr. Cast included Bernice Claire, Alexander Gray and Inez Courtney.

Musical Numbers: Two songs were used: Yours Sincerely; With a Song In My Heart, both sung by Bernice Claire and Alexander Gray. Remaining songs were by Sam Lewis, Joe Young, and Henry Warren.

HEADS UP. A Paramount Picture. Directed by Victor Schertzinger. Screenplay by John McGowan and Paul Gerard Smith. Cast included Charles "Buddy" Rogers, Helen Kane, and Victor Moore.

Musical Numbers: Two songs were used: A Ship Without a Sail (Buddy Rogers); My Man Is On the Make (Helen Kane).

1935

EVERGREEN. A Gaumont British Picture. Directed by Victor Saville. Screenplay by Benn W. Levy. Cast included Sonny Hale and Jessie Matthews.

Musical Numbers: Four songs were used: In the Cool of the Evening; If I Give In to You; Dear, Dear; Dancing on the Ceiling. Additional songs were by Harry M. Woods.

1939

ON YOUR TOES. A Warner Brothers Picture. Directed by Ray Enright. Screenplay by Jerry Wald and Richard Macauley. Adaptation by Sig Herzig and Lawrence Riley. Cast included Vera Zorina, Eddie Albert, James Gleason and Frank McHugh.

Musical Numbers: Four numbers were used: There's a Small Hotel; Quiet Night; On Your Toes; Slaughter on Tenth Avenue.

BABES IN ARMS. A Metro-Goldwyn-Mayer Picture. Produced by Arthur Freed. Directed by Busby Berkeley. Screenplay by Jack McGowan and Kay Van Riper. Cast included Mickey Rooney, Judy Garland, Charles Winninger and Guy Kibbee.

Musical Numbers: Three numbers were used: Where or When? (Betty Jaynes and Douglas McPhail); The Lady Is a Tramp; Babes in Arms (Mickey Rooney, Judy Garland and others). Additional songs were by Nacio Brown and Arthur Freed, Harold Arlen and E. Y. Yarburg.

1940

THE BOYS FROM SYRACUSE. A Universal Picture. Produced by Jules Levy. Directed by Edward Sutherland. Screenplay by Leonard Spiegelgass and Charles Grayson. Cast included Allan Jones, Martha Raye, Joe Penner, Rosemary Lane, and Charles Butterworth.

Musical Numbers: Four numbers were used: Falling in Love with Love (Allan Jones); He and She (Martha Raye and Joe Penner); This Can't Be Love (Rosemary Lane); Sing for Your Supper (Raye). Two additional numbers were written for the picture: Who Are You? (Jones); The Greeks Had No Word for It (Raye).

TOO MANY GIRLS. An RKO-Radio Picture. Produced and directed by George Abbott. Screenplay by John Twist. Cast included Desi Arnaz, Lucille Ball, Hal LeRoy, Eddie Bracken, and Frances Langford.

Musical Numbers: Eight numbers were used: I Didn't Know What Time It Was; Love Never Went to College; I Like to Recognize the Tune; Pottawatomie; 'Cause We Got Cake; Spic and Spanish; Look Out; Heroes in the Fall. An additional number was written for the picture: You're Nearer.

1942

I MARRIED AN ANGEL. A Metro-Goldwyn-Mayer Picture. Produced by Hunt Stromberg. Directed by W. S. Van Dyke II. Screenplay by Anita Loos. Cast included Nelson Eddy, Jeanette Mac-Donald and Edward Everett Horton.

Musical Numbers: Five numbers were used: I Married an Angel; I'll Tell the Man in the Street; Spring Is Here; A Twinkle in Your Eye; At the Roxy Music Hall. Additional songs by Herbert Stothart, Chet Forrest and Bob Wright.

1944

HIGHER AND HIGHER. An RKO-Radio Picture. Directed by Tim Whelan. Screenplay by Jay Dratler and Ralph Spence. Cast included Jack Haley, Michele Morgan, Frank Sinatra, and Leon Errol.

Musical Numbers: Only one number was used: So Disgustingly Rich. A few other numbers from the stage production were used as background music. All other numbers were written for the motion picture by Jimmy McHugh and Harold Adamson.

1955

OKLAHOMA! A Magna Theatre Corporation Picture in the Todd-AO process. Produced by Arthur Hornblow, Jr. Directed by Fred Zinnemann. Screenplay by Sonya Levien and William Ludwig. Dances staged by Agnes de Mille. Cast included Gordon MacRae, Shirley Jones, Gloria Graham, Charlotte Greenwood, Rod Steiger, and Eddie Albert.
Musical Numbers: Virtually the entire score was used.

1956

CAROUSEL. A Twentieth Century-Fox Picture. Produced by Henry Ephron. Directed by Henry King. Screenplay by Henry and Phoebe Ephron. Dances by Rod Alexander and Bambi Linn. Cast included Gordon MacRae, Shirley Jones, Barbara Ruick, Robert Rounseville, Audrey Christie, and Claramae Turner.
Musical Numbers: Virtually the entire score was used.

THE KING AND I. A Twentieth Century-Fox Picture. Produced by Charles Brackett. Directed by Walter Lang. Screenplay by Ernest Lehman. Choreography by Jerome Robbins. Cast included Deborah Kerr, Yul Brynner and Rita Morena.
Musical Numbers: Virtually the entire score was used.

1957

SOUTH PACIFIC (In preparation).
PAL JOEY (In preparation).

𝒱

ORIGINAL SCORES
FOR MOTION PICTURES

1 with Lorenz Hart

1931

THE HOT HEIRESS. A First National Picture. Directed by Clarence Badger. Screenplay by Herbert Fields. Cast included Ben Lyon, Ona Munson and Walter Pidgeon.
Musical Numbers: Like Common People Do; You're the Cats; Nobody Loves a Riveter.

1932

LOVE ME TONIGHT. A Paramount Picture. Directed by Rouben Mamoulian. Screenplay by Samuel Hoffenstein, Waldemar Young, and George Marion, Jr., based on a play by Leopold Marchand and Paul Armont. Cast included Maurice Chevalier, Jeanette MacDonald, Charlie Ruggles, Charles Butterworth, and Myrna Loy.

Musical Numbers: That's the Song of Paree; Mimi; He's Nothing but a Tailor; Isn't It Romantic?; Love Me Tonight; Lover; The Poor Apache.

THE PHANTOM PRESIDENT. A Paramount Picture. Directed by Norman Taurog. Screenplay by Walter de Leon and Harlan Thompson. Cast included George M. Cohan, Claudette Colbert, and Jimmy Durante.

Musical Numbers: Give Her a Kiss; The Country Needs a Man; Somebody Ought to Wave a Flag. George M. Cohan's "A Grand Old Flag" was interpolated for him.

1933

HALLELUJAH I'M A BUM. A United Artists Release. Produced by Joseph M. Schenck. Directed by Lewis Milestone. Screenplay by S. N. Behrman on a story by Ben Hecht. Cast included Al Jolson, Madge Evans, and Frank Morgan.

Musical Numbers: Hallelujah I'm a Bum; You Are Too Beautiful; What Do You Want with Money?; I'll Do It Again; Bumper's Found a Grand; I Got to Get Back to New York; Sleeping Beauty; Laying the Cornerstone.

DANCING LADY. A Metro-Goldwyn-Mayer Picture. Produced by David O. Selznik. Directed by Robert Z. Leonard. Screenplay by Allen Rivkin and P. J. Wolfson, based on a novel by James Warner Bellah. Dances by Sammy Lee and Eddie Prinz. Cast included Clark Gable, Joan Crawford, and Franchot Tone. Fred Astaire and Nelson Eddy played themselves.

Musical Numbers: Only one number was used: That's the Rhythm of the Day. All other songs were by Burton Lane and Harold Adamson, and Jimmy McHugh and Dorothy Fields.

1934

NANA. A United Artists Release. Produced by Samuel Goldwyn. Directed by Dorothy Arzner. Based on the novel of Emile Zola, adapted by Willard Mack and Harry Wagstaff Gribble. Cast included Anna Sten and Phillip Holmes.
Musical Numbers: Only one number was used: That's Love.

MANHATTAN MELODRAMA. A Metro-Goldwyn-Mayer Picture. A Cosmopolitan Production by David O. Selznik. Directed by W. S. Van Dyke. Screenplay by Oliver H. P. Garrett and Joseph L. Mankiewicz. Cast included Clark Gable, Myrna Loy, and William Powell.
Musical Numbers: Only one number was used: The Bad in Every Man.

HOLLYWOOD PARTY. A Metro-Goldwyn-Mayer Picture. Produced by Howard Dietz and Harry Rapf. Screenplay by Howard Dietz and Arthur Kober. Dances by Seymour Felix, George Hale, and David Gould. Cast included Jimmy Durante, Lupe Velez, Polly Moran, and Charles Butterworth. Laurel and Hardy, Frances Williams, and Mickey Mouse played themselves.
Musical Numbers: Hello; Hollywood Party; Reincarnation. All other numbers were by Walter Donaldson and Gus Kahn, and Nacio Herb Brown and Arthur Freed.

1935

MISSISSIPPI. A Paramount Picture. Produced by Arthur Hornblow. Directed by A. Edward Sutherland. Based on an original story by Booth Tarkington, adapted by Herbert Fields and Claude Binyon. Cast included Bing Crosby, W. C. Fields, Joan Bennett, and Queenie Smith.
Musical Numbers: Soon; Easy to Remember; Down by the River.

1936

DANCING PIRATE. An RKO-Radio Picture. A Pioneer Production. Directed by Lloyd Corrigan. Story by Emma-Lindsey Squier. Screenplay by Ray Harris and Francis Faragoh. Cast included Charles Collins, Steffi Duna, Frank Morgan, and Victor Varconi.
Musical Numbers: When You're Dancing the Waltz; Are You My Love?

1938

FOOLS FOR SCANDAL. A Warner Brothers-First National Picture. Produced and directed by Mervyn LeRoy. Screenplay by Herbert Fields and Joseph Fields based on a play by Nancy Hamilton, James Shute, and Rosemarie Casey. Cast included Carole Lombard, Fernand Gravet and Ralph Bellamy.
Musical Numbers: There's a Boy in Harlem; How Can You Forget?; Food for Scandal.

1941

THEY MET IN ARGENTINA. An RKO-Radio Picture. Directed by Leslie Goodwins and Jack Hively. Story by Lou Brock and Harold Daniels. Screenplay by Jerry Cady. Cast included Maureen O'Hara, James Ellison and Buddy Ebsen.
Musical Numbers: Amarillo; Cutting the Cain; Simpatica; You've Got the Best of Me; Never Go to Argentina; Lolita; North America Meets South America.

1948

WORDS AND MUSIC. A Metro-Goldwyn-Mayer Picture. Directed by Norman Taurog. Produced by Arthur Freed. This was a screen biography of Rodgers and Hart, with story by Guy Bolton and

Jean Holloway, and screenplay by Fred Finklehoffe. Musical numbers staged and directed by Robert Alton. Cast included Tom Drake as Richard Rodgers, Mickey Rooney as Larry Hart, Janet Leigh as Dorothy Feiner, Harry Antrim as Dr. Rodgers, and Ilka Gruning as Mrs. Rodgers. June Allyson, Judy Garland, Lena Horne, Gene Kelly, Cyd Charisse, Mel Torme, Vera-Ellen appeared as themselves.

Musical Numbers: There's a Small Hotel; Way Out West; With a Song in My Heart; Where's That Rainbow?; Thou Swell; The Lady Is a Tramp; Where or When?; I Wish I Were in Love Again; Blue Moon; Johnny One Note; Manhattan Mountain Greenery; The Blue Room; Spring Is Here; Slaughter on Tenth Avenue; On Your Toes Ballet; This Can't Be Love Ballet; Lover; You Took Advantage of Me; Ev'rything I've Got Belongs to You; I Married an Angel; My Heart Stood Still.

2 with Oscar Hammerstein II

1945

STATE FAIR. A Twentieth Century-Fox Picture. Produced by William Perlberg. Directed by Walter Lang. Screenplay by Oscar Hammerstein II, based on the novel by Phil Stong.

Musical Numbers: Our State Fair; It Might As Well Be Spring; That's for Me; It's a Grand Night for Singing; Isn't it Kinda Fun; All I Owe Iowa.

"It Might As Well Be Spring" won the Academy Award.

1953

MAIN STREET TO BROADWAY. A motion picture based on a story by Robert E. Sherwood, produced for the Council of the Living Theatre by Lester Cowan and released by Metro-Goldwyn-Mayer. Cast included Rodgers and Hammerstein, Mary Martin, Gertrude Lawrence, Ethel Barrymore, Helen Hayes, Tallulah Bankhead, and many others.

Rodgers and Hammerstein contributed one new song: "There's Music in You," sung by Mary Martin.

3 miscellaneous

1952

VICTORY AT SEA. A documentary film of the naval encounters of World War II presented for twenty-six weeks over the NBC-TV network with the cooperation of the U.S. Navy. Produced by Henry Salomon. Written by Salomon and Richard Hanser.

THE GREATEST SONGS
OF RICHARD RODGERS
(and the stars who introduced them)

1   with Lorenz Hart

Bewitched, Bothered and Bewildered. Introduced by Vivienne Segal in *Pal Joey*.

The Blue Room. Introduced by Eva Puck and Sam White in *The Girl Friend*.

Careless Rhapsody. Introduced by Constance Moore and Ronald Graham in *By Jupiter*.

Dancing on the Ceiling. Introduced by Sonny Hale and Jessie Matthews in *Evergreen*.

Falling in Love with Love. Introduced by Muriel Angelus in *The Boys from Syracuse*.

The Girl Friend. Introduced by Eva Puck and Sam White in *The Girl Friend*.

Have You Met Miss Jones?. Introduced by Joy Hodges and Austin Marshall in *I'd Rather Be Right*.

Here in My Arms. Introduced by Helen Ford and Charles Purcell in *Dearest Enemy*.

I Could Write a Book. Introduced by Gene Kelly and Leila Ernst in *Pal Joey*.

I Didn't Know What Time It Was. Introduced by Marcy Wescott and Dick Kollmar in *Too Many Girls*.

I Feel at Home with You. Introduced by Jack Thompson and June Cochrane in *A Connecticut Yankee*.

I Married an Angel. Introduced by Dennis King in *I Married an Angel*.

I Must Love You. Introduced by Helen Ford and William Williams in *Chee-Chee*.

Isn't It Romantic?. Introduced by Maurice Chevalier and Jeanette MacDonald in *Love Me Tonight*.

It Never Entered My Mind. Introduced by Shirley Ross in *Higher and Higher*.

I've Got Five Dollars. Introduced by Hariette Lake (Ann Sothern) and Jack Whiting in *America's Sweetheart*.

Johnny One Note. Introduced by Wynn Murray and chorus in *Babes in Arms*.

The Lady Is a Tramp. Introduced by Mitzi Green in *Babes in Arms*.

Little Girl Blue. Introduced by Gloria Grafton in *Jumbo*.

Lover. Introduced by Jeanette MacDonald in *Love Me Tonight*.

Manhattan. Introduced by June Cochrane and Sterling Holloway in the first *Garrick Gaieties*.

Mimi. Introduced by Maurice Chevalier in *Love Me Tonight*.

The Most Beautiful Girl in the World. Introduced by Donald Novis and Gloria Grafton in *Jumbo*.

Mountain Greenery. Introduced by Bobbie Perkins and Sterling Holloway in the second *Garrick Gaieties*.

My Funny Valentine. Introduced by Mitzi Green in *Babes in Arms*.

My Heart Stood Still. Introduced by Jessie Matthews and Sonny Hale in *One Dam Thing After Another* and by William Gaxton and Constance Carpenter in *A Connecticut Yankee*.

My Romance. Introduced by Donald Novis and Gloria Grafton in *Jumbo*.

Nobody's Heart Belongs to Me. Introduced by Constance Moore in *By Jupiter*.

On a Desert Island with Thee. Introduced by Jack Thompson and June Cochrane in *A Connecticut Yankee*.

Sentimental Me. Introduced by June Cochrane, James Norris, Edith Meiser, and Sterling Holloway in the first *Garrick Gaieties*.

A Ship Without a Sail. Introduced by Jack Whiting in *Heads Up*.

Spring Is Here. Introduced by Dick Keene and Inez Courtney in *Spring Is Here*.

Ten Cents a Dance. Introduced by Ruth Etting in *Simple Simon*.

There's a Small Hotel. Introduced by Doris Carson and Ray Bolger in *On Your Toes*.

This Can't Be Love. Introduced by Marcy Wescott and Eddie Albert in *The Boys from Syracuse*.

Thou Swell. Introduced by William Gaxton and Constance Carpenter in *A Connecticut Yankee*.

To Keep My Love Alive. Introduced by Vivienne Segal in the 1943 revival of *A Connecticut Yankee*.

A Tree in the Park. Introduced by Helen Ford and Lester Cole in *Peggy-Ann*.

Wait Till You See Her. Introduced by Ronald Graham and chorus in *By Jupiter*.

Where or When?. Introduced by Mitzi Green and Ray Heatherton in *Babes in Arms*.

Where's That Rainbow?. Introduced by Helen Ford and Margaret Breen in *Peggy-Ann*.

With a Song in My Heart. Introduced by Lillian Taiz and John Hundley in *Spring Is Here*.

You Took Advantage of Me. Introduced by Busby Berkeley and Joyce Barbour in *Present Arms*.

Yours Sincerely. Introduced by Glenn Hunter and Lillian Taiz in *Spring Is Here*.

2 with Oscar Hammerstein II

A Fellow Needs a Girl. Introduced by William Ching and Anna-mary Dickey in *Allegro*.

A Lovely Night. Introduced by Julie Andrews in *Cinderella*.

All at Once. Introduced by Bill Johnson in *Pipe Dream*.

Bali Ha'i. Introduced by Juanita Hall in *South Pacific*.

The Big, Black Giant. Introduced by Bill Hayes in *Me and Juliet*.

Do I Love You?. Introduced by Julie Andrews and Jon Cypher in *Cinderella*.

Everybody's Got a Home but Me. Introduced by Judy Tyler in *Pipe Dream*.

Hello, Young Lovers. Introduced by Gertrude Lawrence in *The King and I*.

If I Loved You. Introduced by John Raitt and Jan Clayton in *Carousel*.

I Have Dreamed. Introduced by Doretta Morrow and Larry Douglas in *The King and I*.

I'm in Love with a Wonderful Guy. Introduced by Mary Martin in *South Pacific*.

In My Own Little Corner. Introduced by Julie Andrews in *Cinderella*.

It Might As Well Be Spring. Introduced by Luanne Hogan (singing for Jeanne Crain) in *State Fair*.

It's a Grand Night for Singing. Introduced by the ensemble in *State Fair*.

June Is Bustin' Out All Over. Introduced by Christine Johnson and Jean Darling in *Carousel*.

No Other Love. Introduced by Isabel Bigley and Bill Hayes in *Me and Juliet*.

Oh, What a Beautiful Mornin'. Introduced by Alfred Drake in *Oklahoma!*.

Out of My Dreams. Introduced by Joan Roberts in *Oklahoma!*.

People Will Say We're in Love. Introduced by Alfred Drake and Joan Roberts in *Oklahoma!*.

A Puzzlement. Introduced by Yul Brynner in *The King and I*.

So Far. Introduced by Gloria Wills in *Allegro*.

Soliloquy. Introduced by John Raitt in *Carousel*.

Some Enchanted Evening. Introduced by Mary Martin and Ezio Pinza in *South Pacific*.

Ten Minutes Ago. Introduced by Julie Andrews and Jon Cypher in *Cinderella*.

The Surrey with the Fringe on Top. Introduced by Alfred Drake, Joan Roberts and Betty Garde in *Oklahoma!*.

That's for Me. Introduced by Vivian Blaine and Dick Haymes in *State Fair*.

This Nearly Was Mine. Introduced by Ezio Pinza in *South Pacific*.

We Kiss in a Shadow. Introduced by Doretta Morrow and Larry Douglas in *The King and I*.

What's the Use of Wond'rin'. Introduced by Jan Clayton in *Carousel*.

You'll Never Walk Alone. Introduced by Christine Johnson in *Carousel*.

Younger than Springtime. Introduced by William Tabbert in *South Pacific*.

vii

RECOMMENDED RECORDINGS

1 scores of musical comedies and plays

Babes in Arms. Columbia 3 ML-4488. Mary Martin, Mardi Bayne, Jack Cassidy, with chorus and orchestra conducted by Lehman Engel.

Boys from Syracuse. Columbia 3 ML-4837. Jack Cassidy, Portia Nelson, Bibi Osterwald, Stanley Prager, Holly Harris, Bob Shaver, with chorus and orchestra conducted by Lehman Engel.

Carousel. Decca DL-8003. Original Broadway cast. Also Capitol W-694. Sound track of motion picture.

Cinderella. Columbia OL-5190. Original television cast.

A Connecticut Yankee. Victor LK-1026. Earl Wrightson, Elaine Malbin and Al Goodman Orchestra.

Jumbo. Victor LPM-3152. Lisa Kirk, Jack Cassidy, Jordan Bentley with orchestra conducted by Lehman Engel.

The King and I. Decca DL-9008. Original Broadway cast. Also Capitol. Sound track of motion picture.

Me and Juliet. Victor LOC-1012. Original Broadway cast.

Oklahoma!. Decca DL-8000. Original Broadway cast. Also Capitol. Sound track of motion picture.

On Your Toes. Decca DL-9015. Original Broadway cast of 1954 production.

Pal Joey. Columbia 5 ML-4364. Vivienne Segal, Harold Lang, Beverly Fite, Barbara Ashley, Kenneth Remo, Jo Hurt, with chorus and orchestra directed by Lehman Engel.

Pipe Dream. Victor LOC-1023. Original Broadway cast.

South Pacific. Columbia 5 ML-4180. Original Broadway cast.

2   miscellaneous recordings of musical comedies, plays or motion pictures

Carousel. Orchestral Suite. Victor LM-1884. Morton Gould Orchestra.

Oklahoma!. Orchestral Suite. Columbia AAL-4. André Kostelanetz Orchestra.

On Your Toes. "Slaughter on Tenth Avenue." Columbia CL-806. Philadelphia Pops Orchestra conducted by André Kostelanetz. Also Victor LM-1725. Boston Pops Orchestra conducted by Arthur Fiedler.

South Pacific. Orchestral Suite. Columbia ML-2104. Houston Symphony Orchestra conducted by Efrem Kurtz.

Victory at Sea. Suite arranged by Robert Russell Bennett. Victor LM-1779. NBC Symphony Orchestra conducted by Bennett.

Words and Music. MGM E-3233. Original cast in songs they sang in the motion picture biography of Rodgers and Hart.

3   song collections

Ella Fitzgerald Sings the Rodgers and Hart Song Book. Verve MGV-4002. CONTENTS: A Ship Without a Sail; Bewitched, Bothered, and Bewildered; Blue Moon; The Blue Room; Dancing on the Ceiling; Ev'rything I've Got; Give It Back to the Indians; Have You Met Miss Jones?; Here in My Arms; I Could Write a Book; I Didn't Know What Time It Was; Isn't

It Romantic?; I've Got Five Dollars; I Wish I Were in Love Again; It Never Entered My Mind; Johnny One Note; Little Girl Blue; Lover; Manhattan; Mountain Greenery; My Funny Valentine; My Heart Stood Still; My Romance; Spring Is Here; Ten Cents a Dance; The Lady Is a Tramp; There's a Small Hotel; This Can't Be Love; Thou Swell; To Keep My Love Alive; Wait Till You See Her; Where or When?; With A Song in My Heart; You Took Advantage of Me.

Margaret Whiting Sings Rodgers and Hart. Capitol H-209. Margaret Whiting with Frank De Vol Orchestra. CONTENTS: My Romance; My Heart Stood Still; Little Girl Blue; Lover; I Didn't Know What Time It Was; This Can't Be Love; Thou Swell; My Funny Valentine.

A Symphonic Portrait of Richard Rodgers. Capitol P-278. Arranged and conducted by Guy Luypaerts. CONTENTS: The Lady Is a Tramp; Oh, What a Beautiful Mornin'; Where or When?; My Romance; With a Song in My Heart; My Heart Stood Still; Lover; I Married an Angel; If I Loved You; People Will Say We're in Love; It Might as Well Be Spring; June Is Bustin' Out All Over.

The Music of Richard Rodgers. Columbia 4 ML-4130. CONTENTS: My Heart Stood Still; The Most Beautiful Girl in the World; It Might as Well Be Spring; Blue Moon; Johnny One Note; If I Loved You; Where or When?; The Girl Friend; There's a Small Hotel; Lover; Slaughter on Tenth Avenue.

Richard Rodgers. Columbia CL-810. The Philharmonic-Symphony Orchestra of New York conducted by Richard Rodgers. CONTENTS: Waltz Medley (Lover; The Most Beautiful Girl in the World; Falling in Love with Love; Oh, What a Beautiful Mornin'); March of the Siamese Children; Carousel Waltz; Slaughter on Tenth Avenue; Victory at Sea: Symphonic Scenario.

Rodgers and Hart Musical Comedy Hits. Columbia CL-6074. Lee Sullivan, Deane Janis, with orchestra conducted by Richard Rodgers. CONTENTS: My Heart Stood Still; Thou Swell; You Took Advantage of Me; Do I Hear You Saying I Love You; The Girl Friend; The Blue Room; Where or When?; Johnny

One Note; This Can't Be Love; Sing for Your Supper; With a Song in My Heart; Yours Sincerely; Falling in Love with Love; Lover; There's a Small Hotel; It's Gotta Be Love.

Rodgers for Moderns. London LL-1500. Ted Heath and His Orchestra. CONTENTS: Have You Met Miss Jones?; There's a Small Hotel; It's Easy to Remember; My Heart Stood Still; Down by the River; Thou Swell; The Lady Is a Tramp; Where or When?; This Can't Be Love; I Married an Angel; The Blue Room; Dancing on the Ceiling.

The Wonderful Waltzes of Richard Rodgers. MGM E-3028. Paul Britten Orchestra. CONTENTS: Lover; Carousel Waltz; Falling in Love with Love; Oh, What a Beautiful Mornin'; This Nearly Was Mine; Out of My Dreams; It's a Grand Night for Singing; A Wonderful Guy.

Lee Wiley Sings Rodgers and Hart. Storyville LP-312. Lee Wiley with Jimmy Jones, Ruby Braff, Joe Jones and Bill Pemberton. CONTENTS: My Heart Stood Still; You Took Advantage of Me; My Romance; Glad to Be Unhappy; Mountain Greenery; My Funny Valentine; It Never Entered My Mind; Give It Back to the Indians.

Rodgers and Hart Song Book. Victor LPM-4. Patrice Munsel, Vaughn Monroe, with orchestra conducted by Norman Leyden. CONTENTS: Falling in Love with Love; The Most Beautiful Girl in the World; My Funny Valentine; My Romance; Where or When?; With a Song in My Heart.

Ralph Flanagan Plays Rodgers and Hammerstein—vol. 1. Victor LPM-16. Ralph Flanagan Orchestra with vocal. CONTENTS: Some Enchanted Evening; The Surrey with the Fringe On Top; If I Loved You; Oh, What a Beautiful Mornin'; It Might as Well Be Spring; People Will Say We're in Love.

Ralph Flanagan Plays Rodgers and Hammerstein—vol. 2. Victor LPM-8. Ralph Flanagan Orchestra with vocal. CONTENTS: Oklahoma!; That's for Me; June Is Bustin' Out All Over; The Gentleman Is a Dope; What's the Use of Wond'rin'; Bali Ha'i.

She Dances Overhead. Victor LPM-1065. Matt Dennis with Harry Geller's Orchestra. CONTENTS: Dancing on the Ceiling; Mimi; Nobody's Heart; Blue Moon; Isn't It Romantic?; I Married an

Angel; Mountain Greenery; Give Her a Kiss; Wait Till You
See Her; I Didn't Know What Time It Was; This Funny
World; Have You Met Miss Jones?.
Rodgers and Hart. Walden W-304. Louis Carlyle, Bob Shaver,
with the John Morris Trio. CONTENTS: Did You Ever Get
Stung?; Nobody's Heart; A Tree in the Park; Sentimental Me;
To Keep My Love Alive; Wait Till You See Her; A Ship With-
out a Sail; Any Old Place with You; Easy to Remember; I've
Got Five Dollars.

viii

BIBLIOGRAPHY

1 books

Hammerstein, Oscar. *Six Plays by Rodgers and Hammerstein.* New York: Random House, 1955. CONTENTS: Oklahoma!; Carousel; Allegro; South Pacific; The King and I; Me and Juliet. Original casts and credits, scenes and musical numbers indicated.

Hammerstein, Oscar. *Lyrics.* New York: Simon and Schuster, 1949. An anthology of 71 lyrics.

Rodgers, Richard (editor). *The Rodgers and Hart Song Book.* New York: Simon and Schuster, 1951. With introductions by Rodgers and Hammerstein, illustrations by Doris Lee, arrangements by Dr. Albert Sirmay, and text by Margery Darrell. CONTENTS: Any Old Place with You; Garrick Gaieties Opening; Sentimental Me; Manhattan; Mountain Greenery; Here in My Arms; The Blue Room; The Girl Friend; Where's That Rainbow?; A Tree in the Park; My Heart Stood Still; Thou Swell; On a Desert Island with Thee; To Keep My Love Alive; I Feel At Home with You; You Took Advantage of Me; With a Song in My Heart; Yours Sincerely; A Ship Without a Sail; Ten Cents a Dance; Dancing on the Ceiling; I've Got Five Dollars; Lover; Mimi; Isn't It Romantic?; You Are Too Beautiful; Blue Moon; Little Girl Blue; My Romance; The Most Beautiful Girl in the World; There's a Small Hotel; Where or When?; The Lady Is a Tramp; My Funny Valentine; Johnny One Note; Have You Met Miss Jones?; Spring Is Here; I Married an Angel; Falling in Love with Love; This Can't Be Love; Give It Back to the Indians; I Didn't Know What Time It Was; It Never Entered My Mind; Bewitched, Bothered and Bewildered; I Could Write a Book; Wait Till You See Her; Nobody's Heart.

Taylor, Deems. *Some Enchanted Evenings: The Story of Rodgers and Hammerstein*. New York: Harper and Brothers, 1953.

2 selected magazine articles

Barnett, Lincoln: "With Songs in His Heart—The Story of Richard Rodgers." *Ladies' Home Journal,* November, 1950.

Beiswanger, George: "Richard Rodgers." *Theatre Arts,* December, 1944.

Feldman, Patricia: "Richard Rodgers: Man of the Theatre." *Seventeen,* July, 1950.

Goodman, Eckert: "Richard Rodgers: Still Stagestruck." *Harper's* magazine, August, 1953. Also *Reader's Digest,* November, 1953.

Hamburger, Philip: "The Perfect Glow" [A profile on Oscar Hammerstein II]. *New Yorker,* May 12-19, 1951.

Harriman, Margaret Case: "Words and Music" [A profile on Rodgers and Hart]. *New Yorker,* May 28, June 4, 1938.

Hughes, Carol: "Richard Rodgers: Master of Melody." *Coronet,* January, 1951.

Keating, John: "Mr. and Mrs. Richard Rodgers." *Cue,* May 6, 1950.

McCarthy, Joe: "Mrs. Rodgers and Mrs. Hammerstein." *Good Housekeeping,* November, 1954.

Nichols, Lewis R.: "Rodgers and Hammerstein Co." *Saturday Review,* October 25, 1947.

Porter, Amy: "Words and Music" [Rodgers and Hammerstein]. *Collier's,* May 26, 1945.

Pringle, Henry F.: "Words and Music" [Rodgers and Hart]. *Collier's,* February 18, 1933.

Rice, Charles D. (and Ben Feiner, Jr.): "A Couple of Stage-struck Guys" [Rodgers and Hammerstein]. *New York Herald Tribune Magazine,* November 9, 1947.

Samuels, Gertrude: "Success Story Set to Music" [Rodgers]. *New York Times Magazine,* January 21, 1945.

Taylor, Deems: "The Rodgers and I." *House and Garden,* June, 1952.

Wickware, Francis Sill: "Oscar Hammerstein II." *Life,* May 29, 1944.

Willig, John M.: "One Man's Way With a Melody" [Rodgers]. *New York Times Magazine,* March 18, 1951.

Wittels, David G.: "How to Make $4,000,000 on Broadway" [Oscar Hammerstein II]. *Saturday Evening Post,* October 4-11, 1947.

Index